Teacher Exam Cracker Series

BPSC

BIHAR TEACHER RECRUITMENT

FOR SECONDARY SCHOOL TEACHERS

English

PART I

15 PRACTICE SETS

DR. RANJIT KUMAR SINGH, IAS (AIR-49)

PRABHAT EXAMS

Publisher

PRABHAT EXAMS

Imprint of Prabhat Prakashan Pvt. Ltd.

4/19 Asaf Ali Road, New Delhi–110 002

Ph. 23289555 • 23289666 • 23289777 • Helpline/ 7827007777

e-mail: prabhatbooks@gmail.com • Website: www.prabhatexam.com

Price

One Hundred Seventy Five Rupees

ISBN 978-93-5488-643-0

Printed at

Impressions Printing & Packaging Ltd., Noida

BPSC

BIHAR TEACHER RECRUITMENT

FOR SECONDARY SCHOOL TEACHERS

English Part I

15 PRACTICE SETS

by Dr. Ranjit Kumar Singh, IAS (AIR-49)

ISBN 978-93-5488-643-0

₹ 175.00

CONTENTS

PRACTICE SET–1

1. Which of the following essays is not written by Charles Lamb ?
(A) The Convalescence
(B) Imperfect Sympathies
(C) A Bachelor's Complaint of the Behaviour of Married People
(D) Of Studies

2. Who composed the famous line :
'If winter comes can spring be far behind'?
(A) Shelley (B) Keats
(C) Wordsworth (D) None of the above

3. Who is called the Prince among essayists?
(A) Bacon (B) Addison
(C) Charles Lamb (D) Hazlitt

4. 'Love Song of J. Alfred Prufrock' opens with the line :
(A) 'April is the cruelest month....,
(B) 'Let's go then you and I......,
(C) 'Let me not to the marriage of true minds.....,
(D) 'Under the greenwood true......,

5. Choose the right meaning of the word "Effeminate" from the following :
(A) A man who is womanish in his habits
(B) A man who is devoted to the welfare of woman
(C) A man who amuses himself by love-making
(D) A man who is prone to find fault with women

6. Shakespeare Tragedy is written by ....
(A) Edward Dowden
(B) A. C. Bradley
(C) Dover Wilson
(D) Wilson Knight

7. Who among the following writers has not won the Nobel Prize ?
(A) T. S. Eliot
(B) Mulk Raj Anand
(C) William Faulkner
(D) Earnest Hemingway

8. John Keats died at the age of......
(A) 20 (B) 22
(C) 30 (D) 26

9. Who among the following writers was a University Professor of English ?
(A) Kamala Das (B) Mulk Raj Anand
(C) Nissim Ezekiel (D) None of these

10. Dicken's "A Tale of Two Cities" refers to......
(A) Berlin and London
(B) Paris and Vienna
(C) Berlin and Paris
(D) Paris and London

11. T. S. Eliot migrated to England from.......
(A) USA
(B) France
(C) Germany
(D) Canada

12. "The Lotos-Eaters" was composed by :
(A) P. B. Shelley
(B) Alfred Tennyson
(C) Matthew Arnold
(D) Thomas Hardy

13. Which of the following collections of poems was written by Kamala Das ?
(A) Summer in Calcutta
(B) Gitanjali
(C) Leaves of Grass
(D) Song and Sonnets

14. Which part of the United State has been written in Faulkner's fiction ?
(A) The northern (B) The southern
(C) The eastern (D) The western

15. Trace in the following list the drama which T. S. Eliot did not write :
(A) Cocktail
(B) Family Reunion
(C) Murder in the Cathedral
(D) The Ascent of F6

16. "What the Thunder said" is a section of the poem:
(A) 'Four Quartets'
(B) 'Love Song of J. Alfred Prufrock'
(C) 'Gerontion'
(D) 'The Waste Land'

17. The name of the protagonist of The Mayor of Casterbridge is :
(A) Newson
(B) Clym Yeobright
(C) Alec D'Urbervilles
(D) Michael Henchard

18. 'To strive, seek, to find and to yield' occurs in the Poem :
(A) 'Lotos Eaters'
(B) 'Tears Idle Tears'
(C) 'Ulysses'
(D) 'The Charge of the Light Brigade'

19. In which category will you place Arnold as a critic ?
(A) Romantic (B) Marxist
(C) Aesthetic (D) Classicist

20. One of my friends........a fine collection of postage stamps.
Choose the correct option from the following :
(A) Has (B) Have
(C) Do have (D) None of these

21. Ten pounds.........money :
Fill in the blank space by choosing the right answer:
(A) Are a lot of (B) Is the lot of
(C) Is a lot of (D) None of these

22. Shakespeare's sonnets are in the following form :
(A) Tree quatrains and a couplet
(B) An octave and sestet
(C) Two six-line stanzas and a couplet
(D) None of these

23. The name of Alfred Tennyson's famous elegy is:
(A) 'Lycidas'
(B) 'Adonais'
(C) 'Elegy Written in a Country Churchyard'
(D) 'In Memoriam'

24. 'Break, Break, Break' was written on the death of :
(A) John Keats
(B) William Wordsworth
(C) Leigh Hunt
(D) Arthur Hallam

25. With which of the following poets do we associate the 'pictorial quality' of poetry ?
(A) Wordsworth (B) Keats
(C) Shelley (D) Milton

26. Which of the following epithets brings out the most characteristic quality of David Copperfied pinpointed by the majority of Dickens scholars ?
(A) Autobiographical
(B) Grotesque
(C) Baroque
(D) Lengthy

27. Bathsheba is the heroine of :
(A) Return of the Native
(B) Tess of D' urberville
(C) Far from the Madding Crowd
(D) Jude the Obscure

28. Which of the following writers is noted for what Keats called 'Negative Capability' ?
(A) Milton (B) Shelley
(C) Tennyson (D) Shakespeare

29. Which of the following writers writes uninhibitedly about his or her sexual relationships ?

(A) Mulk Raj Anand
(B) Nissim Ezekiel
(C) Kamala Das
(D) Robert Frost

30. Wordsworth's "The Lyrical Ballads" was published in :
(A) 1789 (B) 1805
(C) 1799 (D) 1798

31. Who asserted himself as "a classicist in literature, royalist in politics and anglo-Catholic in religion" ?
(A) Matthew Arnold
(B) T. S. Eliot
(C) Walt Whitman
(D) None of these

32. "Adonais" by Shelley is an elegy on......
(A) Wordsworth (B) Byron
(C) Keats (D) Coleridge

33. Who called Shelley "a beautiful but an ineffectual angle beating in the void his luminous wings in vain" ?
(A) John Ruskin (B) Mathew Arnold
(C) T. S. Eliot (D) Tennyson

34. The sonnet "The world is too Much with Us" is written by.......
(A) Scott (B) Keats
(C) Shelley (D) Wordsworth

35. The phrase "Willing suspension of disbelief" is associated with........
(A) Byron (B) Keats
(C) Coleridge (D) Wordsworth

36. The Waste Land was published in :
(A) 1915 (B) 1918
(C) 1920 (D) 1922

37. The imaginary county 'Yoknapatawpha' occurs in the novels of :
(A) Hardy (B) Dickens
(C) Faulkner (D) Mulk Raj Anand

38. Which of the following poets wrote the poem entitled 'Dover Beach' ?
(A) Arnold (B) Tennyson
(C) Milton (D) Wordsworth

39. What played the most important part in shaping Ernest Hemingways' literary creations like Farewell to Arms ?
(A) Experiences of war
(B) His friends and relations
(C) His love affairs and marriages
(D) His power of oratory

40. The movement of "Return to nature" has to do with :
(A) The Neoclassical Age
(B) The Romantic Age
(C) The Restoration Age
(D) None of these

41. What figure of speech has been used in the following line ?
"All the perfumes of Arabia cannot sweeten this little hand."
(A) Metaphor (B) Oxymoron
(C) Hyperbole (D) Apostrophe

42. What is the figure of speech when the real meaning is exactly the opposite of that which is expressed by words apparently ?
(A) Satire (B) Irony
(C) Oxymoron (D) None of these

43. What is a direct address to the dead, to the absent, or to a personified object or idea ?
(A) Epigram (B) Personification
(C) Apostrophe (D) None of these

44. What is the name of an implied simple ?
(A) Metaphore (B) Apostrophe
(C) Hyperbole (D) None of these

45. The repetition of vowel sounds in a sequence of nearly words is called :
(A) Rhyme (B) Rhythm
(C) Assonance (D) Casura

46. When the sound of a word resembles the sound it denotes, the figure of speech is :
(A) Synecdoche (B) Onomatopoeia
(C) Prosopopeia (D) Transferred epithet

47. The statement, namely, 'Happiness is but an occasional episode in the general drama of paint', contains the figure of speech called :

(A) Simile (B) Personification
(C) Paradox (D) Metaphor

48. Which of the following words is onomatopoeic ?
(A) Carry (B) Bear
(C) Fear (D) Bug

49. Which of the following sentences has the figure of speech called 'Apostrophe' ?
(A) Man is the measure of all things.
(B) Patriotism, what horrors are done in your name
(C) My Love is Like a Red, Red Rose
(D) All that glitters is not gold

50. Hamlet's question 'To be or not to be......?' means :
(A) To kill Claudius or not to kill him ?
(B) To kill Gertrude or not to kill her ?
(C) To marry Ophelia or not to marry her ?
(D) To live or to die ?

51. Who is known as the fourth-witch among Shakespeare's woman characters ?
(A) Desdemona (B) Gertrude
(C) Lady Macbeth (D) Cordelia

52. Shylock is a character in Shakespeare's......:
(A) Twelfth Night
(B) Merchant of Venice
(C) As You Like It
(D) Commedy of Errors

53. Who said :
"There is no essential difference between the language of prose and that of the metrical composition" ?
(A) Wordsworth (B) Arnold
(C) Eliot (D) Keats

54. "Background, Casually" is written by :
(A) Kamala Das (B) Robert Frost
(C) Whitman (D) Nissim Ezekiel

55. Who among the following writers did recently change his/her religion ?
(A) Mulk Raj Anand
(B) Kamala Das
(C) Nissim Ezekiel
(D) None of these

56. Who wrote the following well-known lines ?
"The woods are lovely dark and deep And I have promises to keep......"
(A) Whitman (B) Emerson
(C) Frost (D) Faulkner

57. Complete the following :
"I Hear America Singing" is a ....lyric.
(A) Patriotic (B) Amorous
(C) Mystic (D) Revolutionary

58. Who is known as 'The Bard of Democracy' among the following ?
(A) Emerson (B) Robert Frost
(C) Walt Whitman (D) Emily Dickinson

59. Who defined tragedy in the following manner ?
"Tragedy is an imitation of an action, that is serious, complete and of a certain magnitude......"
(A) Plato (B) Shakespeare
(C) Aristotle (D) Longinus

60. A long poem telling the story of the leader of the whole community written in a narrative form and lofty style is called :
(A) A drama (B) An epic
(C) A short story (D) A lyric

61. An iambic pentameter line contains :
(A) Five feet (B) Seven feet
(C) Nine feet (D) Six feet

62. How many lines does a sonnet consist of ?
(A) Twenty (B) Two
(C) Nine (D) Fourteen

63. They literary art of diminshing a subject by making it ridiculous and evoking towards it the attitudes of amusement and scron is called:
(A) Allegory (B) Melodrama
(C) Parody (D) Satire

64. A lyric is :
(A) A long poem written in the form of an address
(B) A poem written in praise of God
(C) A short poem in which the poet expresses his intense personl feelings
(D) A triumphal songs

65. A ballad is :

(A) A short poem narrating a tale

(B) A poem written on somebody's death

(C) A prayer song

(D) A marriage song

66. "The talk of memorials to him in statues of bronze or marble or pillars and thus they mock him and belie his message."

What does the writer say ?

(A) Memorials of costly metals are important

(B) The dead person's message is important

(C) The people who build memorials are important

(D) None of the above

67. "I had been part of Nelson's prayer, that the British fleet might be distinguished by humanity in the victory which he expected."

What was Nelson's dream ?

(A) A prayer to God

(B) To serve humanity

(C) Victory of the British fleet

(D) None of these

68. What does the idiom "Be-all and end-all" mean ?

(A) From begining to end

(B) That which begins well

(C) That which ends well

(D) The whole and sole

69. Pick out the right option which expresses the meaning of the word "Jealous" :

(A) Enthusiastic (B) Envious

(C) Proud (D) Popular

70. Choose the right option which expresses the meaning of the word "Invincible" :

(A) Defeated (B) Spoken

(C) Learned (D) Unconquerable

71. Fill in the blank with a suitable preposition or verb. He..........the bus when it came.

(A) Got off (B) Got on

(C) Got in (D) None of the above

72. Read the following passage and answer the qustion that follows it :

"But the ten poets represented in the following pages all share a technical master of English verse and a broad enough thematic concern to make then worthy of the attention of a wide audience."

To which of the following categories does the book alluded to in the above statement belong?

(A) An anthology of poetry

(B) An anthology of critical essays on some poets

(C) A book of English prosody

(D) A treatise on poetry and its nature

73. Read the lines that follow the answer, the question based on them :

Created half to rise and half to fall;
Great lord of all things, yet a prey to all.

Which of the following Statement best articulates the human condition, Suggested in the above lines ?

(A) Man is a mysterious being, defying all logic.

(B) Man's state in the world is paradoxical.

(C) Man is doomed to failure.

(D) Man is a social being.

74. Read the following lines from a poem and answer the question that follows :

And though a single world scatters all doubts
I quake for wonder at your choice of me :
Why, why and why ?

How would you like to characterize the speaker of lines ? (Choose the best option from the following) :

(A) He is a melancholy person.

(B) He was diffident regarding his selection as a lover by his lady-love but is now surprised at her choice of him.

(C) He is sceptical by nature.

(D) He is despondent.

75. Which of the following words is the "Antonym" of the word "Auspicious" ?

(A) Oracular (B) Optical

(C) Ominous (D) Austere

76. Which of the following words is the "Synonym" of "Apathetic" ?
(A) Hostile (B) Callous
(C) Repulsive (D) Ominous

77. Which of the following sentences is not in Passive Voice ?
(A) That nuance of the word was not intended by the speaker in his speech.
(B) I am sure you will be awarded the pulitzer for your novel this year.
(C) My uncle seeks on appointment with you.
(D) We are sure to be punished by the boss.

78. Which of the following sentences is in Passive Voice ?
(A) I want to purchase a plot here.
(B) She knows swimming very well.
(C) You cannot compete in this game this year.
(D) She was awarded the British Council scholarship in 1999.

79. Trace in the following list, the play which does not belong to the category to which the rest do :
(A) Othello (B) King Lear
(C) Hamle (D) The Tempest

80. Which of the folloing words means 'a cure for all ills' ?
(A) Epidemic (B) Didactic
(C) Panacea (D) Diction

81. Which of the following words is mis-spelt ?
(A) Career (B) Creator
(C) Canter (D) Carrier

82. What is the meaning of 'on the alert' ?
(A) Ready to act
(B) Depend on police
(C) Depend on others
(D) None of the above

83. What is the synonym of 'timorous' ?
(A) Up-to-date
(B) Bright
(C) Timid
(D) None of the above

84. What is the synonym of 'elegant' ?
(A) Gentle
(B) Famous
(C) Graceful
(D) None of the above

85. Find out the correct indirect narration of the following direct speech :
He said to me,"what are you doing ?"
(A) He asked me what I was doing.
(B) He asked to me what was I doing ?
(C) He asked me what I was doing ?
(D) None of the above

86. Find out the correct indirect narration of the following direct speech :
He said, "Alas! I am undone".
(A) He exclaimed alas that he was undone.
(B) He told Alas that he was undone.
(C) He exclaimed sadly that he was undone.
(D) None of the above

87. Punctuation of the following sentence :
"As Caesar Loved me i weep for him as he was fortunate rejoice at it as it as he was valient i honour him but as he was ambitious i slew him" is given in following sentences. Find out the correct one.
(A) As Caesar loved me I weep for him, as he was fortunate I rejoice at it, as he was valiant I honour him, but as he was ambitious I slew him.
(B) As Caesar loved me I weep for him. As he was fortunate I rejoice at it. As he was valiant, I honour him. But as he was ambitious I slew him.
(C) As Caesar loved me, I weep for him: as he was fortunate, I rejoice at it: as he was valiant, I honour him: but, as he was ambitious, I slew him.
(D) None of the above

88. What does the abbreviation I. P. C. mean in the context of our Constitution ?
(A) Indian People's Code
(B) Indian Premier Code
(C) Indian Popular Code
(D) Indian Penal Code

89. Select the right meaning of the word "Biography" from the following :
(A) The life-history of a man written by someone else
(B) The life history of a man written by himself
(C) The life history of a man as reflected in his writings
(D) The life-history of a man created in painting by someone else

90. 'It is not necessary says smiles to show that economy is useful.' The sentence wants punctuation. Find out the correctly punctuated sentence from the following sentences :
(A) "It is not necessary", says Smiles, "to show that economy is useful.
(B) "It is not necessary says smiles to show that Economy is useful."
(C) "It is not," Necessary says Smiles, "to show that Economy is useful"
(D) None of the above

91. Find out the Correct sentence :
(A) He is rich enough to starve
(B) He is too rich to starve
(C) He is too rich not to starve
(D) None of the above

92. Which is the alternative to complete the sentence:
If I were the Prime Minister of India.......
(A) I will help the poor
(B) I would helped the poor
(C) I had helped the poor
(D) None of the above

93. Who regarded poetry as the criticism of life ?
(A) Mathew Arnold
(B) Wordsworth
(C) T. S Eliot
(D) None of the above

94. What is the unique quality of Dickens humour?
(A) It blends humour with satire
(B) It blends humour with romantic narration
(C) It blends humour with pathos
(D) None of the above

95. Which of the following novels was written by W. Faulkner ?
(A) For Whom the Bell Tolls
(B) The Portrait of the Artist as a Young Man
(C) Ulysses
(D) The Sound and the Fury

96. Whose novels throw light on the miseries of poor orphan children ?
(A) Dickens (B) Fielding
(C) Jane Austen (D) Thackeray

97. Who composed the famous line :
"Our sweetest songs are those that tall of saddest thought".
(A) Keats (B) Wordsworth
(C) Shelley (D) None of the above

98. Identify the figure of speech in the following line:
The pen is mighter than the sword
(A) Metaphor (B) Simile
(C) Personification (D) Metonymy

99. Choose the meaning of the word "Teetotaller" from the following :
(A) One who drinks only tea
(B) One who takes everything
(C) One who does not take any intoxicating drinks
(D) One who is selective in the matter of drinks

100. Who wrote "The Revolt of Islam' ?
(A) Tennyson (B) Shelley
(C) Arnold (D) None of the above

ANSWERS WITH EXPLANATION

1. (D) 'Of Studies is an essay by Francis Bacon.
2. (A) If winter comes can spring be far behind.
3. (C) The Position of Lamp amongst essayists is the most eminent. In fact, he has after been called the prince of all the essayists England has so far produced.
4. (B) Let us go then, you and I, when the evening is spread out against the sky.
5. (A)
6. (B)
7. (B) Other three have got Nobel prize.
   (1) T. S. Eliot 1948
   (2) William Faulknor 1950
   (3) Earnest Hemingway 1954
8. (B) Keats was born in 1795 and died in 1821.
9. (C) Ezekiel was a professor of english at the university of Bombay.
10. (D) The scene of 'A Tale of two cities' is laid in London and Paris, at the time of French Revolution.
11. (A) T. S. Eliot was born in 1885 at St. Louis in the United State of America.
12. (B)
13. (A) Summer in Calcutta was published in 1965.
14. (B)
15. (D)
16. (D) 'The Waste Land' by T. S. Eliot progresses rather abruptly through five movement as follows:
    (i) The Burial of the Dead
    (ii) A Game of Chess
    (iii) The Fire Sermon
    (iv) Death by water; and
    (v) What the thunder said
17. (D)
18. (C)
19. (D)
20. (A)
21. (C) Ten pounds is a single unit so singular verb is used.
22. (A) Earl of Survey does not follow the Petrarchan model of the sonnet. He divides his sonnets into quatrains, with a couplet in the end, and thus he is the first to use that form of the Sonnet which came to be called Shakespearean from the great dramatistic use of it.
23. (D) Perhaps the most loved of all Tennyson's work is 'In Memorium' which is 'one of the few immoral names that were not born to die.'
24. (D) Tennyson's friend Hallam died in 1833. Tennyson was plunged into a period of gloom and sorrow.
    The sorrow may be read in the exquisite little poem–Break Break Break.
25. (B)
26. (A) Of the novels, 'David Copperfied' is regarded by many as Dickens's masterpiece. It gives the glimpse of author's own boyhood and family.
27. (C)
28. (D) It struck me what quality went to form a man of achievement, especially in literature and which Shakespeare possed so enormously mean Negative capability.
29. (C) In 'My Story' She wrote–In the orbit of illicit sex there seemed to be only crudeness and violence.
30. (D)
31. (B) Eliot had often declared himself the champion of all kinds of conservation-monarchist in politics, dogmatic in religion and classical in literature.
32. (C) Adonais is a wonderful threnody over the death of the poet Keats.
33. (B)
34. (D)
35. (C)
36. (D) The Waste Land first appeared in 'The Sial' and won the magazines award from the poetry, after which it was published in book form in 1922.
37. (C) Sartoris (1929) is the first novel in his long loosely constructed 'Yoknapatawpha'

saga, whose themes include decline of the compson.

38. (A)

39. (A) He was selected as a honorary lieutenant. He was hit by Austrian mortar shell while handling out chocolate to Italian soilders. He was admitted to red cross hospital where he fell in love with a nurse whom he described in.

40. (B) The Romantic Movement in English poetry is generally described as a 'Return to Nature'.

41. (C) **42.** (B)

43. (C)

44. (A) A metaphor is implied simile. Its comparison is not clearly stated.

45. (C)

46. (B) As above in question No. 3.

47. (D) Life is here compared to a drama which is generally painful and happiness is a brief episode.

48. (D) Onomatopoeia is the use of a word or words whose sound itself conveys the sense of the author.

49. (B) Apostrophe is a direct address to the dead, to the absent or to a personified object or idea. Here patriotism is personified.

50. (D) This is the 56th line of Hamlet (Act-III, Sc-I) where Hamlet mases on either to end his existence or still continue to live.

51. (C) There are three witches in 'Macbeth' but lady Macbeth infuses in Macbeth to murder Duncan thus called the fourth witch.

52. (B) Shylock the few is the moneylender in the play 'Merchant of Venice'.

53. (A) In his (Wordsworth) famous preface to the 'Lyrical Ballads' he enunciated his theories. He said that 'there neither is nor can be any essential difference between the language of prose and verse.

54. (D) Background Casually is one of the biographical poems of Ezekiel.

55. (B)

56. (C) The lines are part of a poem Titled 'Stopping by woods on a Snowy Evening' by Robert Forst. These lines were so dear to Pt. J. L. Nehru that they were found after his death on his desk in his own handwrinting.

57. (A)

58. (C) Whitman entered politics as a democrat. He became editor to a democratic newspaper. He believed and showed how man might achieve for himself the greatest possible freedom with in the limits of natural law, for mind and body through democracy.

59. (C) Aristotle defines tragedy as "an imitation of an action, serious, complete, and of a certain magnitude in a language beautified in diffrent parts with different kind of emblishment, through action and not narration and through scenes of pity and fear bringing about the 'Catharsis' of these emotions."

60. (B) It is a long narrative poem on a great and serious subject, related in an elevated style and centered on a heroic or quasi-divine figure on whose action depends the fate of a tribe, a nation or the human race.

61. (A) In iambic metre each foot has two syllables of which the first is unaccented and the second accented. If there are five feet or ten such syllables in a line, it would be known as Iambic Pentametre.

62. (D) Sonnet is a short lyric of fourteen lines and the Italian poet Petrarch was the first to use this form of lyric to express his love for his beloved Laura.

63. (C) Imitative of words, style, attitude, tone and ideas of an author in a way to make them ridiculous.

64. (C) A lyric is always an expression of the moods and emotions of a poets. The best lyrics are emotional in tone.

65. (A) The Ballad presents a short story in verse. It is a song, transmitted orally, which tells a story.

66. (B) Raising memorials of great person is in a way forgetting his/her message which is more important.

67. (B) Nelson's Prayer was not only for victory of the British fleet, infact he was hopeful of the victory, but he wanted that this victory should be recognized by humanity that is it should be useful to humanity.

68. (D)

69. (B) Jealous means envious and zealous means enthusiastic.

70. (D) 71. (B)

72. (A) Passage says the qualities of the poets and the themes of their poetry which win count for their popularity.

73. (B)

74. (B) The Poet seems to be doubtful of being choosen as a lover by his lady love but that doubt vanishes from her reply and now his mind is filled with surprise at his selection.

75. (C) Auspicious means 'Good Omen' Ominus means 'bad omen'.

76. (A)

77. (C) It is to be noted that in passive voice verb is always in its third form. The passive of this sentence is– An appointment is being seeked by my uncle with you.

78. (D) A verb is in the passive voice when its form shows that something is done to the person or thing denoted by the subject. The passive voice is called so beacause the person or thing denoted by the subject is not active but passive, that is, suffers or receive some action. Here 'she' the subject is passive and is awarded action.

79. (D) Othello, King Lear, Hamlet and Macbeth are four major tragedies by Shakespeare where as the Tempest by Shakespeare is a comedy.

80. (C)

81. (C) The correct spelling is 'Centre'.

82. (A) 83. (C)

84. (C)

85. (A) "What are you doing" is a direct question while changing it into indirect, subject is given before the verb as in statement. Question mark is not used.

86. (C) 'Alas' shows that it is an exclamatory sentence. While changing the narration word alas is removed and 'exclaimed with sorrow' or such words are used.

87. (C) 88. (D)

89. (A) 90. (A)

91. (B) If sentence having 'two' contains no negative word the subordinate clause becomes negative. If however there is a negative word in the sentence, the subordinate clause become positive.

92. (B)

93. (A) Arnold as shown in his essay on 'The study of poetry' regarded poetry as "a criticism of life under the conditions fixed for criticism by the laws of poetic truth and poetic beauty."

94. (C) But in one way, at least, Dickens's humour rises above being a flashy, superficial affair and that is its proximity to pathos.

95. (D) The Sound and the Fury' (1929) is a psychological novel, with a strange autobiographical element.

96. (A)

97. (C) This line occurs in "To A Skylark'.

98. (D) In Metonymy, an object is designated by the name of something which is generally associated with it.

99. (C)

100. (B) 'The Revolt of Islam' was published in 1818.

❑❑❑

PRACTICE SET–2

1. About which novel of his own Hardy marked–a war between 'Flesh and spirit' ?
   (A) The Mayor of Casterbridge
   (B) Tess of the d'Urbervilles
   (C) Jude the Obscure
   (D) The Return of the Native
2. Hardy began and ended his career by writing:
   (A) Novel (B) Drama
   (C) Essays (D) Poetry
3. Arms and the Man by G. B. Shaw is divided into :
   (A) Four Acts (B) Five Acts
   (C) Two Acts (D) Three Acts
4. Who wrote 'The habit of freedom, which English room never acquire and never let their children acquire, came to me naturally' ?
   (A) Arnold (B) Eliot
   (C) Shaw (D) Lawerence
5. 'The Old Man and the Sea' fetch Nobel Prize for Hemingway. The Protagonist is :
   (A) A Cuban fisherman
   (B) An American fisherman
   (C) A Mexican fisherman
   (D) A British Naval Officer
6. Who called Wordsworth 'The egotistical sublime' ?
   (A) Lamb (B) Arnold
   (C) Eliot (D) Keats
7. Wordsworth wrote 'The Prelude' in :
   (A) Twelve books
   (B) Fourteen books
   (C) Ten books
   (D) Sixteen books
8. Which of the following is not a poetic play by T. S. Eliot ?
   (A) Sweeney Agonista
   (B) Murder is the Cathedral
   (C) The Family Reunion
   (D) None
9. Where from the epigraph of 'The Love Long of T. Alfred Prufrock' is taken ?
   (A) Illiad (B) Gita
   (C) Inferno (D) Hamlet
10. How is Lamb associated with Christ's Hospital ?
    (A) It was the hospital where he took birth.
    (B) Here he died.
    (C) Here he was educated.
    (D) Many lamb was treated here.
11. Who is called the essayist for excellence ?
    (A) Bacon (B) Lamb
    (C) Arnold (D) None
12. Who termed Shelley as 'Melopoeic' ?
    (A) Keats (B) Arnold
    (C) Eliot (D) G. B. Shaw
13. Where did Shelley settle and wrote his best poetry ?
    (A) Sussex (B) Eton
    (C) France (D) Pisa
14. Shelley wrote a pamphlet at oxford – "The Necessity of Atheism". By whom was he inspired ?
    (A) Kant
    (B) Bergson
    (C) Hume
    (D) Keats

15. Which work of Hemingway was called the Bible of 'Lost Generation'?
(A) The Sun Also Rises
(B) Men Without Women
(C) A Moveable Feast
(D) The Old Men and the Sea

16. Who utter these words – 'I guess I am not a nature poet, I have written only two poems without a human being in them' ?
(A) Wordsworth (B) Keats
(C) Frost (D) Whitman

17. Who is the author of 'A Masque of Mercy' ?
(A) Robert Frost
(B) Earnest Hemingaway
(C) D. H. Lawrence
(D) G. B. Shaw

18. How many times did Robert Frost got Pulitzer Prize ?
(A) One (B) Two
(C) Three (D) Four

19. Kamala Das got 'Kerala Sahitya Akademi Award' in the year :
(A) 1985 (B) 1969
(C) 1964 (D) 1965

20. Which of the following poems by Kamala Das is in dialogue form ?
(A) The Invitation (B) In Love
(C) Composition (D) The Suicide

21. Who wrote these lines "I cannot leave this island I was born here and belong" ?
(A) Kamala Das (B) T. S. Eliot
(C) Whitman (D) Ezekiel

22. Who is of a Jewish origin ?
(A) Kamala Das
(B) R. K. Narayan
(C) Nissim Ezekiel
(D) None

23. Which novel of R. K. Narayan is similar to the 'A Doll's House'?
(A) Mr. Sampath
(B) The Guide
(C) The Dark Room
(D) The Bachelor of Arts

24. Who authored the novel 'The Financial Expert' ?
(A) Mulk Raj Anand
(B) R. K. Narayan
(C) William Faulkner
(D) Hemingway

25. How many books did Mulk Raj Anand Publish before 1935 ?
(A) 10 (B) 6
(C) 4 (D) 5

26. Where was Mulk Raj Anand born ?
(A) Peshawar (B) Lahore
(C) Amritsar (D) Jalandhar

27. Who is the writer of the 'Adventure of Ulysses'?
(A) Charles Lamb (B) Marry Lamb
(C) Both (D) None

28. Which volume of poetry by Keats contained poem 'Hyperion' ?
(A) First volume (B) Second volume
(C) Third volume (D) Fourth volume

29. 'Here lies one whose name was writ in water' who is here spoken of ?
(A) Shelley (B) Arnold
(C) Wordsworth (D) Keats

30. In which of his odes Keats wonders "Do I Wake or Sleep"?
(A) Ode to Grecian urn
(B) Ode to Psyche
(C) Ode to Nightingale
(D) None of these

31. Who Said "Milton ; thou shouldst he living at this hour" ?
(A) Keats
(B) Wordsworth
(C) Arnold
(D) W.B.Yeats

32. Which one is a philosophical work of W. B. Yeats which he wrote with the help of his wife ?
(A) A Vision
(B) The Wandering of Oisin

(C) The Seven Woods

(D) The Celtic Twilight

33. Which one of the following statements is true about D. H. Lawrence's Sons And Lovers ?

(A) Paul's mother dies of cancer

(B) Paul's father is lawyer

(C) Paul marries Gertrude

(D) Paul kills his mother

34. 'The Waste Land' by T. S. Eliot is a poem' of :

(A) 400 lines (B) 370 lines

(C) 800 lines (D) 430 lines

35. Which was Faulkner's last novel ?

(A) The Wild Palms

(B) The Hamlet

(C) The Reivers

(D) Mosquitoes

36. Which work of William Faulkner is also known as 'A Boy's Ambition' ?

(A) Absalom Absalom

(B) Light in August

(C) The Sound and Fury

(D) Mosquitoes

Direction (Q. No. 37 to 46):

Answer the questions based on the following passage :

Educational planning should aim at the educational needs of the entire population of all age groups while the traditional structure of education as a three-layer hierarchy from the primary stage to the university represents the core. We should not overlook the periphery which is equally important. Under modern conditions, workers need to rewind or renew their enthusiasm of strike out in a new direction or improve their skills as much as any university professor. The retired and aged have their needs as well as educational planning in their words, should take care of the needs of every one.

Our structure of education have been built upon the assumption that there is a terminal point of education. This basic defect has become all the more harmful today. A UNESCO report entitled — 'Learning To Be' prepared in 1973 asserts that the education of children must prepare the future adult for various forms of self learning. A viable education system of the future should consist of models with different kinds of functions serving a diversity of constituents. And performance is not the period of study should be the basis for credentials. The writing is already on the wall.

In view of the significance of a commitment of lifelong learning and life time education is being discussed only in recent years even in educationally advance countries. The possibility of the idea becoming an integral part of educational thinking seems to be a for cry. For to more in the direction means much more than some simple rearrangement of the present organization of education. But a good beginning can be made by developing open universities programmes for older tearners of different categories and introducing extensive services in the conventional colleges and schools. Also these institutions should learn to cooperate with the numerous community organizations such as libraries, museums, municipal recreational programmes, health services.

37. Which of the following is most opposite in meaning to phrase – 'a far cry' as used in the passage ?

(A) A reality

(B) A theoretical suggestion

(C) Very funny

(D) Next to impossible

38. Which of the following is nearly the same in meaning as the word 'Terminal' as used in the passage ?

(A) Approaching

(B) Satisfying

(C) Introducing

(D) Find

39. What is the meaning of the sentence 'the writing is already on the wall' ?

(A) Everything is uncertain nowadays

(B) Changes have already taken place

(C) The signs of changes are already visible

(D) It is a mysterious process.

40. The concept of life time is :

(A) As old as traditional education

(B) Still in formative stage

(C) In vogue in advance countries

(D) Not practical

41. Which of the following is not true :

(A) Life long learning is a recent concept.

(B) Workers knowledge and skills also needs to be updated constantly.

(C) 'Learning To Be' defends that there is a terminal point to education.

(D) Schools and colleges should provide extension services.

42. According to the author what should be the basis of awarding credentials ?

(A) Duration of course

(B) Competence of the course teachers

(C) Diversity of the topics covered

(D) Real group of matter or skill

43. According to the author what measures should open universities adopt to meet modern conditions :

(A) Develop various programmes for adult learners.

(B) Open more colleges on traditional lines.

(C) Cater to the needs of those who represents core.

(D) Derecognition numerous community organization.

44. According to the author, educational plan should attempt at :

(A) Train the people at core.

(B) Encourage conventional schools and colleges.

(C) Decide a terminal point of education.

(D) Fulfil the educational needs of everyone.

45. Which of the following best describes the purpose of the author ?

(A) To criticise the present educational system.

(B) To strength the present educational system.

(C) To support non-conventional educational organization.

(D) To present Pragmatic point of view.

46. What is the main thrust of the author ?

(A) Traditional system should be strengthen.

(B) Formal education is more important than non-formal.

(C) One should never cease to learn.

(D) There is no substitute for the extant system of education.

47. Who wrote 'A Tiger's Heart Wrapped in a Player's Hide' about Shakespeare.

(A) Ben Jonson (B) Philip Sidney

(C) Greene (D) Narlowe

48. To which work of his own Shakespeare called 'the first heir of invention' ?

(A) The Rape of Lucrece

(B) Venus and Adonis

(C) As you Like it

(D) Cymbeline

49. "All the World's a Stage,
And all the men and women merely players."
Who is the speaker of these lines ?

(A) Shakespeare (B) Prospero

(C) Hamlet (D) Jaques

50. Stratford-on-Avon is the place where Shakespeare born. Where is it located ?

(A) Warwickshire (B) London

(C) Sussex (D) Edinburgh

Direction (Question Nos. 51 to 53): In the sentences given below mark the part which contains an error. If there is no error, mark '4' as your choice :

51.

Very few	people now believe that
1	2
the wages of sin are death.	No error
3	4

52.

Neither Ram nor his parents	are
1	2
to blame	No Error
3	4

53.

Everyone of us	should do our duty
1	2
to the country	No Error
3	4

Direction: The passage below is followed by Questions on its content. Answer the question on the basis of what is implied or stated in the passage:

The expression 'the rule of law' relates to human association. It purports to stand for human being associated in terms of the recognition of certain conditions of association, namely 'laws': human beings joined in an exclusive, specifiable mode of relationships. I shall begin, therefore, with two brief remarks about human relationship in general.

First, relations between persons are apt to be contingent assemblages of a variety of different modes of association. I mean categorically distinct kind of relationship, specifiable in terms of its own condition, which excludes other modes of association but does not deny them. Thus, two persons may be joined, as husband and wife, in a legal mode of relationship, civil or ecclesiastical, but they may also be related in the categorically different terms of love, affection, friendship and so on and further they may be partners in a business enterprise. And while a teacher and his pupil may have a legal and a commercial relationship, they have also an educational relationship whose terms are neither those of law nor of commerce. In short white persons may have (and, indeed, be largely composed of) a variety of different kinds of relationship with others and move between them without confusion, the subject in a mode of relationship is always the abstraction, a person in respect of being related to there in terms of distinct and exclusive conditions. And 'the rule of law', standing for a mode of relationship, identifies a person related to others of the same modal character. What is the character of this person and what are the conditions of this mode of association ?

Secondly, in spite of their modal diversity, all human relationship have a common character. Human beings are intelligent agents and the terms of all or any of the relationship they enjoy are beliefs and recognitions: not merely what they have learnd and understood (or misunderstood), attributed to or assumed about themselves, but what they have seen fit to require of themselves and one another. Human relationships are human inventions, invented ambulando in the course of living and imposing conditions upon conduct. Here we have to do with artifice, but a particular mode of human relationship, having been imagined, perhaps elaborated and refined and enjoyed as a practice, may then become the subject of reflection in which its terms and conditions are precisely dislinguised. Here, as elsewhere, practice precedes the reflection in which its modal character is formulated.

54. The tone of the passage is :

(A) critical (B) expository

(C) descriptive (D) narative

55. Which of the following statements is true about 'the rule of law'?

(A) In spite of difference, human beings can accept the same modal character.

(B) Human beings cannot be subjected to the same rule of law.

(C) All men and women being alike, the same 'rule of law' is not difficult to endorse.

(D) Human beings are too egoistical to accept a common 'rule of law'.

56. In the phrase 'contingent assemblages', contingent means :

(A) accidental

(B) convenient

(C) specific

(D) representative

57. Throughout the passage, the term 'mode' implies :

(A) style (B) rule

(C) form (D) manner

58. In the context of the passage, which of the following statement is not correct ?

(A) All human relationships are based on laws.

(B) There are different modes of relationships among human beings.

(C) Legal relationship can be indisputably blended with non-legal relationships.

(D) There is no contradiction between a civil and an ecclesiastical relationship.

59. In a state or society, human beings are associated with one another in terms of :

(A) Love

(B) Friendship

(C) Business concerns

(D) Laws

60. Find out the correctly spelt word :
(A) Monstrous (B) Monsterous
(C) Monstorous (D) Monstoros

61. Fill in the blanks with appropriate tense : .
I wish I .... dead.
(A) shall (B) will
(C) may (D) were

62. Which of the following sentences is correct one ?
(A) I went there with a view to meet him.
(B) I went there with a view to meeting him
(C) I went there for a view to meeting him.
(D) I went there with view to meeting him.

63. Fill in the blank in the following sentence with correct preposition :
My friend came all the way from Kathmandu to congratulate me .... my success :
(A) for (B) at
(C) over (D) on

64. The gardens of Srinagar are more beautiful than .... :
(A) this of Mysore
(B) that in Mysore
(C) these of Mysore
(D) those of Mysore

65. I am looking forward to ....
(A) see my friend
(B) seeing my friend
(C) have seen my friends
(D) having been seen my friend

66. Which sentence has an intransitive verb :
(A) He ran a long distance
(B) The boy kicks the football
(C) I feel a severe pain in may head
(D) The driver stopped the train

67. Which one is the correct passive voice of sentence—Help the poor.
(A) Let the poor be helped
(B) The poor should he helped
(C) Poors should be helped
(D) Let the poors be helped

68. Change the narration — You say, 'I cut the finger',
(A) You say that you cut the finger
(B) You say that I cut the finger
(C) You say that he cut the finger
(D) You say that the finger was cut

69. Which one is the correct indirect narration of the sentence — He Said, "Two and three is five"?
(A) He said that two and three are five
(B) He said that two and three is five
(C) He said that two and three was five
(D) He said that two and three were five

70. Which sentence is correct ?
(A) We travelled by auto
(B) We travelled by the auto
(C) We travelled by a auto
(D) We travelled by an auto

71. Which sentence is incorrect ?
(A) They are women teachers
(B) We are Lady-doctors
(C) You all are house-maids
(D) We are woman-doctors

72. Which sentence is grammatically correct ?
(A) I and you have done it
(B) He and you went there
(C) I and he liked it
(D) You, Tom and I ate sweets

73. Which sentence is correct ?
(A) Tom is elder than his friend
(B) My older brother is respected by all
(C) My brother is elder than me
(D) Ravi is older than his friend

74. Find the correct sentence :
(A) Many a man wants to be rich overnight
(B) Many a men want to be rich overnight
(C) Many a men wanted to rich overnight.
(D) None

75. Which sentence is correct ?
(A) I am born in India
(B) I am born at India

(C) I was born in India
(D) I was born at India

76. Which word is correctly spelt ?
(A) Duely (B) Duly
(C) Duley (D) Dully

77. The antonym of 'Familiar' is :
(A) Known (B) Infamiliar
(C) Unfamiliar (D) Unknown

78. The antonym of Advance is :
(A) Follow (B) Submit
(C) Disperse (D) Retreat

79. What is the meaning of Galling ?
(A) Imitation (B) Absurd
(C) Odd (D) Irritable

80. What is the meaning of propensity :
(A) Disposition (B) Prosperity
(C) Nearness (D) Distant

81. Keats was a victim of <u>rap on the knuckles</u>. The underlined idiom denotes :
(A) Appreciation
(B) Support
(C) Severe criticism
(D) Loud approval

82. G. B. Shaw was having the <u>gift of the gab</u>. What does the underlined phrase means ?
(A) Talent for speaking
(B) Outspoken
(C) Over eater
(D) Cynical

83. What do you mean by 'a square meal' ?
(A) A full meal
(B) Unpleasant meal
(C) Alms
(D) None

84. Find the figure of speech in — To err is human to forgive divine :
(A) Simile (B) Metaphor
(C) Apostrophe (D) Antithesis

85. Milton ! thou shouldst be living at this hour. Find the figure of speech.
(A) Oxymoron (B) Apostrophe
(C) Hyperbole (D) Simile

86. What figure of speech is in – The man is no fool ?
(A) Litotes (B) Tautology
(C) Euphemism (D) Epigram

87. "An ambassador is a gentleman who lies abroad for good of his country". Pun is on the word :
(A) Ambassador (B) Gentleman
(C) Lies (D) Good

88. The word 'Picaresque' has been derived from :
(A) Latin word Picaro
(B) Greek word Picaro
(C) Italian word Picaro
(D) Spanish word Picaro

89. What does the term 'Curtain Kaiser' indicates in drama :
(A) One who raises curtains
(B) A modern drama of serious nature
(C) Super natural agency in drama which reveals some tooth
(D) A short play before the main play

90. A 'Ballad Stanza' is of :
(A) Two lines (B) Three lines
(C) Four lines (D) Five lines

91. What problem has been dealt with in Dickens 'The Bleak House' ?
(A) Persecution of poor indebtors
(B) Abuse of charity school
(C) Working condition in work houses
(D) Law's delays

92. Lady Deadlock, a character, occurs in Dicken's:
(A) Bleak House
(B) A Tale of Two Cities
(C) Hard Times
(D) Pickwick papers

93. Which one is Dickens's complete work :
(A) Pickwick Papers
(B) Edwin drood
(C) Dombey and sons
(D) Bleak House

94. When was 'Literature and Dogma' published?
(A) 1869 (B) 1849
(C) 1885 (D) 1873

95. Who is reffered as 'Europe's sagest head'' and 'Physician of the iron age'– by Arnold ?
(A) Wordsworth
(B) Byron
(C) Goethe
(D) Shakespeare

96. Arnold took the theme of his 'The Scholar Gipsy' from Joseph Glanville's book entitled :
(A) The Scholar Gipsy
(B) TheVagabond
(C) The First Mesmerist
(D) None

97. The rhyming scheme of 'In Memoriam' is :
(A) ABAB
(B) AABB
(C) ABC ABC
(D) ABBA

98. Which poem of Tennyson was his favourite ?
(A) Maud
(B) The Princess
(C) In Memorium
(D) Ulysses

99. "To strive to seak, to find, and not to yeild is the last line of a poem by Tennyson, which one is it ?
(A) Crossing the Bar
(B) The Princess
(C) The Lady of Shalot
(D) Ulysses

100. Which one was Hardy's first serial novel ?
(A) A Pair of Blue Eyes
(B) The Trumpet Major
(C) The Woodlander
(D) Far from the Madding Crowd

ANSWERS WITH EXPLANATION

1. (C) Most of Hardy's novels are tragedies, and the Jude the Obscure is most sombre all. The story in Hardy's own words is "of a deadly war waged with old apostolic desperation between flesh and spirit."

2. (D) Hardy is more known for his novels than for his poetry, but surprisingly he began and ended his career with the latter.

3. (D) **4.** (C)

5. (A) 'The Old Man and the Sea' (1952) is a tale of a ritual encounter between the old cuban fisherman, Santiago and the forces of erosion itself.

6. (D) Wordsworth is too preoccupied with his own self to take an objective view of things. Keats rightly called him, 'The egotistical sublime'.

7. (B) 'The Prelude' is an autobiographical poem in 14 books written between 1797 and 1805 but published only in 1850 after his death.

8. (D) All of them are poetic plays. He wrote some seven poetic plays which are : (1) Sweeney Agonists, (2) The Rock, (3) Murder in the Cathedral, (4) The Family Reunion, (5) The Cocktail Party, (6) The Confidential Clerk, (7) The Elder Statesmen. Of all of them 'Murder in the Cathedral' is outstanding.

9. (C) The epigraph of the poem 'Prufrock' is taken from Dante's Inferno, Canto XXVII lines 61-66.

10. (C) At seven years, Charles was sent to the famous "Blue coat" charity school of Christs Hospital.

11. (B) Hugh Walker calls Lamb the essayist 'Par excellence' and another critic, the prince of essayists".

12. (B) Arnold was Shelley's worst critic. He regarded Shelley as master of 'melopoeia' that is the use of musical words whose sound suggests the sense.

13. (D) Shelley went to Italy in 1818. After wandering here and there he finally settled in Pisa. Here he wrote his best poetry.

14. (C) While a student at Oxford Shelley read a scrap of Humes Philosophy and immediately published a pamphlet called — "The Necessity of Atheism".

15. (A) The Sun Also Rises (1926) was his first major novel 'that sets the hags for a generation and thus called the Bible of Lost Generation.

16. (C)

17. (A) A Masque of Mercy (1947) by Robert Frost based on the biblical story of Jonah, the prophet. It's a drama and the setting is a small book store in Newyork.

18. (D) Robert Frost got Pulitzer Prize for four of his works :

(i) In 1924 for 'New Hampshire' – 1923
(ii) In 1931 for 'Collected poems' – 1930
(iii) In 1937 for 'A Further Range' – 1936
(iv) In 1943 for 'A Witness Tree' – 1942

19. (B) Das earned Sahitya Akademi Award in 1985 whereas Kerala Sahitya Akademi Award in 1969 for 'Cold' a collection of short stories.

20. (A) The Invitation is in dialogue form between Das and the sea.

21. (D)

22. (C) Nissim Ezekiel was born in Bombay in 1924 in a Jewish family.

23. (C) One of the masterpices of Narayan is 'The Dark Room' which is sometimes compared to Henric Ibsen play — 'A Doll's House'.

24. (B) In this novel Narayan given us the story of rise and fall of Margaya, who is symbolic of materialistic philosophy.

25. (D) Mulk Raj Anand had published 5 books before 1935 :

(i) Persian Painting
(ii) Curries and other Indian dishes.
(iii) The Hindu view of Art
(iv) The Golden Breath
(v) The Lost Child and Other Stories

26. (A) Mulk Raj Anand was born in 1905 in Peshawar now in Pakistan.

27. (C) Lamb composed with his sister, some 'Tales From Shakespeare'. Followed up in the some kind after words the 'Adventure of Ulysses'.

28. (C) Keats health now began to fail, however, he had time to publish in 1820, a third volume, containing — Lamia. Hyperion and others.

29. (D) These words are inscribe on the epitaph of Keats.

30. (C) This is the concluding line of Keats ode—'To a Nightingale' was it a vision, or a walking dream ? Fled is that music: do I wake or sleep ?

31. (B) This is the opening line of a sonnet by Wordsworth entitled 'London 1802' or To Milton'.

32. (A)

33. (D) Though Paul's mother suffers from cancer but was killed by Paul himself by overdose of morphine because his mother's pain was intolerable for him.

34. (D) Eliot seems to have understood the limitations of the reader. That is why to a poem (The Waste Land) of 430 lines he attached as many as eleven pages of notes.

35. (C) The Reivers 'was Faulkner's last novel which he began in 1940 and finished in 1962.

36. (A) Absalom Absalom (1936) is also known as 'A Boy's Ambition'. It is set in early 19th century.

37. (A) **38.** (D)
39. (C) **40.** (B)
41. (C) **42.** (D)
43. (A) **44.** (D)
45. (D) **46.** (C)

47. (C) Greene in 1592 pointed out to his fellows that there is an upstart crove beautified without feathers that his — A Tiger's

Heart Wrapped in a Player's Hide — supposes he is as well able to bombast out a blank verse as the best of you.

48. (B) Shakespeare calls his Venus and Adonis (1503) 'the first heir of my inventions'. It was dedicated' to Earl of Southampton.

49. (D) These lines are spoken up by Jaques in 'As You Like It' written by Shakespeare.

50. (A) Stratford is a charming little village in beautiful Warwickshire"

51. (C) Wages

52. (D) The sentence is correct as subjects connected by 'Neither/Nor'. The verb always agrees to the second subject.

53. (B 'Everyone' is a singular third person pronoun, so it will take third person singular possession.

54. (B) **55.** (A)

56. (D) **57.** (C)

58. (C) **59.** (D)

60. (A)

61. (D) The verb in an imaginative sentence always takes past plural verb (were)

62. (B) 'With a view to' is a phrase and it will take a gerund (ing).

63. (D) Congratulate always takes the preposition on

64. (D) 'Those of Mysore' means the gardens of Mysore. So, it will take a plural pronoun.

65. (B) 'Looking forward to' is a phrase, and it will take gerund (ing)

66. (A) An intransitive verb is a verb that denotes an action which does not pass over to an object or which expresses a 'state' or 'being'.

67. (B) If the imperative sentence suggest all advice then the passive is not begin by 'Let' but after the subject 'Should' + be + vs from is used.

68. (A) If the subject of the reporting clause is 'You' and that of reported speech is 'I' then in indirect speech I is changed to 'You'.

69. (B) As the reported speech is a universal truth so the tense of the reported speech will not change.

70. (A) We use 'by + noun' when we talk about means of transport, we do not use 'the' or 'a' or' an'.

71. (D) The plural of a compound noun of two nouns is made by making plural of second noun boyfriend as boy-friends ; but, if the first noun of the compound noun is 'Man' or 'Woman' than both nouns are changed into plural eg- man servent as men-servent.

72. (D) Pronoun are always used in the form of 231, i.e. second person, third person and then first person.

73. (D) 'Elder' is used for the member of the same family and is not followed by 'than', whereas 'Older' is used for objects and people and is followed by 'than'.

74. (A) Both 'Subject' and 'Verb' after 'many a' should be singular.

75. (C) 'Was born' is idiomatic so it is used as such without any modification.

76. (B) **77.** (C)

78. (D) **79.** (D)

80. (A) **81.** (C)

82. (A) Gift of gab means talent of speaking.

83. (A) A square meal is a full meal or just sufficient.

84. (D) In antithesis a striking opposition or contrast of words or sentiments is made in the same sentence.

85. (B) "An apostrophe is a direct address to the dead, to the absent or to a personified object or idea."

86. (A) In Litotes, an affirmative is conveyed by negation of the opposite.

87. (C) When we use the same word in two or more senses in order to laugh, we employ the figure of speech called pun.

88. (C) The word 'Picaresque has been derived from the Spanish word 'picaro' which means a 'rogue' and knave'.

89. (D) A curtain raiser is a short dramatic piece performed before the main play in evening.

90. (C) A ballad stanza is a quatrain (four lines) usually rhyming a - b - a - b.

91. (D) Most of Dickens novels belongs decidedly to the class of problem novels. Thus 'The Bleak House attacks the law's delays.

92. (A) Dickens had tenderly or powerfully drawn figure, like lady deadlock of 'Bleak House', and Sydney carton of 'A Tale of Two Cities' which rise to the dignity of true characters.'

93. (B) Dickens died in 1870, over his unfinished 'Edwin Drood', and was buried in Westminister abbey.

94. (D) 'Literature and Dogma' was published in 1873, is in general, a plea for liberty in religion.

95. (C) In 'Memorial Verses' Arnold put his tribute as such-when Goethe's death was told, we said ; Sunk, then, is Europe's sagest head. Physician of the iron age, Goethe has done his pilgrimage.

96. (D) 'The Scholar Gipsy, is based on the legend told by Glanville in his book— The Vanity of Dogmatizing.

97. (D) 'In Memoriam' is written in quatrains using octosyllabic lines with the rhyme ABBA.

98. (A) Maud (1855) is a story of a lover who passes from morbidness to ecstasy, then to anger and murder, followed by insanity and recovery. This was Tennyson's favourite.

99. (D)

100. (A) 'A Pair of Blue Eyes' was the first novel of Hardy to appear in a serial form before published as a book.

❑❑❑

PRACTICE SET–3

1. In which book of Charles Dickens' we find the character called 'Miss Pross' ?
   (A) Oliver Twist
   (B) Great Expectations
   (C) A Tale of Two Cities
   (D) Little Dorrit
2. "Criticism must always profess an end in view,....Its function is to promote the understanding and enjoyment of literature". Who said this ?
   (A) Mathew Arnold
   (B) Dr. Johnson
   (C) T. S. Eliot
   (D) John Keats
3. "I deal with all periods, but I never study any period but the present". Who said this ?
   (A) Joseph Conrad
   (B) H. G. Wells
   (C) George Bernard Shaw
   (D) Mathew Arnold
4. In which year did Yeats receive his Nobel Prize ?
   (A) 1920 (B) 1924
   (C) 1923 (D) 1929
5. Walt Whitman's poem 'O Captain, my Captain' is a sad poem mourning the death of a great man.
   Who was he ?
   (A) Washington Irving
   (B) Abraham Lincoln
   (C) Ralph Waldo Emerson
   (D) Thomas Alva Edison
6. Ernest Hemingway visited Spain during the Civil War and utilised his experiences in the book :
   (A) For Whom the Bell Tolls
   (B) In Our Time
   (C) A Moveable Feast
   (D) The Fifth Column
7. In the year 1872, a week or two weeks before Thomas Hardy' thirty second birthday, one of his books was published which confirmed Hardy in his profession as a writer. Which book was it ?
   (A) Desperate Remedies
   (B) Under the Green Wood Tree
   (C) The Trumpet Major
   (D) Jude the Obscure
8. "I am asked to write my reminiscences of a famous novelist......" About whom does the author Somerest Maugham say this in context of his novel 'Cakes and Ales':
   (A) Donal Praeter
   (B) Thomas Hardy
   (C) W. M. Thackeray
   (D) Charles Dickens
9. Strange friend, past, present and to be loved deeplier understood.
   (A) Formation of comparative adverbs
   (B) The use of archaic words
   (C) Ommission of a part of speech
   (D) The use of the imperative
10. A Paronym is :
   (A) The use of a word in a sence that does not properly belong to it.
   (B) A clause or phrase wedged into a sentence in passing
   (C) A word that is spelt and pronounced in the same way as another but means different context.

(D) A word not spelt as another but pronounced exactly as the other.

11. R. K. Narayan wrote many wonderfull novels which of these is not written by him ?
(A) Coolie
(B) The Guide
(C) Malagudi Days
(D) The English Teacher

12. I am every
women who seeks love...........
These lines are from the poem written by :
(A) Amita Desai (B) Sarojini Naidu
(C) Kamala Das (D) Toru Dutt

13. Which of the poem expresses Frost's statement that 'a poem begins in delight and ends in wisdom' ?
(A) An Old Man's Winter Night
(B) Home Burial
(C) Stopping by Woods on a Snowy Evening
(D) The Hill Wife

14. Which novel of D. H. Lawrence is said to be strikingly autobiographical ?
(A) Rainbow
(B) Women in Love
(C) Lady Chatterley's Lover
(D) Sons and Lovers

15. " I heard a woman call you the winged victory in Sluggish Venice
You turn your head towards your tail, and smile"
What is the title of the poem by D. H. Lawrence?
(A) Mosquito (B) Miss Gee
(C) The Bees (D) The Tiger

16. The author of 'A Reed Shaken by the Wind' is :
(A) W. B. Yeats (B) Thomas May
(C) Walt Whitman (D) G. Maxwell

17. Which one of these is not a poem by Walt Whitman ?
(A) When Lilacs last in Dooryard Bloom'd
(B) Distant Likeness
(C) Song of Myself
(D) Leaves of Grass

18. Catherine Barkley is a character from Ernest Hemingway's famous novel. Which one is it ?
(A) Old Man and the Sea
(B) For Whom the Bell tolls
(C) Farewell to Arms
(D) In Our Time

19. Which of the following Eliots' characters is different from the rest ?
(A) Macavity
(B) J. Alfred Prufock
(C) Sweeney
(D) Bleistein

20. Which of the following plays by G. B. Shaw has been made into a film staring Audrey Hepburn :
(A) Saint Joan (B) Pygmalion
(C) Candida (D) Major Barbura

21. Fill in the blank with the most appropriate preposition:
"Please don't stop. Go...........with your work".
(A) Out (B) In
(C) On (D) Off

22. Which one is the correct sentence ?
(A) Why did they withdraw from the match ?
(B) Why did they withdrew from the match ?
(C) Why do they withdrew from the match ?
(D) Why does they withdraw from the match ?

23. What does Mulk Raj Anand satirize in Coolie ?
(A) Indian imitating English Society and its consequences
(B) Nationalism
(C) Industrialization
(D) Exploitation of the poor people

24. Which one of these is not a novel written by Mulk Raj Anand?
(A) Coolie
(B) Head and Dust
(C) Across the Black Waters
(D) The Untouchable

25. "His poetry comes out of his reactions to his environment, and he juxtaposes old and new by selling peasant superstition against modern scepticism.'' This is common against modern scepticism." This is a comment on Ezekiel and one of this particular poem. Which one is it ?

(A) Mamaji

(B) The Untouchable

(C) The Hill of Devi

(D) Night of the Scorpiot

26. In which of his poem did Nissim Ezekiel talk about love and sex :

(A) Sixty Poems

(B) The Exact name

(C) Hymns in Darkness

(D) Passion Poems

27. Hamlet was written by Shakespeare, The Hamlet was written by :

(A) Melville (B) Galsworthy

(C) Pope (D) Faulkner

28. Faulkner's 'Sound and the Fury' was published in :

(A) 1927 (B) 1929

(C) 1931 (D) 1933

29. 1914—First World War begining, and Robert Frost published his work. Which one is it ?

(A) North of Boston

(B) Three Soldiers

(C) Age of Innocence

(D) This Side of Paradise

30. R. K. Narayan wrote :

(A) 20 novels (B) 12 novels

(C) 11 novels (D) 19 novels

31. What do you mean by "differentiate" ?

(A) Recognize or show the difference between two things

(B) See or understand the difference between two things.

(C) Distinctive or characteristic aspect of something.

(D) Fact or idea that suggests a possible answer to a problem.

32. Which one of the following sentences is correct ?

(A) What a boring task this is :

(B) What a boring task this is ?

(C) What a bornig task this is.

(D) What a bornig task this is !

33. Choose the correct name of the punctuation mark of the sentence given below in brackets.

"God made the country [:] men the town :

(A) Colon (B) Semi-colon

(C) Comma (D) Inverted comma

34. Replace the clause underlined in the sentence below with a suitable phrase begining with 'the words in bracket given below :

"<u>When prabha lost her sight</u> She had to stop attending school".

(A) [At the loss]

(B) [On losing]

(C) [When the loss]

(D) [The loss]

35. Choose the correct idiom for the explanation given :

"Please keep quiet"

(A) Keep in mind

(B) Be over with

(C) Catch the bull by the tail

(D) Hold your tongue

36. Choose the correct explanation of the idiom :

"Do not always pick holes"

(A) Dig holes (B) Pick up a quarrel

(C) Criticize (D) Keep quiet

37. Choose the correct spelling :

(A) arguement (B) argument

(C) argeument (D). arggument

38. "There are.........in the apple."

Given below are jumbled words. Arrange the letter in proper order and fill in the blank.

(A) morsw (B) storf

(C) angit (D) epitor

39. "How are you getting along with your students ?"

getting along can be replaced by :

(A) recovering (B) behaving
(C) progressing (D) continuing

40. "I ran into an old relative yesterday."
(A) met by chance (B) collided
(C) moved (D) hit and ran

41. Find out the correct indirect narration of the following direct speech :
He shouted, "Let me go."
(A) He shouted that let him go
(B) He shouted to them to let him go
(C) He shouted to go
(D) None of the above

42. Which of the following sentence is in Future Imperfect Tense ?
(A) He has stolen my pen
(B) She came late today
(C) I shall kill him
(D) Mrs. Das will soon be visiting us

43. Which of the following sentences has a Transitive verb ?
(A) He knows English very well
(B) The river is flowing fast
(C) She dances very beautifully
(D) My sister is going to her training centre

44. Find out the correct direct speech of the following indirect narration :
He enquired whether his name was not Ashok.
(A) He said to him," Is your name Ashok"
(B) He said to him," Is your name Ashok."
(C) He said to him," Is not your name Ashok."
(D) None of the above

45. What will be the suitable prefix for the word 'decent' ?
(A) un (B) non
(C) not (D) in

46. Replace the underlined words with a phrasal verb.
Choose the correct one from the following :
"Did you <u>refuse</u> the offer."
(A) turn down (B) break down
(C) set off (D) put off

47. A Homonym is :
(A) Opposite words
(B) similar words in meaning and spelling
(C) similar in sound but different in meaning
(D) Different in sound, but similar in meaning

48. Which is a 'sound' word ?
(A) dreamlike (B) peered
(C) sparked (D) chuckle

49. "Fees <u>will not be received</u> after 3 p.m."
The underlined expression is :
(A) Passive sentence
(B) Model passive
(C) Phrasal verb
(D) Intransitive verb

50. Give the correct term for the statement given :
'Set of facts systematically arranged in rows and columns'.
(A) Training task (B) Sequence
(C) Table (D) Key

51. Who used the epithet 'gentle hearted Charles' for Charles Lamb ?
(A) Wordsworth (B) Keats
(C) Browning (D) Coleridge

52. The essay 'South Sea House' has been written by :
(A) Bacon (B) Lamb
(C) Stevenson (D) Addison

53. Who was the father of 'Eassay' ?
(A) Montague (B) Rousseau
(C) Wyatt (D) Dowden

54. For whom Keats used the term 'Egotistical Sublime' ?
(A) Coleridge (B) Shelley
(C) Byron (D) Wordsworth

55. Who was 'Machiavelli' ?
(A) A Florentine Stateman
(B) An American Statesman
(C) An Italian Statesman
(D) A French Statesman.

56. "Under the Greenwood Tree" is a novel by :
(A) Thomas Hardy (B) Charles Dickens
(C) Thackeray (D) George Eliot

57. Who has regarded as a representative victorian novelist ?
(A) Charles Dickens
(B) Charles Reade
(C) Charles Kinsley
(D) Thackeray

58. Who is the author of the poem 'Shakespeare' ?
(A) Tennyson
(B) Browing
(C) Matthew Arnold
(D) Wordsworth

59. "Sir Bedivere" figures in the poem by :
(A) Morte D' Arthur
(B) The Princess
(C) Locksley Hall
(D) Jean. Idle Jean

60. In which poem does the following lines occur ?
"They flash upon that inward eye
Which is the bliss of solitude"
(A) The Education of Nature
(B) Daffodils
(C) The World is Too Much with Us
(D) Tintern Abbey

61. Which play of Shakespeare opens with the line
"If music be the food of loves, play on"?
(A) The Tempest
(B) Twelfth Night
(C) Macbeth
(D) Romeo and Julliet

62. From which poem of Robert Frost are the following lines taken ?
"They click upon themselves
As the breeze rises, and turn many coloured.....,"
(A) Birches
(B) After Apple Picking
(C) Mending Wall
(D) The Road Not Taken

63. From which poem of Whitman are the following lines taken ?
O powerful western fallen star!
O Shades of night-o moody, tearful night!
(A) O Captain ! my Captain
(B) When Lilacs Last in the Dooryard Bloomed
(C) Crossing Brooklyn Ferry
(D) None of these

64. The character 'Robert Jordan' figure in
(A) For Whom the Bell Tolls
(B) The Old Man and the Sea
(C) In Our Times
(D) A Farewell to Arms

65. Ernest Hemingway was awarded the Nobel prize for the novel :
(A) For whom the Bell Tolls
(B) The Old Man and the Sea
(C) A Farewell to Arms
(D) The Sun also Rise

66. To some of his contemporaries, he appear as a member of "the Cockney school of poerty". Who is 'he' ?
(A) Shelley (B) Keats
(C) Byron (D) Southey

67. Shelley's Adonais' is a threnody bewailing the death of :
(A) Harriet Shelley (B) John Keats
(C) Robert Burns (D) William Wordsworth

68. Prometheus Unbound is a :
(A) Poetic Drama (B) Lyrical Drama
(C) Verse Play (D) Dramatic Satire

69. Which of these was written by Shelley ?
(A) The Four Ages of Poetry
(B) Defence of Poesy
(C) Defence of Poetry
(D) Poetry and Anarchy

70. Which of these poem by Shelley is written in Blank Verse ?
(A) The Witch of Atlas
(B) Hellas
(C) The Triumph of Life
(D) The Cenci

71. It is said that Shakespeare based his Julius Caesar on certain incidents of his era. Which of these, is it said to be ?
(A) The Execution of Sir Walter Raleigh
(B) The Formation of trade relation with the East
(C) The rebellion of the Duke of Essex
(D) The supremacy of Spain on land and sea

72. The early plays of Shakespeare were written between :
(A) 1597-1625 (B) 1598-1614
(C) 1590-1595 (D) 1600-1607

73. Which of Shakespeare's tragedies is called the 'tragedy of reflection' ?
(A) King Lear (B) Hamlet
(C) Macbeth (D) Othello

74. In which play of Shakespeare do we find these lines."There needs no ghost, my Lord, come from the grave, to tell in this."
(A) King Lear (B) Macbeth
(C) Hamlet (D) Henry IV

75. Wordsworth's Prelude was completed in :
(A) 1800 (B) 1805
(C) 1822 (D) 1825

76. Apart from Tales of Shakespeare, Lamb's work for children only includes :
(A) Specimen of English Dramatic Poets who lived about the time of Shakespeare
(B) Dream Children
(C) Child Harold
(D) The Adventure of Ulysses

77. Lamb's "Essays of Elia" were written in (1820-23) when were the "Last Essays of Elia" written?
(A) 1827 (B) 1829
(C) 1833 (D) 1835

78. "Mrs Battle's opinions on Whist" is an essay that has delighted generation of readers. We find it in:
(A) Essays of Elia by Charles Lamb
(B) Confression by De Quincey
(C) Imaginary Conversation by W. S. Landor
(D) Essays by Hazlitt

79. Which romantic novel is by Charles Lamb ?
(A) Kloster Lein (B) Rosamund Gray
(C) Absentee (D) Cranford

80. Endymion by Keats is the story of a young Shepherd, loved by the Moon Goddess, Keats took the story from :
(A) Greek Mythology
(B) Highland Love
(C) Kentish Tales
(D) Roman Myths

81. Which is John Keats first Poem ?
(A) Meg Merrilies
(B) On looking at Chapman's Homer
(C) Endymion
(D) When I have Fears

82. F. Scott Fitzgerald was a great admirer of the poetry of John Keats so that he named one of his novels with a line from one of the poems of Keats. Which poem was it ?
(A) Ode to a Nightingale
(B) Ode on a Grecian Un
(C) Ode to Autumn
(D) Ode to Psyche

83. Which of these is not a work by John Keats ?
(A) Ode of Autumn
(B) To Night
(C) Isabella
(D) The Pot of Basil

84. Charles Dickens' marriage was not very successful.
When Dickens was middle aged, his name was linked with an actress, a girl twenty-five year younger than him. What was her name ?
(A) Mary Hogarth
(B) Maria Beadnell
(C) Georgeine Hogarth
(D) Ellen Ternan

85. Which of his own books did Charles Dickens consider to be his best work ?
(A) David Copperfield
(B) Pickwick Papers

(C) Oliver Twist
(D) Nicholas Nickelby

86. When did the last poem of the Idyllus appear ?
(A) 1885 (B) 1844
(C) 1853 (D) 1890

87. Queen Victoria found great solace in her grief from one of Tennyson's poem, what is the title of the poem ?
(A) In Memoriam
(B) Crossing the Bar
(C) The Brook
(D) The Passing of Arthur

88. What is known today as the Idylls of the King began in 1842 with the poem 'Morte D Arthur'. Which is the last poem of the Idylls ?
(A) Eaid
(B) Balin
(C) Vivien
(D) Elaine

89. The question of women's rights and her sphere had been agitating the minds of men for a long time. Tennyson expressed his views on it in :
(A) The Princess
(B) Maud
(C) Tears, Idle Tears
(D) Sweet and Low

90. 'Emotions recollected in Tranquility,' the profound philosophy of Wordsworth's was rejected by :
(A) William Hazlitt
(B) T. S. Eliot
(C) Ezra Pound
(D) Roland Barthes

91. Lyrical Ballads appeared with :
(A) Six poems by Coleridge and fifteen by Wordsworth
(B) Ten poems by Coleridge and ten by Wordsworth
(C) Four poems by Coleridge and fifteen by Wordsworth
(D) Four poems by Coleridge and nineteen by Wordsworth

92. Which of these travel poems belong to William Wordsworth ?
(A) Descriptive Sketches
(B) Sketches of the Natural civil and political state of Switzerland
(C) Sketches of Nature
(D) A vivid sketch and picture of our time

93. "He resembles the animal that brows on thistles."
The above is an example of :
(A) Tautology
(B) Periphrases
(C) Onomato pacia
(D) Litotes

94. "An allegory is a series of metaphors or Symbols continued throughout an entire story so as to represent or describe one series of facts by another series that is analogous to it in its main features". —Nesfield.
Following this, which of the books mentioned below is an allegory ?
(A) Pilgrim's Progress
(B) The Crucifixion of Christ
(C) Gulliver's Travels
(D) Robinson Crusoe

95. Which of these is not a poem by Matthew Arnold ?
(A) The Foresaken Merman
(B) Dover Beach
(C) Tristram and Iseult
(D) The King's Tragedy

96. Thomas Hardy's novel 'Under the Green Wood Tree' is also known by another name. Which of the four below is it ?
(A) The Woodlander
(B) The Mellstock Quire
(C) The Dynasts
(D) Life Little Ironies

97. Which book of Hardy is not pessimistic ?
(A) Jude the Obscure
(B) The Return of the Native
(C) A Pair of Blue Eyes
(D) Tess of the Durbrvills

98. Matthew Arnold's "Rostam and Sohrab" is taken from a story from :
(A) Arabian Nights
(B) Akbarnama
(C) Shahnama
(D) Rubaiyat of Omar Khayyam

99. A well Known English writer wrote for the Morning Chronode under the Pseudonym of 'Boz'. Who was he ?
(A) Joyce Cary
(B) Charles Dickens
(C) Henry James
(D) Thomas Gray

100. The last book that Dickens wrote was :
(A) The Uncommercial Traveller
(B) Bleak House
(C) Great Expectations
(D) A Christmas Carol

ANSWERS WITH EXPLANATION

1. (A) **2.** (C)

3. (C) In explaining why she drew such topsy-turvy pictures of historic characters he said, "I deal with all periods, but I never study any period........ ."

4. (C) Yeats was elected a senator of the Irish free state in 1922. He was awarded the Noble Prize for literature in 1923.

5. (B) "O Captain ! My Captain !' is an elegy on the death of the famous American President, Abraham Lincoln.

6. (A) 'For whom Ten Bell Tolls' (1940) is Hemingway's longest novel and is based on spanish civil war. Robert Jordan is the hero.

7. (B) 'Under the Greenwood Tree : A Rural painting of the Dutch School' was published in 1872.

8. (B) **9.** (C)

10. (D) Paronyms are the words having same pronunciation but different spelling and meaning as: Berth means Seat and Birth means to come to life.

11. (A) 'Coolie' is a novel by Mulk Raj Anand Published in 1936.

12. (C) **13.** (C)

14. (D) The Story of the novel 'Sons and Lovers' is strongly autobiographical, and the Paul Morel is a representation of Lawrence himself.

15. (A)

16. (A) Of his (W. B. Yeats) lyrics and ballads, which have very uneven merit, one can only say to a reader, Dip into his first little volume, The wind among the Reeds (1899).

17. (C)

18. (C) Hemingway fell in love with a nurse when he was hospitalised in red cross Hospital. She has been described by him as British Brett Asheley in 'The sun Also Rises' and as Scottish catherine Barkley in 'Farewell to Arms' (1929).

19. (B) **20.** (D)

21. (C)

22. (A) The sentence is in simple past tense which follows the order as why/where/when + did + subject + first form of verb.

23. (C)

24. (B) Coolie (1936); Across The Black Waters (1940) and Untouchable (1935) were written by Mulk Raj Anand.

25. (C)

26. (A) 'Sixty Poems' (1953) and 'The Third' (1959) are his second and third volume of poetry which deals mainly with sex. So Herman Hesse called him 'a poet of the body'.

27. (D) The Hamlet (1940) by William Faulkner shows the rise to power of the depraved snopes family, espcially Flem Snopes.
28. (B) 'The sound and The Fusy' (1929) is a psychological novel. It contains the story of decline of Compson family, with a strange autobiographical element.
29. (A) 'North of Boston' was first published in London in 1914 and then in U. S. A. It is a 'book of people'.
30. (B) 31. (A)
32. (D) Exclamatory sentences express sudden feeling or strong emotion. In such sentence the subject preceed the verb. It ends with a sign of exclamation.
33. (B) 34. (A)
35. (D) Keep quiet means to be silent that is to hold tongue.
36. (C) Pick up holes means to find out faults of that is to criticize.
37. (B)
38. (A) The ordered word from the jumble word 'morsw' is worms.
39. (C) Get along means to be friendly. Third option is most appropriate.
40. (B) Run into means collided as in the sentence- The bus got of control and ran into a wall.
41. (B) As there is no object in the given sentence so while changing the narration an object is supplied.
42. (D)
43. (A) Transitive verb is one that can have an object and can be changed into passive. Here 'english' is object.
44. (C) 45. (D)
46. (A) Turn down means to refuse.
47. (C) Word is same as another but of different sence.
48. (D)
49. (B) Can , May, Must, Shall, Will, Should, Would, Could and Might are known as modal verbs, into passive we use : model verb + v^3 after subject .
50. (C) 51. (D)
52. (B)
53. (A) The word "Essay" means an attempt.
54. (D) S. T. Coleridge, P. B. Shelley, Byron and William Wordsworth belong to the Romantic Age.
55. (C)
56. (A) Under the Green Wood Tree, The Return of Nature, Far from the Madding Crowd etc.
57. (A) Charles Dickens, Charless Read, Charles Kingsley and Thackeray belong to the Victorian Age.
58. (C)
59. (A) Morte D' Arthur, The Princess, In Memoriam etc.
60. (B) Poem of William Wordsworth. The Education of Nature, The Prelude. The World is Too Much with Us.
61. (B) The Tempest (1610), Twelfth Night (1600-01), Macbeth (1606), Romeo and Juliet (1501).
62. (B) 63. (D)
64. (D)
65. (B) Works of Ernest Hemingway, For Whom Bell Tolls (1940) The Old Man and Sea (1952). A Farewell to Arms (1929), The Sun Also Rises (1926).
66. (B) Keats belonged to what was derisively called the cockney school of poetry, of which Leigh Hunt was chief.
67. (B) 'Adonas' is a wonderful threnody, or a song of grief, over the death of the poet Keats.
68. (B) 'Prometheus Unbound' (1818), a lyrical drama, is the best work of Shelley's revolutionary enthusiasm.

69. (C) 'Defence of Poetry' (1821) is a prose work by Shelley whereas 'The Defence of Poesy' is by Philip Sidney.

70. (A) 'Hellas' is a lyric drama; The Triumph of Life is in terza rima; The Cenci is in blank verse but it is a drama.

71. (C)

72. (C) Shakespeare's literay career has been divided into 4 periods. His first period date from his arrival in London in 1595.

73. (B) Hamlet is called the tragedy of reflection. Infact it is the tragic flow of Hamlet.

74. (C) These lines are spoken by Horatio to Hamlet in Act I Sc. V of Hamlet. [Text]

75. (B) "The Prelude' which records the impresion made upon Wordsworth's mind was completed in 1805, but published after his death.

76. (D) Lamb with his sister composed "Tales From Shakespeare' followed up in the same kind afterwards - 'The Adventure of Ulysses'.

77. (C) Lamb's third literary period includes criticism of life, which are gathered together in his 'Essays of Elia' 1823 and his 'Last Essays of Elia' which were published ten years later.

78. (A)

79. (B) Rosamund Gray' (1798) is Lamb's romance written in his first period of literary career.

80. (A) Keats set himself to task of reflecting in modern English the spirit of the old Greeks. The imperfect results of this attempt are seen in his next volume 'Endymion'.

81. (B) **82.** (B)

83. (B) 'To Night' is a poem by P. B. Shelley Composed in 1824.

84. (D) His relationship with Ellen Ternan his mistress, was as unhappy as was his married life.

85. (C) **86.** (A)

87. (A) Queen Victoria, too treasured 'In Memoriam', and once told Tennyson that next to the Bible his poem was to her the greatest source of comfort.

88. (B) Tennyson began the legends of 'Morte d'Arthur' and later added the stories of "Vivien". "Elaine", Guinevere", untill 'Balin', the last of the Idy"s appeared in 1885.

89. (A) 'The Princess', a Medley' (1847) is Tennyson's answer to the questions of women's sphere, which was then strongly agitating the public mind.

90. (B)

91. (D) 'The 23 Poems' the first edition of 'Lyrical Ballads' contained were the work of Wordsworth and Coleridge. Wordsworth's contribution being nineteen and Coleridge's four.

92. (A) Wordsworth published poem-Descriptive Sketches, An Evening Walk, 1793, and wrote a verse tragedy, the Borderess.

93. (B) Periphrases is round about speech or phrase.

94. (A) John Bunyan's 'Pilgrim's Progress' is an allegory first published in 1678.

95. (D) **96.** (B)

97. (C) A Pair of Blue Eyes (1875) is a pastoral romance and is not tragic.

98. (C) The poem and 'Rostam and Sohrab' is taken from the 'Shahnama' (Book of kings) of the Persian Poet Firdausi.

99. (B) The name of this first sketch was "Mr. Minns and His Cousin', and it appeared with other stories in Dickens' first book, 'Sketches by Boz'.

100. (A) 'A Christmas Carol' was produced between 1843-48. 'Bleak House' in 1852-53. 'The Uncommercial Traveller' and 'Great expectations' were produced in 1861 but 'Great Expectations' was produced later.

❑❑❑

PRACTICE SET–4

1. Which of the following novels of Hemingway deals with his actual disappointing experiences of love and war ?
   (A) A Farewell to Arms
   (B) To Have and Have Not
   (C) Across the River and into the Trees
   (D) The Sun Also Rises
2. "O God ! O God !
   How weary, state and unprofitable seems to me all the uses of this world."
   Which of Shakespeare's tragic heroes utters these words ?
   (A) Hamlet (B) Macbeth
   (C) Othello (D) King Lear
3. To follow knowledge like a sinking star beyond the utmost bound of human thought, who wrote these lines ?
   (A) P.B. Shelley
   (B) William Blake
   (C) Alfred Tennyson
   (D) Robert Browning
4. Which one of the following theatre companies was owned by Shakespeare where his masterpieces were first performed ?
   (A) Wooden O (B) Globe
   (C) Rose (D) Curtain
5. Who first imported sonnet to England ?
   (A) Sir Philip Sidney
   (B) Sir Thomas Wyatt
   (C) Shakespeare
   (D) Milton
6. The figure of speech used in the following sentence is :
   "All the perfumes of Arabia will not sweeten this little hand."
   (A) Antithesis (B) Oxymoron
   (C) Hyperbole (D) Synecdoche
7. The name of Macbeth's wife in the Shakespearen play is :
   (A) Cordelia (B) Calpurnia
   (C) Desdemona (D) None of these
8. Which of the following is a work of Ezekiel ?
   (A) A time to Change
   (B) Rough Passage
   (C) Summer
   (D) None of these
9. "Good fences make good neighbours" This line occurs in which poem of Frost ?
   (A) Birches
   (B) Mending Wall
   (C) Road Not Taken
   (D) Two Tramps in Mud Tune
10. Milton's Samson Agonistes is :
    (A) an elegy
    (B) anode
    (C) a classical epic
    (D) a classical tragedy
11. Essays of Elia is :
    (A) full of didactic sermonising
    (B) practically autobiographical fragments
    (C) remarkable for their terse and aphoristic style
    (D) satirical and critical
12. The Lake District in England is associated with :
    (A) William Blake
    (B) William Collins
    (C) William Shakespeare
    (D) William Wordsworth

13. The Waste Land was first published in the year:

(A) 1922 (B) 1932

(C) 1942 (D) 1912

14. Which of the following works is not associated with Matthew Arnold ?

(A) Culture and Environment

(B) Dover Beach

(C) Thyrsis

(D) Empedocles on Etna

15. The rhetorical device of 'anaphora' implies which of the following ?

(A) A certain metrical arrangement in fines

(B) Use of circumlocution in phraseology

(C) Juxtaposing the abstract with the concrete

(D) Repeating the first word or words of successive sentences or clauses

16. Which work was left incomplete because of Hemingway's sudden death ?

(A) Islands in the Stream

(B) A Movable Feast

(C) The Garden of Eden

(D) The Dangerous Summer

17. The 'iambic pentameter' implies which of the following?

(A) Five Syllables in the pattern unstressed-stressed

(B) Five syllables in the pattern stressed-unstressed

(C) The pattern stressed-unstressed repeated five times

(D) The pattern unstressed-stressed repeated five times

18. "The rest is silence" These are the last words of..........before his death in Shakespeare's play.

(A) Caesar (B) Macbeth

(C) Hamlet (D) Lear

19. How many times did Robert Frost win the prestigious Pulitzer Prize ?

(A) Once

(B) Twice

(C) Thrice

(D) Never

20. The Dance of Eunuchs has been written by :

(A) Sylvia Plath (B) Sarojini Naidu

(C) Kamala Das (D) Nissin Ezekiel

21. The romantic poetry is a revival of :

(A) Classicism (B) Romanticism

(C) Medievalism (D) Humanism

22. Who said, "The poet is a man speaking to men" ?

(A) T. S. Eliot

(B) S.T. Coleridge

(C) Dr. Samuel Johnson

(D) William Wordsworth

23. 'Munoo' is the central character of M. R. Anand's novel :

(A) Coolie

(B) Untouchable

(C) Two Leaves and a Bud

(D) The Village

24. Who has called Shelley a 'perfect singing God' ?

(A) A. C. Swinburne

(B) William Morris

(C) Mathew Arnold

(D) S.A. Brooke

25. In which year did Robert Frost sell his farm in New England and moved to England ?

(A) 1910 (B) 1911

(C) 1912 (D) 1913

26. What was the origin of the race of Nissin Ezeklel ?

(A) Bene Israel (B) Indian Christians

(C) Dravidian (D) Latin American

27. Santiago is the hero of Hemingway's novel:

(A) For Whom the Beil Talls

(B) The Old Man and the Sea

(C) A Farewell to Arms

(D) The Sun Also Rises

28. Who is the author of the Unvanquished ?

(A) F. Scott Fitzgerald

(B) O'Henry

(C) Henry Sinclair Lewis

(D) William Cuthbert Faulkner

29. Fredrick Henry, the hero of Hemingway's novel, A Farewell to Arms, is a driver in :
(A) Italian army
(B) British army
(C) American army
(D) German army

30. Point out the figure of speech in the following: "Life sorrows sit and weep".
(A) Personification
(B) Simile
(C) Pun
(D) Oxymoron

31. Nissim Ezeiel's poem, 'Background, Casually' reflects:
(A) his felling alienation
(B) his love for rural life
(C) his love for religion
(D) None of these

32. Which of the following novels of Dickens was left unfinished ?
(A) A Tale of Two Cities
(B) Bleak House
(C) The Mystery of Edwin Drood
(D) The Old Curiosity Shop

33. Who is 'Thyrsis' in the poem of the same name ?
(A) Percy Bysshe Shelley
(B) Arthur Hugh Clough
(C) Arthur Hallam
(D) Edward King

34. Who praised Shakespeare thus ?
"Others abide our question thou art free We ask and ask - Thou smilest and art still"
(A) Dr. Johnson (B) Mathew Arnold
(C) Coleridge (D) T.S. Eliot

35. Who wrote Sohrab and Rustum ?
(A) Wordsworth
(B) Swinburne
(C) Mathew Arnold
(D) Tennyson

36. To which character in Shakespeare's 'Hamlet' does the following description apply ? "the tedious wiseacre who meddles his way to his doom" :
(A) Claudius (B) Hamlet
(C) Polonius (D) Rosencrant

37. Point out the figure of speech in the following line
"The ploughman homeward plods his weary way."
(A) Metaphor
(B) Personification
(C) Transferred Epither
(D) Hyperbole

38. "The analogy was that of the catalyst. When the two gases, previously mentioned, are mixed in the presence of a filament of platinum, they form sulphurous acid. This acid contains no trace of platinum and the platinum itself is apparently unaffected; has remained inert, neutral and unchanged. The mind of the poet is the shred of platinum."
The above lines are an extract from T.S. Eliot's essay :
(A) Hamlet and his Problems
(B) The Perfect Critic
(C) The Imperfect Critic
(D) Tradition and Individual Talent

39. Ernest Hemingway's 'Men at War' is :
(A) a novel
(B) a collection of short stories
(C) an essay
(D) an autobiography

40. Who has written the essay, The Old Benchers of the Inner Temple' ?
(A) Hazlit
(B) Bacon
(C) Charles Lamb
(D) Mathew Arnold

41. Mathew Arnold's Rughby Chapel commemorates:
(A) the death of his father
(B) the death of his friend
(C) the death of a girl
(D) the death of his relative

42. The term 'essay' is the derivative of the French root 'essai', which means :

(A) to compose (B) to go on a walk

(C) to try (D) to express

43. Which of the following is the first poem of Eliot's first published volume of verse ?

(A) The Waste Land

(B) The Hollow Men

(C) The Love Song of J. Alfred Prufrock

(D) Gerontion

44. In which famous poem does Walt Whitman make a reference to Suez Canal and wire line across the Atlantic ?

(A) O Captain, My Captain !

(B) Passage to India

(C) Earth My Likeness

(D) Prayers of Columbus

45. "No nightingale did ever chaunt More welcome notes to weary bands of travellers in some shady haunt Among Arabian sands" Where from the above quoted lines of Wordsworth?

(A) Solitary Reaper

(B) Ode to a Nightingale

(C) To the Cuckoo

(D) To a Skylark

46. 'Keats' poetry is "abundantly and enchantingly sensous". Who has made this comment about the poetry of Keats ?

(A) Mathew Arnold

(B) H. W. Garrod

(C) Middleton Murry

(D) Oliver Elton

47. In which play of Shakespeare do the characters 'Voltemand' and 'Cornelius' appear ?

(A) The Merchant of Venice

(B) Hamlet

(C) Much Ado About Nothing

(D) Macbeth

48. What can be the best explanation for the character of John Falstaff in Shakespeare's Henry IV ?

(A) Simple (B) Complex

(C) Novics (D) Caricature

49. Who is the most furious character in Fagin's Den in Dickens' Oliver Twist ?

(A) Dodger (B) Chitting

(C) Bates (D) Bill Sikes

50. "Let knowledge grow from more to more But more of reverence in us dwell" In which poem of Tennyson do we find the above quoted lines ?

(A) Ulysses (B) Morte d'Arthur

(C) In Memorium (D) Locksley Hall

51. Find out correct conversion of the following direct speech into indirect narration :

"Please, please, don't drink too much. Remember that you'll have to drive home." She said to him.

(A) She forbade him not to drink too much reminding him that he would have to drive home.

(B) She begged him not to drink too much, reminding him that he would have to drive home.

(C) She requested him again and again that he should not drink too much. She told him to remember that he will have to drive home.

(D) She said to him please did not drink too much and remember that he'll have to drive home.

52. Which of the following sentences is a correct one?

(A) The ship let go its anchor

(B) Let the ship go its anchor

(C) Let its anchor go the ship

(D) Its anchor let the ship go

53. Fill in the blank with appropriate word :

The tree was .... with fruits.

(A) load (B) loaded

(C) laden (D) loading

54. The appropriate meaning of 'EL Dorado' is :

(A) an attainable thing

(B) an approachable thing

(C) an unattainble thing
(D) an invincible thing

55. Which of the following means 'a charlatan'?
(A) who pretends to have more skill than he really has
(B) a modest woman
(C) a gentleman
(D) milkman

56. 'With a high hand' means :
(A) a praiseworthy way
(B) in a dictatorial way
(C) in a nasty way
(D) in an honorable way

57. Select the best choice to replace the underlined expression in the following sentence : Aditya was not selected for the job of a medical officer because he was wet behind the ears.
(A) underage (B) inexperienced
(C) ill-mannered (D) untrustworthy

58. Choose the correct word for the expression given below :
'a room for the display of works of art'
(A) artery (B) artillery
(C) gallery (D) library

59. Choose the most appropirate one-word substitute for the expression given below :
'a supporter of the cause of women'
(A) feminine (B) feminist
(C) effeminate (D) sophist

60. Choose the correct meaning of the following idiom out of the four options given after it :
"Black and Blue"
(A) multicoloured
(B) in a severe manner
(C) in a mixed manner
(D) in an attractive manner

61. Choose the most appropriate one-word substitute for the expression given below :
'an office with good salary but no work'
(A) gratis
(B) honorary
(C) discretionary
(D) sinecure

62. Choose the correct word to fill in the blank in the sentence given below :
Wordsworth was a great lover of natural scenery and ..... .
(A) cite (B) site
(C) sight (D) shite

63. Choose the correct meaning of the word 'persue'.
(A) to lie under oath
(B) to argue convincingly
(C) to read thoroughly
(D) to look for the clues

64. Which of the following is the correct spelling ?
(A) Iriconciliable (B) Irriconcialiable
(C) Irreconcilable (D) Irreconceliable

65. Find out the correct spelling :
(A) rheumatic (B) rhumetic
(C) rhumetic (D) rhumatic

66. Find out the correctly spelt word from the following:
(A) concomitent (B) concupiscence
(C) concordant (D) condescension

67. Choose the mis-spelt word :
(A) Subsistence (B) Mismerise
(C) Anamolous (D) Ninth

68. The synonym of FELICITOUS is :
(A) happy (B) convenient
(C) fervent (D) brittle

69. The synonym of APEX is :
(A) peak (B) underground
(C) qualified (D) greedy

70. The synonym of ADROIT is :
(A) skilful (B) cunning
(C) villainous (D) wicked

71. The synonym of AMNESTY is :
(A) penalty (B) justice
(C) pardon (D) release

72. Give the correct antonym of the word 'prodigal'.
(A) ardent
(B) extravagant

(C) frugal
(D) liberal

73. The antonym of AGILE is :
(A) swift (B) hard
(C) feeble (D) slow

74. The antonym of VOLUNTEER is :
(A) support (B) defeat
(C) conscript (D) provoke

75. The antonym of GENUINE is :
(A) beautiful (B) ugly
(C) brave (D) spurious

76. What is the meaning of the idiom 'ins and outs' ?
(A) outside and back side
(B) internally
(C) full details
(D) partly

77. What does the idiom 'Penelop's web' mean ?
(A) a complicated web
(B) a complicated situation
(C) an unending work
(D) an unending life

78. That which stays for a long time is :
(A) everlasting (B) permanent
(C) durable (D) eternal

79. What does the underlined expression mean : Every verdict that he gave was <u>sui generis</u>.
(A) well-balanced (B) sensational
(C) challengable (D) unique

80. Choose the correct meaning of the following idiom out of the four responses given after it : 'in cold blood'
(A) indifferently
(B) deliberately
(C) unintentionally
(D) in anger

81. The idiom 'double Dutch' means :
(A) language spoken by the Dutch
(B) Unintelligible language
(C) Long distance march
(D) two natives of the Netherlands

82. Which of the following is not an essay by Charles Lamb ?
(A) Night Fears
(B) Christ's Hospital
(C) Going on a Journey
(D) Poor Relation

83. In which poem has Wordsworth described different moods of nature?
(A) The Daffodils
(B) Lines Written above Tintem Abbey
(C) An Evening Walk
(D) The Excursion

84. In which poem does Tennyson commemorate his friend 'Arthur Hallam' ?
(A) The Princess (B) Enoch Arden
(C) In Memoriam (D) Ulyssis

85. The phrase 'stream of consciousness' was first used by :
(A) William Harvey
(B) William James
(C) William Jones
(D) William Porter

86. Who said, "Poetry is not a turning looses or emotion but an escape from emotion" ?
(A) Shakespeare (B) Keats
(C) Eliot (D) Arnold

87. T. S. Eliot declared himself to be a :
(A) romanticist
(B) poetic dramatist
(C) painter
(D) catholic

88. Robert Browning is famous for his :
(A) novels
(B) short stories
(C) dramatic monologues
(D) plays

89. A long romance entitled endymion is written by :
(A) Shakespeare (B) Browning
(C) Keats (D) Shelley

90. 'Lyrical Ballads' was first published in :
(A) 1797 (B) 1798
(C) 1799 (D) 1796

91. Chronicle plays were very popular in :
(A) 19th century (B) 18th century
(C) 17th century (D) 16th century

92. The word 'disparity' means :
(A) inequality (B) irregularity
(C) impoliteness (D) unhappiness

93. PERPETUAL means :
(A) rigid (B) holy
(D) rude (C) eternal

94. Find out the correct meaning of 'stimulate' :
(A) move (B) push
(C) eternal (D) rude

95. The word 'furtive' means :
(A) Stealthy (B) quick
(C) interest (D) pretend

96. Who wrote the poem, The Triumph of Life ?
(A) Keats (B) Tennyson
(C) Shelley (D) Wordsworth

97. 'Philip Prip' is a character in Charles Dickens'
(A) A Tale of Two Cities
(B) Great Expectations
(C) Oliver Twist
(D) David Coppertfield

98. Who coined the phrase "Poetry is the criticism of life" ?
(A) T. S. Eliot (B) F. L. Lucas
(C) P. R. Lavis (D) Mathew Arnold

99. Tennyson's poetry represents :
(A) Victorian prudery
(B) Victorian spirit of questioning and loss of faith
(C) Victorian compromise
(D) Victorian pessimism

100. In Yeats' poem 'Sailing to Byzantium', 'Byzantium' refers to :
(A) Constantinople
(B) Himalayas
(C) Athens
(D) Jerusalem

ANSWERS WITH EXPLANATION

1. (C) Hemingway was an American novelist. He tried to project the reality in his novel or short stories. He is better known as a short story writer.

2. (A) This is the famous soliloquy by Hamlet. Everything seems to him useless. So, he utters this. The play Hamlet is famous for his soliloquies the world over.

3. (C) This line is from the poem 'Ulysses'. In this poem Tennyson has tried best at his level to present the doubt and dilemma prevailent in Victorian society. So, he is known as Victorian representation.

4. (B) Shakespeare wrote his plays on behalf of Lord Chamberlain's Company of actors. He owned Globe Theatre. But it was burned down during a performance of Henry VIII in 1613.

5. (B) The sonnet is a form of the lyric, and of all its forms it is most carefully ordered and bound by definite, rigid rules. The word "Sonnet" is derived from Greek word "Sonneto" meaning "a sound". It has two parts— Octane of eight lines and the sted of six lines, with a pause or ceasura after the eight line. Wyatt introduced it in England.

6. (C) The word 'hyperbole' (Hyper-beyond; ballo - throw) literally, "a throwing beyond" means exaggeration. This figure of speech consists in representing this much greater or smaller than they really are, with the intention of producing a more striking effect than a plain statement can.

7. (D) Cordelia was the daughter of king Lear, Calpurnia was the wife of Caesar. While Des Demona was the wife of Othello.

8. (A) Ezekiel was born in Mumbai in 1924. He was a Jew by birth. He was President of

PEN [India]. He is also an art critic. He is, however, better known as a poet.

9. (B) Robert Frost was born in San Francisco, California on 26th March, 1874. He was one of the most distinguished American Poets of 20th Century. His mother was a poetess herself.

10. (D) Samson Agonistes, which tells of Samson's death while a prisoner of the Philistine, has a curious interest, for in the Biblical hero Milton saw more than one resemblance to himself. In form, the work has the strict unity of time, place and action universal in Greek tragedy.

11. (B) Charles Lamb wrote autobiographical essays. He was a romantic writer. He wrote his essays in disguise of his name Elia.

12. (D) Wordsworth is a romantic poet. He was associated with the Lake District, other places where he resided respectively are — Dove Collage, at town End, Grasmere; Allan Bank; Grasmere; Parsonage and lastly well known residence of Royal Mount.

13. (A) This was written by T.S. Eliot, this is a symbolical book on the modern literature. The protagonist in it is Tiresias.

14. (A) The other three were written by him, Matthew Arnold was a Victorian poet. He threw light on the bad condition, especially on immoral attitude of the people.

15. (D)

16. (C) He could not complete this work as he shot himself with his gun.

17. (A) In this meter each foot has two syllables of which the first is unaccented and the second accented. If there are five feet or ten such syllables in a line, it would be known as iambic pentameter.

18. (C) This line is spoken by Hamlet lo Horatio, his friend in the play Hamlet. This can be found in Act V, scene V, when Hamlet, the hero, was on his death bed - he spoke this line.

19. (C) Actually Robert Frost got Pulitzer Prize four times respectively 1924, 1931, 1937, 1943.

20. (C) She is a well-known Kerala writer who writes equally well both in English and Malyalam. She is a poet, novelist and short story writer. She received the Sahitya Academi Award in 1985.

21. (A) As we well know that the first romantic period was Elizabethan Era. In between these two epochs there were a lot of changes. But with the publication of lyrical Ballads in 1798, the romantic traits were revival.

22. (D) This line depicts that Wordsworth was the supporter of this view that the poet used conversational language in his poetry. But vulgars words should be avoided. He was of this view that poetry is the spontaneous overflow of powerful feeling. So there should be no artificiality.

23. (A) M.R. Anand was born in Lahore. He was a social reformer in the sense that he threw light on social evils rampant at that time. He used his pen for this. 'Munoo' is the mouthpiece of it.

24. (C) P. B.Shelley was born on 4th August, 1792 at Yield Place near Horsham in Sussex. P.B. Shelley was the first child of his parents. As a boy, he had no interest in games and sports.

25. (C) He sold his form. He with his wife and children went to England where they settled in Beacons field, Buckinghamshire.

26. (C) Nissim Ezekiel was born in Mumbai in 1924. He was a Jew by birth. He was fond of realism. He gave a different type of impetus to Indian writing.

27. (B) This novel was a naturalistic novel with humanistic outcome. He was born in oak park, Illinois, U.S.A. Hemingway showed a great promise as a writer of short stories.

28. (D) Faulkner was an American novelist. He was born in New Albany, Mississippi in 1897. When he was five years old his family shifted to nearby Oxford, and he continue to reside there till his death.

29. (A) Actually, the hero Freedrick Henry was of an American origin. But during First World War he drived ambulance in Italy. He is the hero of the novel 'A Farewell to Arms'.

30. (A) Here, 'sorrow' has been personified. We know well that this word is abstract noun, and an abstract 'noun' has no 'form' stature. But in this line sorrow has been made sit and weep.

31. (C) He was born in Mumbai in 1924. He was a Jew by birth. He was fond of realism, in his creative writing we can easily trace realism.

32. (C) Dickens was a Victorian novelist. He threw light on the social unrest, and miserable condition of the downtrodden.

33. (B) 'Arthur Hugh Clough' was Arnold's bossom friend. He died early, His sudden death coerced Matthew Arnold to write this beautiful elegy. Here, we find that this piece of poem is the example of pastoral elegy.

34. (B) This line is from the poem "On Shakespeare" by Matthew Arnold. He wrote this poem to praise the qualities of Shakespeare.

35. (C) Matthew Arnold wrote this long poem. To write long poems in Victorian period was in vogue. Soharab was very brave. This has been depicted in the poem.

36. (A) Claudius is the villain of Hamlet. He murdered the father of Hamlet, and married his mother. At last, both Hamlet and Claudius fought with each other and were killed.

37. (C) In the first case weary has been transferred from the ploughmn 'to' the 'way'. And in the second case 'sleepless' has been transferred from he to 'bed'.

38. (D) This line shows how the impersonal theory of Mr. Eliot is formed. This line has been taken from his collection of essays "The Sacred Wood".

39. (C) Ernest Hemingway was an American writer. This war anthology was published on October 22, 1942.

40. (C) Lamb was a romantic prose writer. His collection of essays is known as 'Essays of Ellia'. This particular essay is the part of it. His whole collection of essays is full of autobiographical elements.

41. (A) Matthew Arnold was a Victorian poet. He wrote an elegy to commemorate his father's death. Elegy is a form of poetry which is used to lament the near and dear ones. It is the personal elegy.

42. (C) French root 'essai' means - to try. Any short composition in prose that undertakes to discuss a matter, express a point of view is called "Essay." There are two types are essays — formal essay or informal essay (or familiar or personal essay).

43. (C) It is the manifesto of the modern English poetry. It broke away itself from the tradition form, style, imagery and so on so forth. Eliot used everything new in this volume of verse. It compelled modern writers to think in a different way.

44. (A) Walt Whitman was born on May 31, 1819 at West Hills, Long Island, New York. With no formal education he trained himself to read and write. His 'Leaves of Grass', a collection of poems, is of great value; which was published in July 1855, and found instant admiration all around. He was a visionary. O Captain ! My Captain is an elegy on the death of the famous American President, Abraham Lincoln.

45. (A) Wordsworth was a great romantic poet. And in his poetry each and every trait of romanticism can be traced. This poem is about a lonely lad who reaps on the highlands. The poet shows how the nature is sympathetic with her in her sufferings and sorrows.

46. (A) Keats was a sensous poet. He has given great importance to the senses. This particular trail coerced Matthew Arnold to write something about his sensousness. This line has been taken from Matthew Arnold's "Essays in Criticism".

47. (C) In the Merchant of Venice, the main characters are Portia & Shylock. In Hamlet the main characters are Hamlet, Clodius and Ophelia. In Mackbeth the main characters are Hamlet, Clodius and Ophelia.

48. (D) Shakespeare is related to Elizabethan period of English literature. This play is a historical play. This type of play throws light on the historical facts of great significance. Shakespeare has projected this character for comic relief. So, that the monontony should be avoided.

49. (D) Charles Dickens was a Victorian novelist. He throws light on the social unrest prevailed in Victorian society. He used his pen and notes for social upliftment of the downtrodden. It included each strata of society.

50. (C) Tennyson is known as the Victorian poet. He represents doubt and faith rampant in Victorian poetry. To commemorate his friend's death he wrote "On Memorium". This line has been taken from this book. The name of his friend is Aurthur Henry Hallam.

51. (B) When the direct narrative is changed into indirect one in an imperative sentence, 'Let' me also changes the reporting verb into beg/request.

52. (B) In an imperative sentence 'Let' is always followed by an object + V.

53. (C) Laden is an adjective which means heavily.

54. (C)

55. (A) A person who claims to have knowledge or skills that they do not really have.

56. (B) [In a dictatorial way]

Using authority in an unreasonable way, without considering the opinions of other people.

57. (B) [Inexperienced] young and without much experience.

58. (C) Artery means a large and important road river, railway. Artillery means large, heavy guns which are often moved on wheels. Library means a room in a large house where most of the books are kept.

59. (B) Feminine means having the qualities or appearance considered to be typical of women. Effeminate means a man or a boy looking, behaving or sounding like a woman or a girl.

60. (B) Black and blue means to hit somebody until they are covered with bruises means to beat somebody in a severe manner.

61. (D) Gratis means done or given without having to be paid for. Honorary means not paid (of a position in an organization). Discretionary means not decided by rules.

62. (C) Sight means the area or distance within somebody can see or something can be seen.

63. (C) To read something, especially in a careful way.

64. (C) All the four options are wrong. The correct spelling is irreconcilable.

65. (A) Rheumatic

66. (B) The correct spelling should be concomitant, concordant, condescension. The correct answer is concupiscence.

67. (C) The correct spelling is anomalous.

68. (B) Felicitous means very suitable or giving a good result. Its synonym is Convenient.

69. (A) Apex means the top or highest part of sth. Its synonym is peak.

70. (A) Adroit means skilful and clever, especially in dealing with people. Its synonym is skilful.

71. (B) Amnesty means an official statement that allows people who have been put in prison for crimes against the state to go free. Its synonym is pardon.

72. (C) Prodigal means too willing to spend money or waste time, energy or materials.

Its antonym is frugal which means using only as much money or food as is necessary. Extravant is synonym of prodigal.

73. (D) Agile means able to move quickly and easily. Its antonym is slow which means not moving, acting or done quickly.

74. (C) Volunteer means a person who chooses to join the armed forces without being forced to join. Its antonym should be conscript, it means to make sb join the armed forces.

75. (D) Genuine means real, exactly what it appears to be, not artificial. Its antonym is spurious. It means false although seeming to be genuine.

76. (C) All the details especially, the complicated or difficult ones. Example - He quickly learned the ins and outs of the problem.

77. (B) Penelop's web means a complicated situation.

78. (C) 'Durable' means likely to last for a long time without breaking or getting breakes. Permanent means existing all the time. 'Eternal' means without an end ; existing or continuing forever.

79. (D) Sui generis is a Latin word. It means different from all other people or things.

80. (B) Acting in a way that is deliberately cruel ; with no pity.

81. (B) Speech or writing that is impossible to understand, and that seems to be nonsense.

82. (C) Charles Lamb was a great essayist. His pen name was 'Elia'. His essays are autobiographical. He was of romantic age.

83. (B) Wordsworth was a great poet of Nature. He was a romantic poet. He with Coleridge Published the Lyricals Ballads in 1798. In this poem he described three moods of nature.

84. (C) In 'In Memoriam' Tennyson commemorate his friend Aruthur Hallam. It is a personal elegy, In the personal the poet lament the death of his near and dear one.

85. (B) Stream of consciousness was a phrase used by William James in his "Principles of Psychology" (1890) to describe the unbroken flow of perceptions, thoughts and feeling in the waking mind; it has since been adopted to describe a narrative method in modern fiction.

86. (C) This line explains T.S. Eliot's theory of "impersonal poetry". He contradicted words with theory - "the spontaneous overflow of powerful feelings".

87. (D) T.S. Eliot was born in U.S.A. He declared himself to be royalist in politics; Anglo catholic in religion and classicist in literature.

88. (C) Dramatic monologue is a type of lyric poem that was perfected by Robert Browning. This is the self revelation of the speakers. The speaker is patently not the poet.

89. (C) Keats was born at Finsbury, in London in 1795. His father a stable-keeper, was a man of commonsense and business ability. When endymion was published it was savagely criticised by Black Wood Magazine and Quarterly Review.

90. (B) Lyrical Ballads is considered to be the manifesto of romantic period. It ushered itself in a new type of thinking. Specially the ship feet and language of poetry and other forms of literature were changed.

91. (D) Chronicle plays were dramatic works based on the historical materials in English Chronicles by Raphael Holinshed and others. They achieved high popularity late in 16th century.

92. (A) Disparity (Inequality).

93. (C) Continuing for a long period of time without interruption.

94. (C) The correct meaning of stimulate is rouse interest. Stimulate means to make something develop or become more active, to encourage something.

95. (A) It means behaving is a way that shows you want to keep something secret, and do not want to be noticed.

96. (C) P.B. Shelley was born on 4th August 1792, at Field Place near Horrsham in Sussex. He had an inevitable mind for stories and poems and had strong likes and dislikes. He wrote "The Necessity of Atheism" for which he was expelled from the University.

97. (B) 'Charles Lamb' was a social reformer. He used his pen for the upliftment of the society. Each and every character in his novel is the mouthpiece of his personality: so is Philip Prip.

98. (D) This line explains that the poetry represent everything that happens in society, it is the mirror. In other words, we can say that literature is the mirror of society.

99. (C) Tennyson is known as representation of victorian poetry. The victorian compromise was the compromise between aristocracy and democracy; between morality and sexuality ; between doubt and faith.

100. (A) W. B. Yeats was a modern writer. His poetry is full of symbolism. He was born in Dublin. Yeats was educated in London. He returned to Dublin in 1880. He founded the Irish Literary Society. And he was responsible for the revival of the Irish drama. He was awarded the Nobel Prize for literature in 1923.

❑❑❑

PRACTICE SET–5

1. Which one of the following is the correct spelling ?
   (A) Ceasarean (B) Caesaraen
   (C) Caesarean (D) Ceasaraen
2. Which one of the following is the correct spelling ?
   (A) Haemorrhage (B) Haemorhage
   (C) Heamorrhage (D) Heamorhage
3. Change the following into an indirect statement and indicate the correct one :
   He said to me, "What are you doing ?"
   (A) He said to me that what he was doing.
   (B) He said to me that what I was doing.
   (C) He asked me what I was doing.
   (D) He asked me what he was doing.
4. Change the correct figure of speech in the following sentence:
   "The quality of mercy is not strained,
   It droppeth as the gentle rain from heaven."
   (A) Metaphor (B) Hyperbole
   (C) Synecedoche (D) Simile
5. Choose the correct figure of speech in the following sentence :
   "The camel is the ship of desert."
   (A) Metaphor (B) Simile
   (C) Hyperbole (D) None of these
6. Fill in the blank with suitable adjective. The book contains many.................quotations.
   (A) Martial (B) Ambitious
   (C) Biblical (D) Ulterior
7. Fill in the blank with correct pronoun : Our soldiers are better than............ of the enemies.
   (A) those (B) these
   (C) that (D) themselves
8. Which of the following sentences is correct ?
   (A) The meeting was adjourned owing to the want of quorum.
   (B) The meeting was adjourned due to want of quorum.
   (C) The meeting was adjourned for want of quorum.
   (D) None of these.
9. Which of the following sentences is correct :
   (A) He entered into the room.
   (B) He entered the room.
   (C) He entered in the room.
   (D) He entered to the room.
10. Fill in the blank with suitable conjunction : Though he is suffering much pain........... he does not complain.
    (A) yet (B) but
    (C) else (D) as
11. An imaginary name assumed by an author for disguise is called
    (A) Pseudonym (B) Neologism
    (C) Loquacious (D) Veteran
12. One who eats everything is called
    (A) Herbivorous (B) Gregarious
    (C) Credulous (D) Omnivorous
13. A speech which is delivered without any previous preparation is called
    (A) Maiden (B) Extempore
    (C) Meticulous (D) Matin
14. A person who hates the institution of marriage is called
    (A) Misogamist
    (B) Pacifist
    (C) Philogynist
    (D) Pessimist

15. Choose the most appropriate preposition :
The doctor advised him to abstain............all alcoholic drinks.
(A) at (B) from
(C) by (D) in

16. The meaning of the idiom "a brain wave" is
(A) a wave passing through one's brain
(B) sudden inspiration
(C) a big fuss
(D) an invention

17. The antonym of ESOTERIC is
(A) clear (B) transparent
(C) simple (D) apparent

18. The synonym of SARDONIC is
(A) miserable (B) cruel
(C) scornful (D) noisy

19. "See the" suggests
(A) spill (B) catch
(C) dry (D) boil

20. Choose the most appropriate preposition: The Indian magpie indulges.......... a long flight.
(A) with (B) in
(C) at (D) on

21. What is the meaning of the idiom "a flying visit" ?
(A) A very short visit
(B) A visit to the space
(C) A visit by an aeroplane
(D) A visit on a gas-filled balloon

22. The synonym of AVIARY is
(A) prison
(B) reformatory
(C) large cage for birds
(D) zoo officer

23. The antonym of ALACRITY is
(A) inaptitude (B) hesitation
(C) uncertainty (D) inability

24. Mark the part which contains an error in the following sentence. If there is no error in it, mark (D) as your choice :
The great poet and dramatist, the Kalidas, (A) is regarded (B) as the Shakespeare (C) of India. No error (D)

25. Mark the part which contains an error in the following sentence. If there is no error in it, mark (D) as your choice :
One should (A) take advantage of opportunities to talk with native orators if one wants (B) to improve his (C) English. No error (D)

26. The idiom 'hush money' means
(A) the money spent at midnight
(B) the bribe paid to keep some matter secret
(C) the money received in a dark room
(D) the money received in paper currency

27. Who has penned the following lines ?
I am sinner,
I am saint. I am the beloved and the Betrayed.
(A) Rabindranath Tagore
(B) Nissim Ezekiel
(C) Kamala Das
(D) Sarojini Naidu

28. Point out the figure of speech in the following line:
Where Beauty cannot keep her lustrous eyes.
(A) Pun (B) personification
(C) Simile (D) Oxymoron

29. T.S. Eliot's "The Waste Land" was published in
(A) 1910 (B) 1918
(C) 1930 (D) 1922

30. Hemingway, the novelist was
(A) an American (B) a British
(C) a Canadian (D) a South-African

31. Who has composed the following line ?
To me that cup has been dealt in another measure.
(A) John Keats
(B) Shakespeare

(C) Robert Southey
(D) P.B. Shelley

32. Michael Henchard began his life as a
(A) driver (B) carpenter
(C) weaver (D) hay-trusser

33. Who is the author of "Tinitern Abbey" ?
(A) Matthew Arnold
(B) John Keats
(C) William Wordsworth
(D) Coleridge

34. Point out the figure of speech in the following line: O World ! O Life ! O Time !
(A) Apostrophe (B) Climax
(C) Pun (D) Personification

35. One of the characters of Shakespeare has been called the fourth witch. She is
(A) Ophelia (B) Lady Macbeth
(C) Emilia (D) Juliet

36. When was T.S. Eliot born ?
(A) 1888 (B) 1905
(C) 1906 (D) 1907

37. Who has written the book, 'The Art of T.S. Eliot' ?
(A) Elizabeth Drew
(B) Helen Gardner
(C) T.S. Eliot
(D) Grover Smith

38. Which one of the following is not a drama by Eliot?
(A) Ash Wednesday
(B) Murder in the Cathedral
(C) The Family Reunion
(D) The Cocktail Party

39. What is the title of Hardy's epic drama ?
(A) The Dynasts
(B) The Mayor of Casterbridge
(C) Far from the Madding Crowd
(D) None of these

40. Which is/are the novel/novels by Hardy ?
(A) The Trumpet Major
(B) Desperate Remedies
(C) Jude the Obscure
(D) All of these

41. Which of the following is not correctly matched ?
(A) Thomas Gradgrind—Hard Times
(B) Richard Carstone—Bleak House
(C) Ada Clare—Bleak House
(D) Abel Magwitch—Oliver Twist

42. Which of the following is not by Dickens ?
(A) The Cricket On the Hearth
(B) The Old Curiosity Shop
(C) Barnaby Rudge
(D) Old Fortunatus

43. Which the following is not correctly matched ?

(A)	When the lips have Spoken. Loved accents are soon forgot	–	When the Lamp is Shattered
(B)	Nothing beside remains Round the decay Of that colossal wreck. boundless and bare, The tone and level sands stretch far away	–	Ozymandias
(C)	Oh. lift me as a wave, a leaf, a cloud ! I fall upon the thorns of life ! I bledd !	–	Ode to the West Wind
(D)	A heavy weight of hours has chained and bowed One too like the: tameless, and swift, and proud.	–	Adonais

44. Whose death is mourned by Shelley in Adonais ?
(A) Keats (B) Wordsworth
(C) Coleridge (D) None of them

45. Shelley's 'Alastor' is also called
(A) The Spirit of Solitude
(B) Queen Mab

(C) Stanzas Written In Dejection Near Naples
(D) None of these

46. Keats passed away in the year :
(A) 1795 (B) 1789
(C) 1821 (D) 1777

47. Which work was described by Keats as 'a feverish attempt rather than a deed accomplished' ?
(A) Endymion
(B) Hyperion
(C) The Even of St. Agnes
(D) None of these

48. In 'Three Years She Grew', the little girl will be sportive as
(A) The Lawn (B) The Fawn
(C) Stars (D) Rivulets

49. To whom is Wordsworth's autobiographical poem the Prelude addressed ?
(A) Jane Austen (B) Coleridge
(C) Pope (D) Dr. Johnson

50. When did the first edition of Lyrical Ballads appear ?
(A) 1698 (B) 1798
(C) 1898 (D) 1794

51. Choose the correctly spelt word :
(A) souvenir (B) suvenire
(C) suvenir (D) souvenire

52. Choose the most appropriate preposition :
Your conduct smacks .... recklessness.
(A) in (B) from
(C) with (D) of

53. The antonym of UNIMPEACHABLE is
(A) corruptible (B) blameworthy
(C) calculating (D) mysterious

54. The synonym of VANGUARD is
(A) watchmen (B) protectors
(C) security men (D) forefront

55. Choose the most appropriate preposition
The patient was disappointed .... not finding the doctor in his seat.
(A) at (B) on
(C) from (D) in

56. The synonym of PONTIFICAL is
(A) boastful (B) wordy
(C) splendid (D) advisory

57. "Impromptu" means
(A) unimportant (C) offhand
(B) unreal (D) effective

58. "Goulash" stands for
(A) top (B) stew
(C) shoe (D) play

59. "Harangue" implies
(A) lecture (B) quarrel
(C) beautify (D) run

60. "Abysmal" means
(A) vigour (B) explosion
(C) horrifying (D) mixed

61. Mark the part which contains an error in the following sentence. If there is no error in it, mark (D) as your choice :
<u>Although there are some similarities in</u>
(A)
<u>the qualifications of the two condidates the</u>
(B)
<u>differences among them are quite pronounced</u>.
(C)
<u>No error</u>
(D)

62. Choose the most appropriate preposition :
A good judge never jumps .... the conclusion.
(A) to (B) into
(C) on (D) for

63. The antonym of BELLIGERENT is
(A) cooperative (B) peaceful
(C) revolutionary (D) uninterested

64. "Archaic" means
(A) decent (B) clumsy
(C) modern (D) primitive

65. Choose the correctly spelt word :
(A) farenheit
(B) ferenheit
(C) fahrenheit
(D) fahrenheight

66. Which of the following is a poem by Wordsworth ?
(A) Daffodils
(B) On first looking into Chapman's Homer
(C) The Forsaken Mesman
(D) The Last Ride Together

67. Who has spoken the following words in Shakespear's Macbeth ?
The sleeping and the dead
Are but as pictures; 'tis the eye of childhood
That fears a painted devil
(A) First witch (B) Second witch
(C) Third witch (D) None of them

68. When was Shakespeare born ?
(A) 1564 (B) 1616
(C) 1671 (D) 1713

69. Which of the following is correctly matched ?
(A) Hyperbole - A figure of speech in which emphasis is achieved by deliberate exaggeration.
(B) Oxymoron - A figure of speech consisting generally of two apparently contradictory terms that express a startling paradox.
(C) Metaphor - A figure of speech in which two unlike objects are compared by identification or by the substitution of one for the other.
(D) All of three options are matched correctly

70. Which one of the following is not a pastoral elegy?
(A) Melton's Lycidas
(B) Shelley's Adonais
(C) Arnold' Thyrsis
(D) Pope's The Rape of the Lock

71. How may acts are there in Shelley's lyrical drama Prometheus Unbound ?
(A) One (B) Three
(C) Four (D) Five

72. Which of the following is not a work by Lamb ?
(A) John Woodvil
(B) The Old Familiar Faces
(C) Hester
(D) Lalla Rookh

73. Which pseudonym was adopted by Lamb for his essays?
(A) Elia (B) Charles
(C) Lamb (D) None of these

74. When was Lamb born ?
(A) 1775 (B) 1834
(C) 1744 (D) 1829.

75. Which poem of Keats has the following lines ?
Heard Melodies are sweet, but those unheard
Are sweeter; therefore, ye soft pipes, play on.
(A) Ode on a Grecian Urn
(B) Ode to a Nightingale
(C) Ode on Melancholy
(D) None of these.

76. Which poem of Tennyson contains the following lines ?
Yet all experience is an arch wherethro'
Gleams that untravelled world, whose margin fades
For ever and for ever when I move.
(A) Crossing the Bar
(B) Ulysses
(C) Tears. Idle Tears
(D) The Lotos-Eaters

77. In whose memory was 'In Memoriam' written ?
(A) Arthur H. Hallam
(B) Alexander Pope
(C) Robert Browning
(D) None of them.

78. Arnold's celebrated poem "The Scholar Gipsy' is based on an old legend, narrated by Glanvil in
(A) The Schoolmaster
(B) Palmerin of England
(C) The Vanity of Dogmatizing
(D) The Shepherd of Salisbury Plain.

79. Whose death was commemorated by Arnold in Thyrsis ?
(A) Arthur Hugh Dough
(B) Tennyson
(C) Edwin Arnold
(D) None of them

80. Who was the father of Matthew Arnold ?
(A) Edwin Arnold (B) Thomas Arnold
(C) A. H. Clough (D) None of them

81. Which of the following novels is not by Mulk Raj Anand ?
(A) Untouchable
(B) Coolie
(C) Two Leaves and a Bud
(D) The Second Wife

82. Point out the figure of speech in the following line: Like a patient etherised upon a table.
(A) Metaphor (B) Climax
(C) Simile (D) Personification

83. Who among the Indian politicians was inspired by the following lines ?
The woods are lovely, dark and deep,
But I have promises to keep,
And miles to go before I sleep,
And miles to go before I sleep.
(A) Pt. Jawaharlal Nehru
(B) Dr. Rajendra Prasad
(C) M. K. Gandhi
(D) Dr. S. Radhakrishnan

84. "The Old Playhouse" by Kamala Das is a poem of
(A) surrender to male domination
(B) protest against male domination
(C) harmony between husband and wife
(D) jealousy

85. Keats dropped the first stanza of one of his 'Odes'. It was from
(A) Ode to Psyche (B) Ode to Melancholy
(C) Ode to Apollo (D) Ode on Indolence

86. When was Robert Frost born ?
(A) 1874 (B) 1963
(C) 1706 (D) 1790

87. Which poem of Kamla Das has the following expression ?
"Why not leave
Me alone, critics, friends, visiting cousins, Every one of you ? Why not let me speak in Any Language I like ?"
(A) The Maggots
(B) The Doubt
(C) An Introduction
(D) Luminol

88. What is the title of Kamala Das' autobiography?
(A) Summer in Calcutta
(B) The Descendants
(C) My Story
(D) None of these

89. In which critical essay did Eliot make the following statement ?
"The historical sense compels a man to write not merely with his own generation in his bones, but with a feeling that the whole of the literature of Europe from Homer has a simultaneous existence and composes a simultaneous order."
(A) Tradition And The Individual Talent
(B) The Metaphysical Poets
(C) Both of these
(D) None of these

90. Which is the first section of Eliot's The Waste Land ?
(A) The Burial of the Dead
(B) A Game of Chess
(C) The fire Sermon
(D) Death By Water

91. Whitman's poem 'Crossing Brooklyn Ferry' contains
(A) nine sections
(B) eleven sections
(C) thirteen sections
(D) none of these

92. The theme of alienation is central to the poetry of
(A) Nissim Ezekiel (B) Kamla Das
(C) Robert Frost (D) Wall Whitman

93. Who is the author of the poem 'Enterprise' ?
(A) Kamla Das
(B) Ezekiel
(C) Ramanujan
(D) None of them

94. Nissim Ezekiel is a born
(A) British (B) American
(C) Swiss (D) Jew

95. What is the real name of the poetess Kamala Das ?
(A) Madhavi Kutty (B) Rutnavalli
(C) Kalluri Devi (D) None of these

96. Who wrote the following line for Shelley ?
" ... he is a beautiful and ineffectual angle, heating in the void his luminous wings in vain."
(A) Compton Rickett
(B) Walter Pater
(C) Dr. Johnson
(D) Matthew Arnold

97. By whom Shelley has been culled as 'perfect singing God' ?
(A) Rossettee (B) Arnold
(C) Swinburne (D) Morris

98. In which poem of Shelley do the following lines occur?
"Alas! I have no hope nor health Nor peace within nor calm around ...."
(A) Ode to West Wind
(B) Stanzas Written in Dejection
(C) To a Skylark
(D) Adonais

99. French revolution broke out in the year
(A) 1789 (B) 1798
(C) 1880 (D) 1785

100. In which Magazine were published the first series of "The Essays of Ella"?
(A) British Magazine
(B) Swiss Magazine
(C) American Magazine
(D) London Magazine

ANSWERS WITH EXPLANATION

1. (C) Caesarean word is given in dictionary.

2. (A) Haemorrhage means discharge of blood from blood-vessels.

3. (C) If reported speech is in double interrogative, wh-form is used us conjuction and 'said to' is changed into asked. You is changed according to the object of the reporting verb.

4. (D) Simile is introduced by words as; like, as....so, so....as.

5. (A) Definition - Metaphor is a figure of speech in which two objects are compared but words 'like', 'as', 'so' are not used.

6. (C)

		Meaning
(A) Martial	–	Warlike
(B) Ambitious	–	Full of ambition
(D) Ulterior	–	Beyond what is obvious

7. (A)

8. (C)

9. (B) 'In' is not used with some verb as enter etc.

10. (A) After though/although, use of yet is correct according to grammar.

11. (A)

		Meaning
(A) Pseudonym	–	Fictituous name esp. one assumed by author.
(B) Neologism	–	New word
(C) Loquacious	–	Talkative
(D) Veteran	–	A person who has grown old in semice or occupation

12. (D)

		Meaning
(A) Herbivorous	–	A person who eats herbaceous plant
(B) Gregarious	–	A person who is fond of company
(C) Credulous	–	A person who is very simple and easily believes whatever is told
(D) Omnivorous	–	A person who eats everything

13. (B)

14. (A) **Meaning**

(A) Misogamist – A person who hates all women

(B) Pacifist – Person opposed to war

(C) Philogynist – Scientist of language

(D) Pessimist – A person who looks to the dark side of things

15. (B) **16.** (B)

17. (C)

18. (D) 'Sardonic', full of scorn.

19. (D) 'See the' means boil bubble, be agitated.

20. (B) **21.** (A)

22. (C) (A) Prison means a place where criminal is confined, (B) Reformatory means improving.

23. (B) 'Alacrity' means readiness and hesitation means a use.

24. (A) 'The' is used before proper Noun only when any adjective adds the value of proper Noun.

25. (C) If one is used in nominative case, one's will be used in progressive case, so his is wrong with one.

26. (B) Hush money means bribe given for hiding a crime.

27. (C) **28.** (B)

29. (D)

30. (A) Works of Earnest Hemingway — The Sun also Rises (1926), A Farewell to Arm (1924), To have and Have Not (1937) etc.

31. (D) Works of P.B. Shelley - Prometheus Unbound, Cency (dramas) and to a Skylark and to the Westwind etc.

32. (D) Works of Hardy- (1) Hinder the Greenwood Tree (1872) for from the madding crowd (1874) the Mayor of Casterbridge Michael Henchard is hay-trusser, the hero of the mayor of easterbridge.

33. (C) Works of William Wordsworth (1) Tintern Abbey (2) The Prelude (3) To a Skylark etc.

34. (A) An apostrophe is direct address to the dead, to the absent, or to a personified object - ideas,

35. (B) There are only three supernatural witches described in Macbeth. Shakespear's major tragedies are Hamlet (1602), Othello (1604), Kinglear (1605), Mackbeth (1606).

36. (A) **37.** (B)

38. (A) **39.** (A)

40. (D) Works of Thomas Hardy; The Trumpet Major, Desperate Remedies etc.

41. (D) **42.** (A)

43. (D) **44.** (A)

45. (A) Alastor or the spirit of solitude, is a long narrative poem, lyrical in spirit.

46. (C) John Keats was born in 1795 and died in 1821.

47. (D) **48.** (B)

49. (B) Works of William Wordsworth's; Tintern Abbey, The Prelude, The World is Too Much With Us etc.

50. (B) A long step forward in the history of romanticism was taken with the publication of the Lyrical Ballads in 1798.

51. (A) Correct spelling is 'souvenir'.

52. (D) **53.** (B)

54. (D) 'Vanguard' means foremost part of army or fleet, etc moving forward.

55. (B) **56.** (C)

57. (C) "Impromptu" means an extempose composition.

58. (B) "Goulash" means stew of meat and vegetables seasoned with paprika.

59. (B)

60. (C) 'Abysmal' means pertaining to depth of ocean of lower word.

61. (C) 'Between' is used for two persons while among for more than two.

62. (A)

63. (B) 'Belligerent' mean engendered in war.

64. (D) 'Archaic' means primitive.

65. (C) Correct spelling, fahrenheit.

66. (A) John Keats's poems, Endymion, Hyperiod, On first Looking into Chapman's Homer, the Human Season etc.

67. (D)

68. (A) Shakespeare was born at Startford-upon-Avon in Warwickshire in 1564 and died in 1616.

69. (D) **70.** (D)

71. (C)

72. (D) Works of Charles Lamb, John Woodvil, The Old Family Faces, Hester etc.

73. (A) Lamb's essays first appeared in the London Magazine 1821-22 under the name of Elia.

74. (A) Charles Lamb's essays are, the Old and The New School Master, My Relations all Fool's Day etc.

75. (A) Poems of John Keats, Endymion Ode on Grecian Urn, Ode to a Nightingale etc.

76. (B) Alfred Tennyson's poems, Marie all Arthur, Dora, Ulysses etc.

77. (A) Works of Alfred Tennyson, The Princes (1847) In Memoriam (1850), The Lady of Shalott etc.

78. (C) Works of Matthew Arnold, Culture and Anarchy (1869), Literature and Dogma (1872), God and the Bible (1875) etc.

79. (A)

80. (B) Works of Matthew Arnold—The Strayed Traveller (1849), Resigration (1849) Tristram and I Seult (1852) etc.

81. (D) Mulk Raj Anand's novels are, Untouchable (1935), Two Leaves and Bud (1937), Coole (1936) etc.

82. (D) **83.** (A)

84. (B) Works of Kamala Das—The Looking Gloss, An Introduction, In Love etc.

85. (C)

86. (A) Poems of Robert Brost—Mending Wall, After Apple - Ticking, The Code etc.

87. (C) Kamla Das's poems—The Sun House Cat, Composition etc.

88. (C) Works of Kamala Das — Summer In Calcutta, the Descendents and My Story.

89. (A) Prose works of T.S. Eliot—The Second Wood 1920, Homage to John Dryden 1924, Poetry and Drama etc.

90. (A) There are sections in the Wasteland (1922)-(A) The Burial of the Dead (B) A Game of Chess (C) The Fire Sermon (D) Death by Water (5) What the Thunder Said.

91. (D) **92.** (A)

93. (B) **94.** (B)

95. (D)

96. (D) The work of Samuel Johnson—Dictionary of the English Language.

97. (B) Works of Arnold, Thyrsis, Scholar Gypsy, Dover Beach etc.

98. (B) Works of P.B. Shelley—Necessity of Atheism, Prometheus Unbound, Westwind etc.

99. (A) French Revolution (1789-1709), Battle of Waterloo and the Defeat of Napolean 1875.

100. (D) Charles Lamb's essays—The Old and New School Master, My Relations, The Convalescent.

❑❑❑

PRACTICE SET–6

1. The poetry of Romantic Revival is a revolt against :
(A) ways of country life
(B) bondage of classical rules of poetic diction
(C) gravity of governmental actions
(D) beauty of verbal and written English

2. Which among the following is the hero of Coolie ?
(A) Munoo
(B) Oliver
(C) Raju
(D) Shankar

3. Charles Dickens, novel deals largely with :
(A) War affairs
(B) Divine matters
(C) Contemporary social conditions
(D) Business matters

4. The concept of 'objective co-relative' was propounded by :
(A) John Dryden
(B) S. T. Coleridge
(C) Matthew Arnold
(D) T. S. Eliot

5. Who is called the representative Victorian poet ?
(A) Wordsworth
(B) Alfred Tennyson
(C) Robert Browning
(D) John Keats

6. Hardy is called a :
(A) Classical novelist
(B) Ideal novelist
(C) Regional novelist
(D) Experimental novelist

7. Who wrote the poem, The Lady of Shalott ?
(A) Keats (B) Tennyson
(C) Shelley (D) None of these

8. "And miles to go before I sleep,
And miles to go before I sleep".
In which poem of Robert Frost do the above lines occur ?
(A) Mending Wall
(B) Birches
(C) Stopping by Woods
(D) The Read Not Taken

9. William Shakespeare's Measure for Measure is a :
(A) Tragedy
(B) Comedy
(C) History play
(D) Tragi-comedy

10. Mulk Raj Anand passed away in the year :
(A) 1998
(B) 2000
(C) 2002
(D) 2004

11. In the poem O Captain! My Captain! the captain is :
(A) George Washington
(B) Abraham Lincoln
(C) J. F. Kennedy
(D) L. B. Johnson

12. Which of the following statements is correct ?
(A) Ernest Hemingway committed suicide
(B) Ernest Hemingway was killed in a battle
(C) Ernest Hemingway was murdered in a street brawl
(D) None of the above

13. Who wrote the line, "God's not in his heaven; all's wrong with the world" ?
(A) Robert Browning
(B) Thomas Hardy
(C) G. B. Shaw
(D) P. B. Shelley

14. Who wrote the poem The Defence of Lucknow?
(A) Alfred Tennyson
(B) Mulk Raj Anand
(C) Rudyard Kipling
(D) E. M. Forster

15. In Matthew Arnold's Culture and Anarchy the term 'Philistines' is used for :
(A) the English working class
(B) the English middle class
(C) the English aristocratic class
(D) the people of Palestine

16. Which character in Dickess keep on waiting for 'something to turn up' ?
(A) Mr. Micawber
(B) Sydney Carton
(C) Oliver Twist
(D) Miss Havisham

17. Who is called "the prince of English essayists' ?
(A) Francis Bacon
(B) Joseph Addison
(C) Charles Lamb
(D) R. L. Stevenson

18. Who said about Keats
"He is; he is with Shakespeare" ?
(A) P. B. Shelley
(B) S. T. Coleridge
(C) Walter Pater
(D) Matthew Arnold

19. "To me the meanest flower the blow can give Thoughts that do often lie too deep for tears." Who said it ?
(A) John Keats
(B) Alfred Tennyson
(C) P. B. Shelley
(D) None of the above

20. Venus and Adonls is a poem written by :
(A) John Keats
(B) P. B. Shelley
(C) William Shakespeare
(D) Matthew Arnold

21. Who of the following has written : 'Earth's the right place for love' ?
(A) Walt Whitman (B) Robert Frost
(C) Hemingway (D) Faulner

22. Who is bitten by the scorpion in Night of the Scorpion ?
(A) The poet (B) The narrator
(C) The mother (D) The father

23. When was Mulk Raj Anand's novel, Untouchable, Published ?
(A) 1934 (B) 1935
(C) 1936 (D) 1937

24. The tern 'negative capability' is given by :
(A) Wordsworth (B) John Keats
(C) Byron (D) P. B. Shelley

25. Who is the heroine in Shakespeare's The Tempest ?
(A) Viola (B) Portia
(C) Miranda (D) Beatrice

26. Who, among these, is called a 'home-spun philosopher' ?
(A) Arnold (B) Robert Frost
(C) Raja Rao (D) Walt Whitman

27. When was Charles Dickens born ?
(A) 1820 (B) 1888
(C) 1812 (D) 1825

28. Who said, "My heart aches and a drowsy numbness pains" ?
(A) Shelley
(B) Tennyson
(C) Keats
(D) Wordsworth

29. Shelley's Adonais is :
(A) a tragedy
(B) an epic poem
(C) a pastoral elegy
(D) a poem in blank verse

30. William Shakespeare was born in :
(A) 1575 (B) 1564
(C) 1512 (D) 1616

31. The title of Wordsworth's first poetical volume is :
(A) Descriptive Sketches
(B) Lyrical Ballads
(C) Intimations of Immortality
(D) Prelude

32. The title of Shelley's incomplete dream-allegory is :
(A) Mont Blanc (B) Revolt of Islam
(C) Hellas (D) The Triumph of Life

33. Tennyson's elegy In Memoriam is in memory of :
(A) Queen Victoria
(B) Arthur Hallam
(C) William Wordsworth
(D) Charles Darwin

34. The Dynasts is Thomas Hardy's :
(A) Novel
(B) Autobiography
(C) Lyric
(D) Verse Drama

35. Which one of these is not of the five sections of T. S. Eliot's The Wasteland?
(A) "The Burial of the Dead"
(B) 'A Game of Chess'
(C) 'The Hollow Men'
(D) 'The Fire Sermon'

36. The original title of Mulk Raj Anand's Gauri was :
(A) The Women and the Cow
(B) The Village
(C) Across the Black Waters
(D) Untouchable

37. Which among the following is the author of The Barder's Trade Union ?
(A) R. K. Narayan
(B) Mulk Raj Anand
(C) Shashi Deshpande
(D) Raja Rao

38. Which among the following is the novel by William Faukner ?
(A) The Grapes of Wrath
(B) The English teacher
(C) The Dark Holds No Terrors
(D) The Sound and the Fury

39. In which poem of Shelley do the following lines occur ?
"Oh, lift me as a wave, a leaf, a cloud!
I fall upon the thorns of life! I bleed!"
(A) Adonais
(B) To a Shylark
(C) Ode to end West
(D) Lament

40. In which poem of Keats does the following line occur ?
"A thing of beauty is a joy for ever".
(A) Endymion
(B) Hyperion
(C) Lamia
(D) Sleep and Beauty

41. Who wrote Tales from Shakespeare ?
(A) Charles Lamp
(B) William Hazlitt
(C) Leigh Hunt
(D) Charles and Mary Lamb

42. In which year did Wordsworth add his Preface to the Lyrical Ballads ?
(A) 1798 (B) 1800
(C) 1802 (D) 1803

43. The number of sonnets authored by Shakespeare is :
(A) 154 (B) 156
(C) 148 (D) 160

44. Which play of Shakespeare is regarded as the tragedy of overleaping ambition ?
(A) King Lear (B) Macbeth
(C) Hamlet (D) Othello

45. What is the name of the hero of Hemingway's The Old Man and the Sea ?
(A) Tom Sawyer (B) Santiago
(C) Henry (D) None of these

46. When did W. B. Yeats receive Nobel Prize for literature ?

(A) 1920 (B) 1921
(C) 1922 (D) 1923

47. Biographia Literaria was written by :

(A) Hazlitt (B) Keats
(C) Wordsworth (D) Coleridge

48. In which country is the story of Othello set ?

(A) Denmark (B) Venice
(C) Greece (D) England

49. From which play of Shakespeare is the following line taken ?

"Life is a tale told by an idiot full of sound and fury....."

(A) Hamlet (B) The Tempest
(C) Macbeth (D) Romeo and Juliet

50. Arnold mourns whose untimely death in his elegy entitled, Thyrisis ?

(A) Arthur Hugh Clough
(B) Arthur Hallam
(C) Mr. W. H. Auden
(D) None of these

51. What is figure of speech in the following sentence ?

"Authority forgets a dying king".

(A) Personification (B) Apostrophe
(C) Hyperbole (D) Metaphor

52. Which figure of speech is used in the following lines ?

Alone, alone, all all alone
alone, on a wide wide sea!

(A) Personification (B) Apostrophe
(C) Alliteration (D) Pun

53. A verse of two lines of equal length rhyming with each other at the end is called :

(A) quatrain (B) terza rima
(C) couplet (D) ottava rima

54. Choose the word that is closet in meaning to 'immunity' :

(A) freedom
(B) tolerance
(C) disinclination
(D) apathy

55. Complete the sentence with appropriate word from the choices given below :

Which is the shortest...........to Delhi,

(A) root (B) rout
(C) route (D) roots

56. Choose the word that is closest in meaning to 'connive" :

(A) instigate (B) disregard
(C) shield (D) threaten

57. Complete the sentence with the appropriate word from the choices given below :

All of his efforts were in_____

(A) wane (B) vain
(C) vein (D) van

Direction (Q. Nos. 58-62): Read the following passage carefully and answer the questions given below :

Just as some men like to play football or cricket, so some men like to climb mountains. This is often very difficult to do, for mountains are not just bill hills. Paths are usually very steep. Some mountain sides are straight up and down, so that it may take many hours to climb as little as one hundred feet. There is always the danger that you may fall off and be killed or injured. Men talk about conquering a mountain. It is a wonderful feeling to reach the top of a mountain after climbing for hours and may be, even for days. You look down and see the whole country below you. You feel god-like. Two Italian prisoners of war escaped from a prison camp in Kenya during the war. They did not try to get back to their country, for they, knew that was impossible. Instead, they climbed to the top of Mount Kenya, and then they came down and gave themselves up. They had wanted to get that feeling of freedom that one has after climbing a difficult mountain.

58. Mountaineering is not a very popular sport like football or cricket, because :

(A) there are no spectators in this sport
(B) it may not take many hours or even days
(C) many people are prepared to risk their lives
(D) people don't want to enjoy a god-like feeling

59. Why did two Italian prisoners escape from the camp and climb to the top of Mount Kenya ?
(A) To escape to Italy
(B) To come down and give up
(C) To get the feeling of freedom
(D) To gain fame as mountaineers

60. "It is a wonderful feeling." 'It' refers to :
(A) the steep path
(B) the prisoner
(C) climbing a mountain
(D) mountaineering

61. To claim mountains is often difficult, because :
(A) mountains are bill hills
(B) it consumes less time
(C) prisoners often escape from camps and settle there
(D) path are steep and uneven

62. Some men like to climb a mountain, because :
(A) they like to play football or cricket
(B) they know the trick to climbing
(C) they want to have a wonderful feeling
(D) they like to face danger

Direction (Q. Nos. 63-67) : A brief passage with five questions based on it is given below. Read the passage carefully and choose the most appropriate answer to each question :

Philosophy teaches us to feel uncertain about the things that seem to us self-evident. Propaganda, on the other hand, teaches us to accept as self-evident matters about which it would be reasonable to suspend our judgement or to feel doubt. The propagandist must therefore be consistently dogmatic. All his statements are made without qualification. There are no greys in his picture of the world. Everything is either diabolically black or celestially white. He must never admit that he might be wrong or that people with a different point of view might be even partially right. Opponents should not be argued with: they should be attacked, shouted down, or if they become too much of a nuisance, liquidated.

63. The author is of the view that an opponent should be:
(A) attacked (B) shouted down
(C) liquidated (D) argued with

64. A philosopher :
(A) never admits that he might be wrong
(B) never admits that the propagandist might be right
(C) is willing to admit that he might be wrong
(D) none of the above

65. Black, white and grey are mentioned as representing:
(A) bad, good and doubtful matters
(B) the basic colours in the world around us
(C) propagandists, philosophers and the common people
(D) none of the above

66. Propaganda teaches us :
(A) to feel doubt about matters that are self-evident
(B) to accent without question even those matters which are not self-evident
(C) to accept as reasonable those matters which are self-evident
(D) none of the above

67. Philosophy teaches us :
(A) to feel certain only about things which seen self-evident
(B) to feel certain only about those things which do not seem self-evident
(C) to feel uncertain about even those things which are supported by acceptable evidence
(D) none of the above

68. What is the correct term for the statement given below ?
"A place that provides refuge"
(A) Sanatorium (B) Shelter
(C) Orphanage (D) Asylum

69. Choose the term that is most opposite in meaning to 'shrill':
(A) weak
(B) muffled
(C) inaudible
(D) bluted

70. Choose the correct antonym of the word "feed" from the following :

(A) nourish (B) foster
(C) sustain (D) starve

71. Complete the following sentence with the most appropriate choice :

My parents were away visiting relatives, so I____to cut classes.

(A) decided (B) had decided
(C) have decided (D) decide

72. Choose the correct antonym of the word 'parsimonious' :

(A) economical (B) frugal
(C) niggardly (D) prodigal

73. Which of the following sentences is grammatically correct ?

(A) Unless he will study regularly, he will not pass
(B) Unless he does not study regularly, he will not pass
(C) unless he studies regularly, he will not pass
(D) None of the above

74. Complete the following sentence by most appropriate choice :

If the patient____enough money, she could have gone to consult a specialist.

(A) had (B) had had
(C) would have (D) was having

75. Complete the following sentence with most appropriate choice :

But, I____the tickets by four o'clock tomorrow.

(A) will have bought
(B) have bought
(C) bought
(D) shall buying

76. Which of the following sentences has a transitive verb ?

(A) He runs very fast
(B) He speaks French very fluently
(C) The dog has been barking for an hour
(D) The boys jumped up and down in excitement

77. Fill in the blank with the appropriate preposition :

This book consists____ten chapters.

(A) in (B) of
(C) off (D) with

78. Choose the mis-spelt word from the following :

(A) believe (B) receive
(C) conceive (D) bereive

79. Choose from the following the word which is correctly spelt :

(A) begining (B) explaination
(C) garage (D) maintainace

80. Which one the following is the correct spelling ?

(A) Limousine (B) Limuosine
(C) Limousane (D) Limozene

81. Find out the mis-spelt word :

(A) Supplementary
(B) surfiet
(C) suppurate
(D) surgery

82. Fill in the blank with an appropriate noun :

He saw a..........of fish.

(A) shoal (B) pack
(C) school (D) bunch

83. Fill the blank with an article :

India today needs..........Gandhi.

(A) the (B) a
(C) an (D) none of these

84. Fill in the blank with an appropriate preposition :

He knows how to play...........words.

(A) into (B) on
(C) up (D) over

85. He said to them all, "Goodbye my friends."

The correct indirect narration of the above direct speech is :

(A) He bade goodbye to all his friends
(B) He said to his friends 'good bye'
(C) He told his friends to goodbye
(D) He suggested goodbye to all his friends

86. Change the following into an indirect statement and indicate the correct one :
"I have bought a house," he said.
(A) He said that he had bought a house
(B) He said that he has bought a house
(C) He said that he would buy a house
(D) He said that he would buy a house

87. Choose the correct explanation of the idiom :
'Hand in hand'
(A) very intimate (B) mutual adjustment
(C) close fight (D) close together

88. 'To tread on someone's tone' meants to :
(A) flatter someone
(B) follow someone
(C) upset someone
(D) satisfy someone

89. Select the correct meaning of the idiom :
'To make both ends meet'
(A) to move between two opposite poles
(B) to meet the needs of the body and the soul
(C) to live within one's income
(D) to do somethine impossible

90. What is the meaning of the phrase ?
'Dispence with the books'
(A) Distribute the books
(B) Do away with the books
(C) Protect the books
(D) Investigate through the books

91. 'Bad blood' means :
(A) a disease
(B) unfriendliness
(C) unwelcome relatives
(D) impure blood

92. The practice of marrying more than one wife at a time is called :
(A) monogamy
(B) bigamy
(C) polygamy
(D) polyandry

93. Replace the underlined portion in the following sentence with one word :
<u>Putting off for tomorrow what can be done today</u> is the surest way to failure.
(A) proclamation
(B) procrastination
(C) profanation
(D) proliferation

94. Give the correct term for the statement given below :
"The part of a government which is concerned with making of rules"
(A) Court
(B) Tribunal
(C) Bar
(D) Legislature

95. A Turncoat is :
(A) a man of principles
(B) a poor man
(C) a man who changes his opinions
(D) a man who does not change his opinions

96. The substitution of part for the whole is :
(A) synecdoche (B) imagery
(C) metaphor (D) symbol

97. 'Lucy poems' by William Wordsworth refer to :
(A) Wordsworth's early poems
(B) a group of five lyrics by Wordsworth
(C) poem by Wordsworth in collaboration with Coleridge
(D) Wordsworth's humorous poems

98. Hemingway's A Farewell to Arms is set in :
(A) Italy (B) Switzerland
(C) USA (D) England

99. Which is the figure of speech used in the following sentence ?
"Friendship is a sheltering tree."
(A) Simile (B) Apostrophe
(C) Hyperbole (D) Metaphor

100. Which movement of the Victorian Age has influenced the novels of Charles Dickens ?
(A) Liberalism
(B) Pre-Raphaelite Movement
(C) Oxford Movement
(D) Aesthetic Movement

ANSWERS WITH EXPLANATION

1. (B) Classical Age or Augustan Age was Characterized by respect for rules, insistence on a set of poetic style.......... As a result against the classical school, strated the Romantic. Revival in English poetry.
2. (A)
3. (C) There is not any in justice to Dickens in going straight to the central feeling which gives life to his work and that feeling is social.
4. (D) It is a term rather casually introduced by T. S. Eliot in an essay on 'Hamlet and his problems (1919).
5. (B) In the wonderful variety of his verse he suggests all the qualities of England's greatest poets. The dreaminess of Spense. The majesty of milton simplicity of Wordsworth, fantasy of Blake and Coleridge..........

   As a poet, therefore, who expresses not so much a personal as a national spirit, he is probably the most representative literary man of victorian era.
6. (C) Thomas Hardy is the most important of the regional novelists of England. His wessca stretches from the English Channel in the south, to Cornwall in the west, and as for as Oxford to the north. It is this limited region which forms the scenic background to each of his "wessed novels"
7. (B) The Poem was published in 1842 along with other poems in the volume - 'Poems'.
8. (C) These lines occur in Robert Frost's famous poem 'Stopping by woods on a snomy evening'. These lines are famous in Indian context because over late Prime Minister Pandit Nehru was a great admiror of the poem and kept these lines written in his own writing on his table.
9. (B)
10. (D) Vivas Panorama Annual Current Affairs.
11. (B) The poem- O Captain! My Captain! is written by Walt Whitman who is considered as one of the best American poets. The poem is an elegy on the death of the famous American President, Abraham Lincoln.
12. (A) Earnest Hemingway (1898-1961) got Nobel Prize for literature in 1954 whose famous works are, Farewell to Arm, The Old Man and the Sea etc. He committed suicide by gun shot.
13. (B)
14. (A) Tennyson's later volumes, like the Ballads' (1880) and Demeter (1889), should not be overlooked, since they contained some of his best work. The former contains stirring war songs, like "The defence of Lucknow".
15. (B) Arnold believes in formulae and employs them unreservedly. The English aristocracy is 'barbarian' to him, the middle class are 'Philistim', while the people are a 'Populace'.
16. (A) History of English Literature, T. Singh.
17. (C) As an essayist, Lamp occupies a place among the great masters of this genre like Montaigne, Sir Thomas Browne, Steel and Addison. He has righty been called the "Prince of English Essayists". Bacon is called the 'Father of essays in English.
18. (D)
19. (D) These lines occurs in the poem— Ode : Intimations of Immortality by Wordsworth.
20. (C)
21. (B)
22. (C) 'The Scorpion' published 'in the exact Name' Presents a common Indian situation. It is a narrative poem. The poem describes a scorpion that stings Geah Laxmi, the poets mother.
23. (B)

24. (B) His letters are among the first in English not only for their discussion of his aesthetic ideas (negative capability', the chameleon poet) but also simple for their humanity, spontancita and humour. He gave this term in a letter.

25. (C) Miranda is the heroine of Shakespear's 'The Tempest' whereas Viola, Portia and Beatrice are heroines of 'Twelfth Night,' 'Merchant of Venice' and 'Much Ado About Nothing'.

26. (D) **27.** (C)

28. (C) These lines are the opening lines of 'Ode to a Nightingale'.

29. (C) Adonias is a wonderful threnody, over the death of poet Keats. I holds its place with Milton's 'Lycidas' and Tennyson's 'In Memorium' as one of the three greatest elegies.

30. (B) From the register of the little parish church at stratford on-Avon we learn that William Shakespeare was baptized there on the twenty-sixth of April, 1564. As it was customary to baptize children on the third day after birth, the twenty third of April is generally accepted as the poet's birthday.

31. (A) The very first poem of Wordsworth (Descriptive sketches, etc.) had borne testimoney to the wealth of his sensory notations.

32. (D) 'Triumph of life' was a unfinished poem and was his Dream poem in tersa rhyma with echoes of Italian poets.

33. (B) Perhaps the most loved of all Tennysons work is 'In Memorium', which on account of both its themes and its exquisite, workmanship, is. "One of the few immortal names that were not born to die." The immediate occasion of this poem was Tennyson's profound personal grief at the death of his friend Arthur Hallum.

34. (D) The Dynastas is a Drama of the Napoleonic wars in 3 parts, completed in 1908.

35. (C) 'The Hollow Men' is a famous poem by T. S. Eliot, Waste Land written in 1922. is a important work in the history of 20th century as Lyrical Ballads was in the history of 19th. The poem progresses rather abrupty through five movement as follows -

(i) The Burial of the Deal (ii) Game of Chess (iii) The Fire Sermon (iv) Death by Water (v) What the Thunder Side.

36. (A) **37.** (B)

38. (D)

39. (C) These lines are taken from the poem 'Ode to the west wide wind' by Shelley. These lines occur towards the end of fourth stanza.

40. (A) ....Endymion, which is the story of a young shephered by a moon Goddess. The poem begins with a striking line, A thing of beauty is a joy for ever.

41. (D) The Tales from Shakespeare (1807) was written by Charles and Mary Lamb, the former reproducing the tragedies, and the latter the comedies.

42. (B) In 1800 a second and enlarged edition of the Lyrical Ballads was Published, with a valuable preface, containing an outline of his poetical theory.

43. (A) Total number of sonnets by Shakespeare is 154 published collectively in 1609.

44. (B)

45. (B) Text of the old Man and the sea.

46. (D) By 1922, Yeats had become quite prosperous and renowned. He was elected a senator of the Irish free state. He was awarded the Nobel Prize for literature in 1923.

47. (D) Of Coleridge's prose works, the 'Biographia Literario' is an explanation and criticism of Wordsworth's theory of poetry, and contains more sound sense and illuminating ideas on the general subject of poetry than any other book in English Language.

48. (B) Othello's setting in Venice, a famous town of Italy, famous for its culure and art. Shakespeare made if the setting of his other novels too. Very first scene of Act I opens in a street of Venice.

49. (C) These lines are taken from Macbeth and told by Macbeth after hearing the news of his wife's death. It occurs in Act.V; SceneV; Lines 26, 27 and 28.

50. (A) ....All these of careful reading, but the best is 'Thyrsis', a lament for the poet clough.

51. (A) In personification inanimate objects and obstract notions are spoken of as having life and intelligence. e.g. Death lay his icy hand on kings.

52. (C) Alliteration consists in the repetition of the letters or syllable, or the same sound at the beginning of two or more words in a line. For example, How high has honour holds his haughty head.

53. (C) A quatrain is of four lines, terza rima of three lines, couplet of two lines and ottava rima of eight lines.

54. (A) **55.** (C)

56. (B) **57.** (B)

58. (C) **59.** (C)

60. (C) **61.** (D)

62. (C) **63.** (D)

64. (C) **65.** (A)

66. (B) **67.** (C)

68. (D)

69. (B) Shrill means 'Piecing'; 'Sharp in tone '. So its antonym is muffled which means low avaible voice.

70. (D) **71.** (A)

72. (D) Parsimonious means rigardly; undue economic, thus its antonym is prodigal that is spend thrift.

73. (C) Unless means 'if not', so no or not is not used after it as unless you work hard you will fail.

74. (B) **75.** (A)

76. (B) **77.** (B)

78. (D) Correct spelling is 'Bereave' which means to rob.

79. (C)

80. (A) Limousine means, clossed type of motor car.

81. (B) Correct spelling is Surfeit which means - Excess; Disgust caused by excess or feed to excess.

82. (A) Group of fish is called shoal of fish.

83. (B) **84.** (B)

85. (A) **86.** (A)

87. (D) **88.** (C)

89. (C) **90.** (B)

91. (B) **92.** (C)

93. (B) **94.** (D)

95. (C)

96. (A) In Synecdoche a part is used to designate the whole to designate a part.

97. (B) Wordsworth wrote and get published Lucy poem around 1800. All these poems are about a girl Lucy whose identity is never mentioned.

Lucy poem are -

(i) Strange Fits of Passion have I Known

(ii) I Travelled among unknown men

(iii) The Dwelt among untrodden ways

(iv) Three Years She Grew

(v) A Slumber did my spirit seal

98. (A)

99. (D) In metaphor, there is comparison between two things without using words-like, as etc. it is implied simile. The word metaphor comes from the Greek 'meta' - over; pheo - carry. By this figure of speech a word is transferred, or carried over, from the object to which it belongs to another in such a matter that a comparison is implied, though not clearly stated.

100. (A)

❑❑❑

PRACTICE SET–7

1. Which is Galsworthy's first play ?
   (A) Loyalties (B) Justice
   (C) Silver Box (D) Jocelyn
2. Which novel of Galsworthy is considered to be his masterpiece ?
   (A) The Pigeon
   (B) Flowering Wilderness
   (C) Island Pharisees
   (D) Indian Summer of A Forsyte
3. The first successful novel of John Galsworthy was :
   (A) The Man of Property
   (B) Fraternity
   (C) Silver Box
   (D) Strife
4. Several of Galsworthy's early novels, were written under a pscudonym of :
   (A) Juhnsin (B) Issac
   (C) John Sinjohn (D) Elia
5. When was 'The Prelude' published ?
   (A) 1805 (B) 1832
   (C) 1853 (D) None of these
6. ....Nature never did betray
   The heart that loved her........
   These lines exist in :
   (A) Immortality Ode
   (B) Michael
   (C) Ode to Duty
   (D) Tintern Abbey
7. Where from these lines have been taken ?
   Our birth is but a sleep and a forgetting :
   The soul that rises with us, our life's star,
   Hath had elsewhere its setting,
   (A) Tintern Abbey
   (B) Intimation of Immortality
   (C) To a Skylark
   (D) None of these
8. When was Wordsworth Laureated ?
   (A) 1798 (B) 1805
   (C) 1843 (D) Posthumously
9. The 'Lyrical Ballads' were better appreciated in America than in England. The first edition published in America in year :
   (A) 1798 (B) 1805
   (C) 1801 (D) 1802
10. Whom Milton considered his master in poetry ?
    (A) Chaucer (B) Shakespeare
    (C) John Donne (D) Spenser
11. The literary form of 'Comus' is :
    (A) A masque (B) A pastoral elegy
    (C) An epic (D) A sonnet
12. 'Nothing is here for tears, nothing to wail Or knock the breast, no weakness, no contempt Dispralse or blame,—nothing but well and fair And what may quiet us in death so noble' where from these lines taken ?
    (A) Paradise Regain
    (B) Paradise Lost.
    (C) On His Blindness
    (D) Samson Agonistes
13. Which one was Milton's favorite ?
    (A) Paradise Lost
    (B) Samson Agonistes
    (C) Paradise Regain
    (D) None of these

14. Theme of Areopagitica is :
(A) Liberty of women
(B) Freedom of press
(C) Sanction on press
(D) Sanction on polygamy

15. When was 'Paradise Lost' Published ?
(A) 1657 (B) 1671
(C) 1637 (D) 1667

16. The age of Milton when he wrote-'On the morning of Christ's Nativity' was :
(A) 20 (B) 23
(C) 43 (D) 47

17. Who wrote and about whom ?
'Thy soul was like a star, and dwelt a part'
(A) Milton about Shakespeare
(B) Keats about Milton
(C) Wordsworth about Milton
(D) Milton about Spencer

18. Lycidas was written in the memory of :
(A) Sir Christopher Milton
(B) Edward King
(C) Arthur Hugh Clough
(D) Arthur Hallam

19. John Milton was blinded in the year 1652, what other event is peculiar in the year ?
(A) Published-Comus
(B) Married
(C) His wife died
(D) Started Paradise Lost

20. Milton was born in Bread Street London in the year :
(A) 1616 (B) 1620
(C) 1608 (D) 1643

21. The line 'This is the noblest Roman of them all'—is said by :
(A) Cleopatra (B) Brutus
(C) Antonio (D) Caesar

22. Hermia is a character in Shakespeare's :
(A) Midsummer Night's Dream
(B) Romeo and Juliet
(C) Two Gentlemen of Verona
(D) Merry Wives of Windsor

23. Who expresses the common judgement of whom when he says, ''I do not remember that any book or person or event in my life ever made so great an impression upon me as the plays of Shakespeare''.
(A) Dante (B) Goethe
(C) Keats (D) Wordsworth

24. Where from these lines have been taken?
Fear no more the heat of the sun,
Nor the furious winter's rages;
Thou thy worldly task has done.
Home art gone and taken thy wages:
(A) Cymbelien
(B) Midsummer Night's Dream
(C) King Lear
(D) Hamlet

25. Where from these lines have been taken ?
"Good friend, for Jesus' sake forbear to dig the dust enclosed hearer Bleste be the man that spares these stones And curst be he that moves my bones".
(A) Cymbeline
(B) As You Like It
(C) Much Ado About Nothing
(D) Shakespeare's Tomb

26. Shakespeare was not of an age, but for all time was uttered by :
(A) John Milton (B) Mathew Arnold
(C) Ben Jonson (D) T.S. Eliot

27. From where these lines have been taken and who is the speaker ?
We or such stuffs
As dreams are made on; and our little life is rounded with a sleep.
(A) Macbeth, Macbeth
(B) Hamlet, Hamlet
(C) Twelfth Night, Malvolio
(D) Tempest, Prospero

28. Who called Shakespeare—'Sweetest Shakespeare, Fancy's child'?
(A) Milton
(B) Coleridge
(C) Ben Jonson
(D) Arnold

29. Which one is the right chronological order of Shakespeare's major tragedies ?

(A) Hamlet, Othello, King Lear, Macbeth,

(B) Hamlet, King Lear, Macbeth, Othello

(C) Hamlet, Macbeth, Othello, King Lear.

(D) Macbeth, King Lear, Hamlet, Othello.

Direction: Answer the questions (30) to (34) based on the passage given below—

It is difficult to believe, that any man can be so spiritually dead as to have no love for his native country after travelling in foreign lands. But if such an unpatriotic person does exist, take careful note of his career, and you will find that he will never inspire poets to celebrate him in deathless songs. He may be a man of high rank, of noble family and of riches beyond the dream of avarice, but these great advantages will not' save him from oblivion. In spite of them all, he will win no fame during his life time, and when he dies he will die in a double sense. His body will return to the dust whence it came, and his name will be forgotten. None will weep for him, non will honour him, and no poet will keep his name alive in immortal poetry.

30. The people who does not love their country are :

(A) In majority (B) None

(C) Very few (D) Not clear

31. In the passage, man is said to die in double sense; Which death is repentable ?

(A) Physical (B) Oblivion

(C) Can't be said (D) None

32. Passage deals with the problem of :

(A) Brain drain (B) Corruption

(C) Treason (D) None

33. Such a man described in the passage will not achieve fame if he is :

(A) Not of a noble family

(B) Not a rich man

(C) Not a great poet

(D) In no condition

34. An unpatriotic man, who not loves his country, will be treated by poets :

(A) Hated

(B) Ridicule

(C) Not immonalize

(D) Not say any thing

35. Who is the author of the line

'Tyger's heart wrapt in a player's hide'—about Shakespeare ?

(A) Ben Jonson

(B) Christopher Murlowe

(C) Mathew Arnold

(D) Robert Greene

36. It is believed that Shakespeare was found guilty of deer poaching in the garden of :

(A) William Herbert

(B) Robert Greene

(C) Thomas Lucy

(D) Thomas Thorpe

37. Which drama of Shakespeare was not included in the first folio of 1623 by Hemiage and Condell ?

(A) Pericles (B) Titus Andronicus

(C) Cymbeline (D) Winter's tale

38. Venus and Adonis by Shakespeare was written in stanzas of :

(A) Four lines (B) Six lines

(C) Seven lines (D) Nine lines

39. Best works of Shakespeare was done :

(A) Before 1595 (B) Before 1601

(C) After 1612 (D) After 1603

40. Who is the author of 'Robinson Crusoe' ?

(A) Daniel Defoe (B) Samuel Richardson

(C) Henry Fielding(D) John Galsworthy

41. What is closet drama ?

(A) Drama to be acted in open

(B) Drama to be read

(C) Drama to be acted indoor

(D) Drama to be performed in streets

42. A character which remains almost unchanged throughout the story is called :

(A) Round character

(B) Dynamic character

(C) Caricature

(D) Flat character

43. What is the theme of the proletarian novel ?
(A) Aristocratic class
(B) Warriors
(C) Middle class
(D) Working class

44. Who is the father of the term "Objective correlative"?
(A) T.S. Eliot (B) Mathew Arnold
(C) John Keats (D) Wordsworth

45. The term Dystopia implies :
(A) Pleasant imaginary world
(B) Unpleasant real world
(C) Pleasant real world
(D) Unpleasant imaginary world

46. What is meant by Catharsis ?
(A) Tragic flaw in the antagonist
(B) Tragic flaw in the protagonist
(C) False step taken in dark
(D) Purgation of emotion of pity and fear

47. The unbroken flow of thought and awareness in the waking mind is called :
(A) Stream of consciousness
(B) Epiphany
(C) Negative capability
(D) Objective correlative

48. Period between 1700-1745 in English literature is called :
(A) The Restoration Period
(B) Caroline Age
(C) The Augustan Age
(D) The Age of Johnson.

49. What is poetic license ?
(A) Poetry written to establish rules and regulations of verification
(B) Royal permission to write poetry
(C) Liberties with language and facts in poetry
(D) Poetic norms of a particular period

50. The type of fiction whose setting is in the medival period, often in a gloomy castle reptele with dungeons subterranean passages and use of ghosts and mysteries is called :
(A) Picaresque novel
(B) Gothic novel
(C) Epistotary novel
(D) Historic novel

51. Transform the following sentence into exclamatory sentence.
He leads a most unhappy life.
(A) What an unhappy life he leads !
(B) What an unhapply life he leads !
(C) What an unhappy life he was leading!
(D) Why he leads a most unhappy life ?

52. Who has written 'Ruth' ?
(A) Milton
(B) Shakespeare
(C) Galsworthy
(D) Wordsworth

53. Who asked, 'How many children had Lady Macbeth' ?
(A) D.C. Knights (B) A.C. Bradley
(C) Rymer (D) Wilson

54. Fill in the blank with an appropriate preposition : She is ignorant .... what she pretends to know.
(A) in (B) of
(C) with (D) for

55. What could be the 'tragic flaw' in Hamlet ?
(A) Noble
(B) Oedipus Complex
(C) Vaulting ambition
(D) None of these

56. What is soliloquy ?
(A) an actor's secret thought uttered aloud
(B) secret speech
(C) an actor's speech not to be heard by audience
(D) an actor's speech meant for other characters also

57. Who considered romanticism, "liberalism in literature" ?
(A) Wordsworth
(B) Plato
(C) Theodore Watts-Dunton
(D) Victor Hugo

58. Fill in the gap.
Galsworthy's famous play. The Silver Box deals with.................. .
(A) the inequality of power
(B) the inequality of justice
(C) the inequality of labour
(D) the inequality of money division

59. Wordsworth has expressed his views on transmigration of the soul in his poem
(A) The Prelude
(B) Ode to Duly
(C) Ecclesiastical Sketches
(D) Ode on the intimations of Immortality

60. Complete the sentence
The term 'Novel' was taken from the Italian word:
(A) novella (B) novelle
(C) novelette (D) noval

61. Who has written *Peter Bell* among the followings?
(A) William Wordsworth
(B) Shakespeare
(C) John Galsworthy
(D) John Milton

62. Who is Hamlet's beloved in Hamlet ?
(A) Olivia (B) Portia
(C) Ophelia (D) Cordelia

63. What is 'Aside' ?
(A) Addressed in words that the other actors are not supposed to hear
(B) Addressed in words that the other actors are supposed to hear
(C) Looking behind when one speaks
(D) Not paying attention

64. Fill in the gap.
The public are cautioned ....pickpockets.
(A) to (B) for
(C) with (D) against

65. "Take O take those lips away,"
The above line occurs in ....
(A) Midsummer Night's Dream
(B) Twelfth Night
(C) Antony and Cleopatra
(D) Measure For Measure

66. Point out the figure of speech-
To err is human, to forgive is divine :
(A) Antithesis (B) Apostrophe
(C) Metaphor (D) Simile

67. Change the voice—Where did Sita buy the hat ?
(A) Where sita bought the hat?
(B) From where did sita bought the hat?
(C) Where was the hat bought by sita?
(D) None of these

68. Change the voice—We may finish the work soon.
(A) The work may be finished soon.
(B) The work might be finished soon.
(C) The work might finish soon.
(D) None of these

69. Change the voice—The news pleased him :
(A) He was pleased by the news
(B) He was pleased with the news
(C) He was pleased to the news
(D) None of these

70. Pick out the most implying meaning—Ingenvity
(A) Skillfulness (B) Bullness
(C) Sentimental (D) Certainly

71. In which sentence 'As' is used as conjuction ?
(A) We walked as fast as we could.
(B) She likes the same colour as I do.
(C) As he was poor I helped him.
(D) None of these

72. In which sentence 'above' is used as adverb ?
(A) The moral law is above the civil.
(B) Analyse the above sentence.
(C) Our blessing come from above.
(D) The heavens are above.

73. The correct sentence is :
(A) The bag together with the books are lost.
(B) The bags together with the book is lost.
(C) The bag together with the books is lost.
(D) The bags together with the books is lost.

74. Choose the correct sentence :
(A) Two hundred rupees is not a big sum.
(B) Two hundred rupee are not a big sum.
(C) Two hundred ruppee are not a big sum.
(D) Two hundred ruppes is not a big sum.

75. Find the correct sentence
(A) He is one of those boys who are wicked.
(B) He is one of those boys who is wicked.
(C) He is one of those boy who is wicked.
(D) He is one of those boy who are wicked.

76. Which sentence is correct ?
(A) The news of the train accident are shocking.
(B) The news of the train accident is shocking.
(C) The news of the train accidents is shocking.
(D) None of the above

77. Which one is the correct sentence ?
(A) He said that earth was round.
(B) He said that earth is round.
(C) He said that earth has been round.
(D) None of the above

78. Change the narration of the sentence :
You say, 'I cut the finger'.
(A) You say that you cut the finger.
(B) You said that you had cut the finger.
(C) You say that I cut the finger.
(D) You said that I had cut the finger.

79. What is the meaning of imminent ?
(A) Famous (B) Crafty
(C) Near at hand (D) Rare

80. What is the meaning of pertinent ?
(A) Narrow minded
(B) Relevance
(C) Curious
(D) Upside down

81. A cure for all diseases is :
(A) Panacea (B) Gratis
(C) Temporal (D) None

82. Antonym of Zenith is :
(A) Nadir (B) Important
(C) Summit (D) Heaven

83. What is the meaning of Indigent ?
(A) Rich (B) Brave
(C) Intellectual (D) Poor

84. The meaning of Liaison is :
(A) Hatred (B) Love
(C) Rough (D) Intimacy

85. Correctly punctuated sentence is :
(A) The other boy (Mukul (alias Munna)) was there.
(B) The other boy (Mukul [alias Munna]) was there.
(C) The other boy (Mukal (alias munna)] was there.
(D) Two brackets are not used in a single sentence.

86. Which sentence has a transitive verb ?
(A) He was looking at me.
(B) Don't interfere in the quarrel.
(C) He has gone to Patna.
(D) He treated her badly.

87. Find the correct sentence :
(A) Tom, I and you ate sweets.
(B) I, you and tom ate sweets.
(C) I. Tom and you ate sweets.
(D) You, Tom and I ate sweets.

88. Find out the correct sentence :
(A) Alm is given to the beggar.
(B) Alms is given to the beggars.
(C) Alms are given to the beggars.
(D) None of these.

89. His courage won him honour. The word 'honour' is :
(A) Adjective (B) Adverb
(C) Noun (D) Verb

90. How many parts of speech are there in number ?
(A) 6 (B) 7
(C) 8 (D) 10

91. Find the correctly spelt word :
(A) Gramar
(B) Havene
(C) Haven
(D) Macaber

92. The misspelt word is :
(A) Comitte (B) Nursery
(C) Miscellaneous (C) Occurrence

Direction: Answer the questions (93-97) based on the passage given below :

We are all short-sighted, and very often see but one side of a matter; our views are not extended to all that has a connection with it. From this defect I think, no man is free. We see but in part, and we know but in part, and therefore it is no wonder we conclude not right from our partial views. This might instruct the proudest esteemer of his own parts how useful it is to talk and consult with others, even such as come short of him in capacity, quickness, and penetration; for since no one sees all and we generally have different prospects of same thing, according to our different, as I may say, positions to it. It is not incongruous to think, not any man to try, whether another man may not havenotions of things which have escaped him, and which his reason would make use of if they came his mind.

93. Suggestion and consultation can be made only with our superior in ability. The statement is :
(A) Incorrect (B) Comet
(C) Not clear (D) None

94. What is the meaning of 'Incongruous'?
(A) Appropiate (B) Dignified
(C) Absurd (D) Useful

95. How can one amend and improve his judgment of things ?
(A) Its not possible
(B) By consulting other imperfect people
(C) By avoiding it
(D) By forcing one's judgment

96. As it is not in our capacity to sec the things as whole so making a partial judgment is :
(A) Justified (B) Not Justified
(C) Partially Justified (D) None

97. Since no one is perfect and whole-sighted so its of no use taking suggestions from other such people to reach a conclusion
(A) Incorrect
(B) Correct
(C) Cannot be said confirmly
(D) None of these.

98. Which drama of Galsworthy deals with the conflict between capitalists and labourers ?
(A) Strife (B) Silver Box
(C) Loyalties (D) The Skin Game

99. 'The Dark Flower' by John Galsworthy is :
(A) A love drama (B) A tragic play
(C) A love novel (D) A comic play

100. When was John Galsworthy awarded Nobel Prize for literature ?
(A) 1933 (B) 1932
(C) 1930 (D) 1929

ANSWERS WITH EXPLANATION

1. (D) All other three—'Loyalties', 'Justice' and 'Silverbox' are plays whereas 'Jocelyn' is a movel written in 1899.

2. (D)

3. (A) 'The Man of Property' (1906) raised Galsworthy to the front rank of living novelists. In this first, successful work he created a new type of fiction by 'balancing', as he said, 'the virtues and vices of his hero Soames Forsyte, against the vices and virtues of other members of the same family.

4. (C)

5. (D) The Prelude was published after Wordsworth's death in 1850.

6. (D) In 'Tintern Abbey' Wordsworth says to his sister to have company with nature which is a true friend and guide to every heart. In fact this is the philosophy of Wordsworth of Nature.

7. (B) Text.

8. (C) On the death of Soutney (1843), Wordsworth was made poet laureate, against his own inclination.

9. (D)
10. (D) Milton, while deep in classics, had yet a greater love for his native literature. Spenser was for years his master.
11. (A) The 'Masque of Comus', written in 1634 to be performed at Ludlow Castle before the earl of Bridgewater and his friends.
12. (D) 13. (C)
14. (B) Milton's Areopagitica—So called from the Arepagus or Forum of Athens, the place of public appeal, and the Mars Hill of St. Paul's address-is the most famous pica in English for the freedom of the press.
15. (D)
16. (A) After some interesting essays, some fine verses to Shakespeare and the superb 'At a Solemn Music' which weds Voice and verse, he wrote, in 1629, his first masterpiece, the ode, 'On the Morning of Christ's Nativity'. Milton was born in 1608.
17. (C) This line is a part of a sonnet entitled 'London-1802' or 'To Milton'. This is the 9th line that is to say the first Sine of the sestet.
18. (B) Lycidas is a pastoral elegy written in 1637. A college friend, Edward King has been drowned in the Irish sea, find Milton follows the poetic custom of his age by representing both his friend and himself in the guise of shepherds leading the pastoral life.
19. (C) Milton lost his eyesight in the same year in which his first wife died that is 1652 and married a second time in 1656.
20. (C) Milton was a Londoner by birth and was born in Bread Street on 9th December 1608, but his family belonged to Oxfordshire.
21. (C) This line is said by Antony in 'Julius Caesar' in Act V; Sc-V at the death of Brutus because he knew that Brutus was the single person in the side of conspirator who participated in the conspiracy against Caesar for the love of his country rather than personal ends.
22. (A) Hermia is daughter of Egues who chooses demetrius for her husband but she elopes with her lover Lysander. In the forest they find Helena who loves Demetrius and is friend of Hermia and a lot of complications amuse the reader.
23. (B)
24. (A) When Tennyson died in 1892 'Cymbelien' by Shakespeare was open at his table where these lines form their existence.
25. (D) And in the sad irony of fate, the broad stone that covered his tomb—now an object of veneration to the thousands that yearly visit the little church —was thus inscribed.
26. (C) 27. (D)
28. (A) Milton echoed his loving praise of Shakespeare, calling him 'sweetest Shakespeare, Fancy's child', who warbled borth his 'native wood notes wild'.
29. (A) 30. (C)
31. (B) Physical death is not in our hand to avoid but we may keep our name worth remembering through our deeds.
32. (D) 33. (D)
34. (C)
35. (D) Greene in a Pamphlet wrote this line out of jealousy.
36. (C) Tradition there is though of no great age and of exceedingly slight authority as to his (Shakespeare) leaving Stratford for London, perhaps in 1585, 1586 or 1587, and perhaps in consequence of a deer steal by prank in the neighouring park of Sir Thomas Lucy.
37. (A) The first printed collection of Shakespeare's plays, now called the first folio 1623, was made by two actors, Heminge and Cordell. This contains 36 of the 37 plays generally attributed to Shakespeare, pericles being omitted.
38. (B) Venus and Adonis is in six lines stanzas and Rape of Lucerce is in 7 lines stanzas.

39. (D) A considerable part of Shakespeare's work was done before 1603. But certainly the best part was not.

40. (A)

41. (B) A closet drama is written in the form of drama, but is intended to be read rather than to be performed in the theatre; e.g. Milton's— Samson Agonistes and Shelley's—'Prometheus Unbound'.

42. (D) **43.** (D)

44. (A) T.S. Elliot used this term is his essay 'Hamlet and His Problems', to explain how emotion is best expressed in poetry. It cannot be simply transmitted from the mind of the poet to the mind of the reader. It has to turn itself into something concrete—a picture of a person, place, or things suggestion of it—to evoke the same emotion in the reader.

45. (D) It means 'bad place'. Its examples, One Aldous Huxley's 'Brave New Worlds' and George Orwels '1984'.

46. (D) The purgation of the emotions of pity and fear aroused by the actions of the tragic hero.

47. (A) It presents supposedly random flow of thoughts through the mind of characters.

48. (C) The period between 1700-1745 is also known as the Age of Pope.

49. (C) The phrase implies that while writing poetry poet can take liberty with facts and events to give vent to his own imagination.

50. (B) The term originally referred to the 'Goths', a Germanic tribe, then came to signify 'Gramanic' then 'medieval'. The term Gothic has also been extended to denote a type of fiction which lacks the medieval setting but develops a brooding atmosphere of gloom or terror, represents events which are uncanny or nacabre.

51. (A) **52.** (D)

53. (A)

54. (B) The following adjectives and participles take the preposition 'of' after them.

Accused, acquitted, afraid, apprehensive, apprised, assured, aware, bought. Cautious, certain, composed, confident, conscious, convicted, convinced, covetous, defraud, deprived, desirous, destitute, devoid, diffident, distrustful, dull, easy, envious, fearful, fond, greedy, guilty, ignorant, innocent, lame, lavish, negligent, proud, sanguine, sick, sure, vain, weary worthy.

55. (D)

56. (A) An actor's secret thought uttered aloud Soliloquy- Theatrical device whereby an actor expresses his thoughts to the audience alone. It is spoken by one person that is alone on the stage.

57. (D) **58.** (A)

59. (D) Ode on the Intimations of immortality

60. (A)

61. (A) William Wordsworth

Peter Bell, a poem written as a reply (or rather a rival) to Coleridge's The Ancient Mariner. Like Coleridge's poem, it is the story of, the redemption of a human soul. About Peter Bell Grierson and Smith write." Wordsworth was so bent on teaching on tracing as he put it, the manner in which we associate ideas in state of excitement that he sometimes forgot in practice the maxim which he acknowledge in theory' the poesy onto instructs as it delightes. Peter Bell does not delight".

62. (C) Ophelia

Characters of Hamlet

Hamlet-Prince of Denmark

Claudius-Hamlet's Uncle

The Ghost of the late king

Gertrude the queen

Poloniun-Councillor of state

Laertes-Polonius's son

Ophelia-Polonius's daughter

Horatio : friend and confident of Hamlet

Rosencrantz and Guidenstern-Courtiers

Fortinbras-Prince of Norway

63. (A) Addressed in words that the other actors are not supposed to hear.

Aside-Theatrical device whereby the audience is directly addressed in words the other actors are not supposed to hear.

64. (A) **65.** (D)

66. (A) **67.** (C)

68. (C)

69. (B) Pleased is a verb showing 'State' rather than action so 'with' will be used.

70. (A) **71.** (C)

72. (D)

73. (C) Here "The bag" and "the books" are subjects, so will be verb accordingly.

74. (A) Two hundred rupees is a single unit hence, singular verb is used.

75. (A) There is boys, a plural, before who, so the verb after it will also be plural.

76. (B) News is a singular noun so with singular subject singular verb is used.

77. (B) Though the verb of principal clause is in past tense yet as there is a universal truth in the subordinate clause so the verb in the subordinate clause will be in present tense.

78. (A) When the subject of reporting clause is 'you' and that of reported speech is 'I' then in Indirect speech 'I' is changed into 'you'.

79. (C) **80.** (B)

81. (A) **82.** (A)

83. (D) **84.** (D)

85. (B) When we have to add something in round brackets ()—we use square brackets [ ].

86. (D) A transitive verb is one that can have an object.

87. (D) The use of first, second and third person pronouns always follows the order of—second, third then first.

88. (C) 'Alms' is always used in the plural form and take a plural verb.

89. (C) **90.** (C)

91. (C)

92. (A) The correct spelling is committee.

93. (A) **94.** (C)

95. (B) **96.** (B)

97. (A)

98. (A) 'Strife' deals with the conflict between the capitalists and the labourers. A long-standing strike that has been going on at the Trenartha Tin Plate Works seems to come in sight by a settlement arrived at between the labourers and the capitalists.

99. (C) **100.** (B)

❑❑❑

PRACTICE SET–8

Direction (Q. No. 1 to 4): Each of the following sentences is divided into three parts (A), (B) and (C). Some of the sentences have errors in one part and some have none. Find out which part of the sentence has an error.

1. I could not convince them/because they persisted (A) (B) to suggest/that I was lying/No error (C) (D)

2. Without a moment's hesitation/the Principal (A) (B) agreed to write/a foreward to my book/No error. (C) (D)

3. My sister and her husband/broke out/When (A) (B) they heard the bad news./No error. (C) (D)

4. He could not do/other wise but/to obey the (A) (B) (C) orders./No error. (D)

5. Whom does Milton accuse in 'Paradise Lost' as "The Sans of Belian flown with insolence and wine"?

(A) The Anglican clergy
(B) The Cavelier poets
(C) The opponents of the commonwealth
(D) All of the above

6. Who is the author of 'Lyrical Ballads'?

(A) Keats
(B) Wordsworth
(C) Dryden
(D) Pope

7. When was 'Paradise Lost' completed by Milton?

(A) 1640 (B) 1665
(C) 1641 (D) 1660

8. 'Lucydes' is Milton's:

(A) A Pastoral Elegy (B) General poem
(C) An Ode (D) None of these

9. Shakespeare's 'Merchant of Venice' was produced in:

(A) 1597 (B) 1598
(C) 1599 (D) 1596

10. What is the year of death of Shakespeare?

(A) 1624 (B) 1616
(C) 1611 (D) 1610

11. One of the best-plays, 'The Tempest' is the last of Shakespeare's plays. He was inspired to write it by which incident?

(A) Sinking of a ship
(B) The defeat of Armada
(C) Return of the sailors of a ship that had disappeared
(D) None of the above

12. Recollect 'Romeo and Juliet', and state the meaning of "My life is my foe's debts":

(A) That he had to marry someone from whose father he had taken a loan
(B) That someone was trying to kill him
(C) That he loved Juliet who was the daughter of the enemy of his family
(D) None of the above.

13. Which of the following was an epic?

(A) Wordsworth's 'Daffodils'
(B) 'Paradise Lost'
(C) Coleridge's 'Kubla Khan'
(D) Keat's 'Hyperian'.

14. Who possesses the natural simplicity of Wordsworth, the fantasy of Coleridge, the melody of Keats and Shelley, the narrative vigour of Scott?

(A) John Masefield (B) Alfred Tennyson
(C) Robert Browning (D) W.B. Yeats

15. "In Milton there is always an appearance of effort; in Shakespeare, scarcely any" This remark has been made by:

(A) Thomas Hardy (B) Nissim Ezekiel
(C) William Hazlitt (D) Mathew Arnold

16. Iliad was first translated into English by:

(A) Dryden (B) Pope
(C) Jone King (D) None of them

17. A Sonnet consists of:

(A) 18 lines (B) 20 lines
(C) 14 lines (D) 12 lines

18. "The fault dear Brutus is not in our stars. But in ourselves, that we are underlings."

Cassius made this remark before Brutus because:

(A) He loves Brutus and wanted to see him on the top
(B) He hates Brutus and wanted to kill him
(C) He hates Caesar and wanted to kill him
(D) He was jealous of growing power of Caesar and wanted to incite Brutus against Caesar.

19. Punctuate the following sentences:

'I went up to him and held out my hand how are you I asked I am not in hilarious spirits he answered,"

Find out the correct one:

(A) I went up to him and held out my hand how are you I asked. I am not in hilarious spirits, He answered.
(B) I went up to him and held out my hand, how are you, I asked, I am not in Hilarious spirits, He answered.
(C) I went up to him and held out my hand. "How are you, I asked, I am not in hilarious spirits, he answered."
(D) I went up to him and held my hand. "How are you?" I asked, I am not in hilarious spirits, he answered.

20. Which of the following words means "Talking to one's self"?

(A) Soliloquy (B) Spokesmen
(C) Garrulity (D) None of these

21. Who set the style for modern English prose?

(A) Chaucer (B) Lamb
(C) Dryden (D) Swift

22. The writer of 'Coriolanus' is:

(A) Christopher Marlowe
(B) P. B. Shelly
(C) William Shakespeare
(D) John Milton

23. 'Paradise Lost' consists of....... books.

(A) 10 (B) 12
(C) 06 (D) 08

24. Select the right meaning of the word 'Omnipotent' from the following:

(A) One who is all powerful
(B) One who is intelligent
(C) One who loves mankind
(D) One who believes in the existence of God

25. Find out the correct sentence:

(A) My son is desirous in joining the Army.
(B) My son is desirous on joining the Army.
(C) My son is desirous of joining the Army.
(D) My son is desirous for joining the Army.

26. Shakespeare was born in:

(A) 1564 (B) 1464
(C) 1664 (D) 1364

27. 'Gitanjali' in English was published in:

(A) 1911 (B) 1912
(C) 1913 (D) 1914

28. Which of the following phrases are Personified:

(A) Revenge is kind (B) Swift as a wind
(C) Thirsty earth (D) Honest thief

29. Who quoted these lines about tragedy? "The plot, then is the first principle and soul of tragedy, and character hold the second place,"

(A) Plato
(B) Aristotle
(C) Shakespeare
(D) Longinus

30. Punctuate the following lines:
The old man chuckled and said you have yet to learn how to fly a kite properly my child.
Find out the correct one.
(A) The old man chuckled and said, you have yet to learn how to fly a kite properly my child.
(B) The Old man chuckled and said, you have yet to learn-How to fly a kite properly my child?
(C) The old man chuckled and said, you have yet to learn "How to fly a kite properly my child?"
(D) The old man chuckled and said," You have yet to learn how to fly a kite properly, my child."

31. Which word is mis-spelt:
(A) Zealous (B) Opposite
(C) Empirical (D) Rhytoric

32. Fill in the blank with a suitable word:
Use of this .... for seven days will cure you of your illness.
(A) Physic (B) Physique
(C) Physics (D) Physical

33. "Cowards die many times before their death. The valiant never taste of death but once," These lines have been taken from:
(A) The Tempest
(B) Julius Caesar
(C) The Merchant of Venice
(D) Othello

34. Correct form of the sentence, 'I bear no malice ......anybody,' is:
(A) I bear no malice on anybody.
(B) I bear no malice against anybody.
(C) I bear no malice in anybody.
(D) I bear no malice over anybody.

35. Fill in the blank with in a suitable preposition:
'Distribute the sweets........Rain and Suresh.'
(A) with (B) between
(C) to (D) for

36. What figure of speech has been used in the following lines?
'O World!O Life !O Time!
O Julius Caesar, thou art mighty yet.'
(A) Oxymoron (B) Rethoric
(C) Personification (D) None of these

37. The most appropriate one word substitute for "A person living at the same time as another" is:
(A) Archaic (B) Nostrum
(C) Contemporary (D) None of these

38. Which of the following sentences has the figure of speech called "Apostrophe"?
(A) I am the monarch of all I survey.
(B) O Solitude! Where are thy charms?
(C) Anxiety is sitting on her face.
(D) I wondered lonely as a cloud.

39. Arnold wrote: "With him is born our real poetry". The word "him" refers to:
(A) Milton (B) Shakespeare
(C) Wordsworth (D) None of them

40. The poet of the famous poem 'Daffodils' is:
(A) J. Keats (B) A Pope
(C) P. B. Shelly (D) W. Wordsworth

41. Who states: "He found English a dialect and left it a Language."
(A) W. Shakespeare (B) J. Milton
(C) M. Arnold (D) None of them

42. 'Macbeth' sees the ghost of:
(A) Banquo (B) Duncan
(C) lago (D) Hamlet

43. Who states these words for Shakespeare?
"Soul of the Age. The applause! the delight! the wonder of our stage."
(A) Matthew Arnold (B) T.S. Elliot
(C) Ben Jonson (D) T. Eagllion

44. Read the following lines and answer the question that follows it:
"O Julius Caesar, thou are might yet! Thy spirit walks abroad and turns, our swords in our proper external."
What is the essence of this statement?
(A) Brutus was too mighty.
(B) Caesar was mighty even after his death.
(C) Antony was mighty.
(D) Cassius was mighty.

45. Who changed his/her religion some years ago?
(A) M.R. Anand (B) Kamala Das
(C) Nissim Ezekiel (D) None of them

46. Autobiography means:
(A) The life history of a person written by someone else.
(B) The life history of a person written by himself.
(C) The life history of a person as reflected in his writings.
(D) The life history of a person created in painting by himself.

47. Who is the heroine in Shakespeare's 'The Tempest'?
(A) Portia (B) Neresia
(C) Desdemona (D) Miranda

48. Which of the following words is mis-spelt?
(A) Gregarious (B) Fatalist
(C) Philistine (D) Celebasy

49. The correct term for "A person of a material outlook and indifferent to culture" is:
(A) Philistine (B) Barbarous
(C) Nomad (D) Anarchist

50. The figure of speech in which we describe intelligence and personality to inanimate things is known as:
(A) Metaphor (B) Personification
(C) Oxymoron (D) None of these

Direction (Q.No. 51 to 55): In these questions, three words having different meaning of a certain word are given, select that word from the answer choices given under each set of words.

51. Tender, Loving, Warm
(A) Fond (B) Affectionate
(C) Lukewarm (D) Control

52. Bribe, Inducement, Carrot
(A) Sweetener (B) Saltiness
(C) Somber (D) Almond

53. Pavement, Roadway, Concrete
(A) Beach (B) Street
(C) Park (D) Border

54. Cheer, Encourage, Warm
(A) Exhilarate (B) Fame
(C) Defame (D) Courageous

55. Haste, Hurry, Promptness
(A) Worry (B) Carelessness
(C) Speed (D) Immediate

Direction (Q.No. 56 to 65): Three of the four items in these questions are alike, in a certain way and so form a group. Choose the one which does not belong to the group.

56. (A) Oyster (B) Snail
(C) Alligator (D) Tortoise

57. (A) Investigation (B) Deliberation
(C) Exploration (D) Probe

58. (A) Globe (B) Sphere
(C) Spectre (D) Ball

59. (A) Violet (B) Indigo
(C) Pink (D) Green

60. (A) Ring (B) Ornament
(C) Bangle (D) Necklace

61. (A) Seminar (B) Semicircle
(C) Semifinal (D) Semiliquid

62. (A) Rain (B) Mist
(C) Cloud (D) Fog

63. (A) Panther (B) Whale
(C) Lion (D) Crocodile

64. (A) Town (B) Village
(C) Home (D) Metropolis

65. (A) Apple (B) Orange
(C) Pineapple (D) Tomato

66. Read the following lines of poem and answer the question that follows:
"Yes I must pass them for a noble life where I may find agonies, the strife of human heart". Which characteristics of the poet's creation do you find in these lines?
(A) Romantic quality (B) Humanitarian
(C) Melancholy (D) Sensuousness

67. Pick out the correct word to complete the given proverb:
The empty vessel ....much.

(A) sounds (B) weights
(C) sells (D) costs

68. What is the antonym of 'Stigma'?
(A) Stain (B) Blot
(C) Smelly (D) Distinction

69. 'Romanticism' and 'Idealism' are the main features of:
(A) Romantic Literature
(B) Victorian Literature
(C) Elezabethan Literature
(D) Augustan Literature

70. What figure of speech has been used in the following line?
'Let not Ambition mock their useful toil'.
(A) Personification (B) Oxymoron
(C) Metaphor (D) Implied Simile

71. The figure of speech which consists in the use of word which suggest the sense by their sound is called:
(A) Onomatopoeia (B) Apostrophe
(C) Hyperbole (D) None of these

72. A .... is a small descriptive poem in which the machinery and conventions of epic proper are used in the treatment of previous themes,
(A) Dramatic Monologue
(B) Ballad
(C) Mock epic
(D) None of these

73. Choose the response which gives the correct spelling to the word:
(A) Dispassonate (B) Dispassionate
(C) Disfasionate (D) Dispassionet

74. "A savage place! as holy and enchanted As e'er beneath a waning moon was haunted! By women wailing for demon lover?" These lines throw light on:
(A) Shakespeare's supernatural element
(B) Coleridge's supernatural element
(C) Wordsworth's passion of nature
(D) Keats hellenism

75. What is the antonym of 'Insolvent'?
(A) Bankrupt (B) Wealthy
(C) Intuition (D) Translate

76. Find out the correct indirect narration of the following direct speech:
He said to them all. "Good-bye, my friends!"
(A) He told to them good-bye.
(B) He said to his friends good-bye.
(C) He bade good-bye to all his friends.
(D) None of these.

77. Select the right meaning of the word 'Linguist' from the following:
(A) One who knows only one language
(B) One who knows two languages
(C) One who knows more than two languages
(D) One who knows several languages

78. Punctuate the following sentences:
'The creator answered yes but by accepting the burden you will show your greatness of heart' is given in following sentences. Find out the correct one.
(A) The creator answered "yes but by accepting the burden you will show your greatness of heart".
(B) The creator answered "yes". But by accepting the burden you will show your greatness of heart.
(C) The creator answered, "Yes, but by accepting the burden you will show your greatness of heart."
(D) None of these

79. Which of the following words means "a hater of learning"?
(A) Misologist (B) Misogamist
(C) Aesthetics (D) Cynic

80. What does the idiom "Hue and Cry" means:
(A) to keep aloof from
(B) to create crisis
(C) a general outcry of alarm
(D) to conclude

81. Pick out the right option which express the meaning of the word 'Disposition':
(A) Position
(B) Charm
(C) One's nature of temper
(D) Affidavit

82. Romanticism is basically a movement that reacted against various aspects. In philosophy, the Romanticism reacted against:
   (A) The rationalism of the eighteenth century
   (B) The view of physical world dominated by science
   (C) The theories of John Lock
   (D) All of these

83. What is a Caesura in poetry?
   (A) A line containing consonance
   (B) Sprung Rhythm
   (C) A pause indicated by a comma
   (D) None of these

84. What figure of speech has been used in the following lines?
   "Even thus last night, and now night more , I lay and could win thee, sleep ! by and stealth."
   (A) Hyperbole
   (B) Onomatopeia
   (C) Apostrophe
   (D) Oxymoron

Direction (Q. No. 85-94): In questions 85 to 94 you have a brief passage with 10 questions. Read the passage carefully and choose the best answer to each question out of the four alternatives.

It is strange that, according to his position in life, an extravagant man is admired or despised. A successful businessman does nothing to increase his popularity by being careful with his money. He is expected to display his success, to have a smart car, an expensive life, and to be lavish with his hospitality. If he is not so, he is considered mean, and his reputation in business may even suffer in consequence. The paradox remains that if he had not been careful with his money in the first place, he would never have achieved his present wealth.

Among the low income group, a different set of values exists. The young clerk who makes his wife a present of a new dress when he hasn't paid his house rent, is condemned as extravagant. Carefulness with money to the point of meanness is applauded as a virtue. Nothing in his life is considered more worthy than paying his bills. The ideal wife for such a man separates her housekeeping money into joyless little piles – so much for rent, for food, for the children's shoes; she is able to face the milkman with equanimity every month, satisfied with her economising ways, and never knows the guilt of buying something she can really afford.

As for myself, I fall into neither of these categories. If I have money to spare, I can be extravagant, but when, as is usually the case, I am hard up, then I am the meanest man imaginable.

85. Which of the following would be the most suitable title for the passage?
   (A) Extravagance leads to poverty
   (B) Miserly habits of the poor
   (C) Extravagance in the life of the rich and the poor.
   (D) Extravagance is always condemnable

86. As far as money is concerned, we get the impression that the writer:
   (A) is incapable of saving anything.
   (B) is never inclined to be extravagant.
   (C) would like to be considered extravagant.
   (D) doesn't often have any money to save.

87. The statement "she is able to face the milkman with equanimity" implies that:
   (A) She is not upset as she has been paying the milkman his dues regularly.
   (B) She loses her nerve at the sight of the milkman who always demands his dues.
   (C) She manages to keep cool as she, has to pay the milkman only a month's dues.
   (D) She remains composed and confident as she knows that she can handle the milkman tactfully.

88. Which of the following is opposite in meaning to the word 'applauded' in the passage?
   (A) Humiliated
   (B) Decried
   (C) Cherished
   (D) Suppressed

89. How does the housewife, described by the writer, feel when she saves money? She:
   (A) is content to be so thrifty.
   (B) wishes life were less burdensome

(C) is still troubled by a sense of guilt

(D) wishes she could sometimes be extravagant

90. The word 'paradox' in the last sentence of the first paragraph means:

(A) Statement based on facts

(B) That which brings out the inner meaning.

(C) That, which is contrary to received opinion.

(D) Statement based on the popular opinion

91. It seems that low paid people should:

(A) Not pay their bills promptly

(B) Not keep their creditors waiting

(C) Borrow money to meet their essential needs

(D) Feel guilty if they overspend

92. We understand from the passage that:

(A) All mean people are wealthy

(B) Wealthy people are invariably successful

(C) Carefulness generally leads to failure

(D) Thrift may lead to success.

93. The phrase "lavish with his hospitality" in the third sentence of the first paragraph signifies:

(A) Miserliness in dealing with his friends

(B) Considerateness in spending on guests and strangers

(C) Extravagance in entertaining guests.

(D) Indifference in treating his friends and relatives

94. In the opinion of the writer, a successful businessman.

(A) is more popular if he appears to be doing nothing.

(B) should not bother about his popularity

(C) must be extravagant before achieving success.

(D) is expected to have expensive tastes.

Direction (Q. No. 95 to 99): The following sentences are given with a blank. Choose the correct alternative to fill in the blanks.

95. He managed to ....several times but was finally..........by the police.

(A) abscond, freed (B) deceive, cheated

(C) cheat, chased (D) escape, nabbed

96. Chastity is the greatest....... of a woman.

(A) possession (B) treasure

(C) ornament (D) property

97. Some people .... themselves into believing that they are indispensable to their organisation.

(A) fool (B) delude

(C) deceive (D) denigrate

98. The clerk was.........by the officer for his negligence.

(A) pulled down (B) pulled up

(C) pulled off (D) pulled in

99. A..........has a strong dislike for women.

(A) misanthropist (B) philologist

(C) misogynist (D) polygamist

100. The following sentence is divided into three parts (A), (B) and (C). Find out which part has an error.

Most politicians are now/interested in
(A) (B)
feathering/their own pockets/No error
(C) (D)

ANSWERS WITH EXPLANATION

1. (B) Suggest is not the proper word in the context.

2. (D)

3. (B) There should be break down which means temporary emotional collapse, whereas broke out means sudden spread.

4. (D)

5. (D) This is the 502nd line of "Paradise Last". Belie is the Hebrew word for worthlessness and he is of the cavalier type.

6. (B) Lyrical Ballads published in 1798 written by William Wordsworth and S.T. Coleridge.

7. (B) 'Paradise Lost, was started in 1658 and finished in 1665 after 7 years of labour in darkness.

8. (A) 'Lucydes', is a pastoral elegy, written in 1637, in memory of a college friend Edward King.

9. (D)

10. (B) Shakespeare died on the probable anniversary of his birth, April 23, 1616.

11. (C) In 1609, however, occurred an event which gave Shakespeare his change for a farewell to the public. An English ship disappeared, and all on board were given up for last. A year later the sailors returned home, and their arrival created intense excitement. Shakespeare took this story and wave it into The Tempest.

12. (C)

13. (B) Paradise Lost by Milton is an epic.

14. (B) Tennyson possesses the dreaminess of Spenser, the majesty of million, All natural simplicity of Wordsworth, all fantasy of Blake and Coleridge, the Melody of Keats and Shelley the narrative vigour of Byron of Scott.

15. (D) **16.** (B)

17. (C) Sonnet is a lyric stanza, written in 14 lines with an elaborate rhyme scheme.

18. (D) **19.** (D)

20. (A) **21.** (D)

22. (C) Coriolanus is a play by William Shakespeare written in the fourth period of his career.

23. (B) In 1658, Milton in his darkness, sat down to dictate the work (Paradise Lost) which he had planned 30 years before. It consists of 12 books.

24. (A) **25.** (C)

26. (A)

27. (B) Gitanjali was translated in English in 1912 by Rabindra Nath Tagore. He won Nobel Prize for it in 1913.

28. Options are improper. Both (A) and (C) are correct.

29. (B) Aristotle quoted these lines about tragedy in his 'Poetics'.

30. (D)

31. (D) The correct spelling is 'Rhetoric' which means – art of effective speaking or writing.

32. (A)

33. (B) These lines are spoken by Julius Caesar in Act II Sc.2.

34. (B) **35.** (B)

36. (D) Here the figure of speech is Apostrophe.

37. (C)

38. (B) An Apostrophe is a direct address to the dead, to the absent or to a personified, object or idea.

39. (D) Here 'him' refers to Chaucer.

40. (D) The poem was written in 1802. Its other title was 'I Wandered Lonely As a Cloud'.

41. (C) The statement is about Shakespeare.

42. (A) Banquo was invited by Macbeth to the royal feast but was murdered and so appeared his ghost and occupies Macbeth's seat.

43. (C)

44. (B) These lines are uttered by Brutus towards the end of Julius Caesar.

45. (B) **46.** (B)

47. (D) Miranda, daughter of Prospero is the heroine of The Tempest.

48. (D) The correct spelling is celebacy which means – single life or unmarried stale.

49. (B) In Culture and Anarchy (1869), Arnold had described the aristocratic class as Barbarian who are essentially crude in soul.

50. (B) In personification, inanimate objects and abstract notions are spoken of as having life and intelligence.

51. (B) **52.** (A)

53. (B) **54.** (A)

55. (C) **56.** (C)

57. (B) Except 'deliberation' all three shows some form of enquiry.

58. (C) All other except spectre are circular in form.

59. (C) All other three are colour of rainbow except pink.

60. (B) All other three are some peculiar ornaments.

61. (A) In all the other three words 'semi' is used as prefix.

62. (A)

63. (D) Crocodile is a reptile, but all others are mammals.

64. (C) All the three have their definition based on population and other mode of living etc. but home, anywhere is a place where we live with our family.

65. (D) Tomato is vegetable whereas all other are fruits.

66. (B) These lines reminds us of Tennyson's Ulysses where Ulysses leaves his Kingdom to explore the new world. It reflects the passion for knowledge and had a masculine vigour and sympathy for humanity.

67. (A) Since it is a proverb so the words cannot be changed even with a meaningful word.

68. (D) **69.** (C)

70. (B) It is a figure of speech in which inanimate objects and abstract ideas are spoken of, as if they were persons or human beings.

71. (A) Onomatopoeia is the use of a word or words whose sound itself conveys the sense of the author.

72. (B) The English Ballad is a tale related in a simple and plain manner. It is characterised by a number of things. It is like the epic in its origin, growth and theme.

73. (B) The correct spelling is Dispassionate which means – unswayed by passion; calm, impartial.

74. (D) Keat's Endymion, which is the story of a young shepherd beloved by a moon Goddess.

75. (B) Insolvent, means debtor who is unable to pay off his debts that is a bankrupt so its antonym will be wealthy.

76. (C) **77.** (D)

78. (C) **79.** (A)

80. (C) Hue and cry means 'General Outcry' as the villagers raised a hue and cry to see the dacoits.

81. (C)

82. (A) The domination of science in views was the trait of Victorian period and the theories of John Lock were democratic and much like that practiced in the Romantic period.

83. (C) Petrarch had divided his sonnets into two parts: the octave of 8 lines and the sestet of 6 lines, with a pause or caesura, after the eighth line.

84. (C) An apostrophe is a direct address to the deads, absent or abstract objects.

85. (C) **86.** (D)

87. (A) **88.** (B)

89. (A) **90.** (C)

91. (D) **92.** (D)

93. (C) **94.** (D)

95. (D) **96.** (C)

97. (B)

98. (B) Pulled up means reprimand.

99. (C) **100.** (B)

❑❑❑

PRACTICE SET–9

Direction (Q. No. 1 to 2): Choose the correct form of narration (reported speech) of the following direct speeches :

1. "I am going to Delhi," he declared.

(A) He said that he was going to Delhi.

(B) He was going to Delhi he declared.

(C) He declared that he was going to Delhi.

(D) He declares that he is going to Delhi.

2. He said," I want to talk to you,"

(A) He said he wanted to talk to you,

(B) He said that he wanted to talk to him.

(C) He says that he wanted to talk, to you.

(D) He had said that he wanted to talk with him.

3. Galsworthy is:

(A) a pessimist, both cynical and demotivating

(B) a passivist

(C) a realist, both minute and delicate

(D) a reactionist revolutionary

Direction (Q. No. 4 to 8): Read the following passage and answer the questions given below:

The sad demise of Mother Teresa left the world weighed down by an unprecedented grief. The Yugoslav-born nun was the first person in India after M.K. Gandhi to be given a state funeral despite never holding any public office. What she will be remembered for is what she stood for. She symbolised the ultimate indestructible memorandum of love lying beyond all contentions.

The saint of the gutters was almost synonymous with the slums and the poverty of Calcutta. She adopted and loved the city as her own. She managed to make shrines out of the grimmest of penurial circumstances. Her saintliness did not have the conventional detachment from society. She waxed a personification of mercy and charity. Her charity was sublime and mellow, never keen to project godliness. She spurred us on to be simply humane. She held the human life with all its trauma in a compassionate embrace. A realisation dawned on her early that love and the assurance of being cared for were what people needed most. Here was a simple message of concern, hope and new life for the unfed, unclothed and the unsheltered. It was her conviction that all is willed by God and it is our duty to serve Him by serving humanity.

Malcolm Muggeridge, one of Mother Teresa's early biographers, was so moved by the mission which cuts across all limitations that he told the whole world about her. Thus, she was catapulted to fame. People responded warmly and her arduous struggle to keep going was considerably eased as funds poured in. It was also the time that Mother started travelling to places in order to meet people and spread her word of God. Dominique Lapierre went about making a film on her and this hurt her very much.

This great woman could not avoid eyebrows beings raised at her. She disapproved of abortion because it signified killing of the fetus and the conscience of the mother. She took children to be the gift of God. She was also accused of almost making a fetish of human misery and using it as a ploy to raise funds, It is always simpler to criticise, it is much harder to defend; Mother did it unequivocally in her own fashion.

4. Mother Teresa understood that people had utmost need for:

(A) hearth and home

(B) food and clothing

(C) monetary help and protection

(D) love and care

5. Mother Teresa was not an advocate of abortion:
(A) because it kills the fetus
(B) because it does not affirm the mother's love for children
(C) because it involves killing of the fetus and the mother's conscience
(D) because it kills the conscience of the mother

6. Mother Teresa identified herself with :
(A) the poverty-stricken slum-dwellers of Calcutta
(B) the Christian community of Calcutta
(C) the foreign visitors to Calcutta
(D) the elite of Calcutta

7. Mother Teresa was :
(A) indifferent to criticism
(B) defenceless against criticism
(C) above criticism
(D) the target of criticism

8. Mother Teresa :
(A) was the first to be given a state funeral in spite of holding no public office.
(B) was the first to be given a state funeral for holding a public office.
(C) was the second unofficial person to be given a state funeral.
(D) was given a state funeral next to Gandhi.

9. The finest of Galsworthy's later dramas is :
(A) Escape (B) The Pigeon
(C) The Skin Game (D) Loyalties

10. The influence of class is depicted in :
(A) Escape (B) the Pigeon
(C) The Skin Game (D) Loyalties

11. Match the meaning with the idiom 'to put off':
(A) to instigate (B) to irritate
(C) to turn down (D) to be very angry

12. Commence the statement with a distributive adjective:
.... boy was excused.
(A) Neither (B) Each
(C) One (D) Excellent

13. The word 'sadism' is derived from :
(A) A Greek pathological term
(B) A native cult in medieval Florence
(C) Notorious French erotic writer Marquis de Sade
(D) A Scottish secret society

14. Use the correct phrasal verb in the gap in the following sentence:
The audience .... the speaker.
(A) turned out (B) turned on
(C) turned in (D) turned off

15. What should be the statement to the interrogative: "Does he run a hotel in Delhi ?"
(A) He is running a hotel in Delhi.
(B) He does run a hotel in Delhi.
(C) He does run a hotel at Delhi.
(D) He runs a hotel in Delhi.

16. Ues the Future Perfect Tense to complete the sentence.
.... this embroidery by evening.
(A) I will finish
(B) I have finished
(C) I will have finished
(D) I shall have finished

17. The Excursion, dated 1814, marks the beginning of :
(A) Wordsworth's growing sensibility to natural phenomena.
(B) the decline of Wordsworth's poetic genius
(C) the height of Wordsworth's ascent to fame
(D) Wordsworth's friendship with Coleridge

Direction (Q. No. 18-22): Pick the sentences which is correctly punctuated:

18. (A) By Heaven, I've done it at last.
(B) By Heaven, I've done is at last !
(C) By Heaven; Ive done it at last!
(D) By Heaven - I've done it at last

19. (A) "You see, she can't forget, sir !"
(B) "You see, she can't forget, sir."
(C) "You see she can't forget, sir."
(D) "You see she can't forget-sir"

20. (A) It could lead to the kind of good life, both spiritual and material, that was once the privilege of a lucky few.
(B) It could lead to the kind of good life both spiritual and material – that was once the privilege of a lucky few.
(C) It, could lead to the kind of good life; both spiritual and material that was once the privilege of a lucky few.
(D) It could lead to the kind of good life, both spiritual, and material that was once the privilege of a lucky few.

21. (A) If properly used however, those very skills could help.
(B) If properly used, however those very skills could help.
(C) If, properly used; however, those very skills could help.
(D) If properly used, however, those very skills could help.

22. (A) Oh no ! I forgot. I'll phone her now.
(B) "Oh no, I forgot. I'll phone her now.
(C) "Oh no. I forgot. I'll phone her now ? "
(D) Oh no ! I forgot ? I'll phone her now !"

23. Shakespeare's sonnets (1 to 126) generally show a re-enaction of :
(A) general philosophy on life
(B) dramatic interchange between lovers
(C) personal relationship with a young, rich patron
(D) dramatic argument with the dark lady

24. The language used by Shakespeare in his dramas for the most part is :
(A) poetic prose (B) blank verse
(C) narrative prose (D) dramatic verse

25. The total number of Shakespearean sonnets is:
(1) 152 (B) 156
(3) 150 (D) 154

26. Galsworthy's masterpiece is:
(A) The Patrician (B) The Free lands
(C) The Forsyte Saga (D) Fraternity

27. Galsworthy's The Country House presents :
(A) the upper class (B) the lower class
(C) the middle class (D) the industrial class

Direction (Q. No. 28-29): Find the appropriate words for the following :

28. .... the shower was over, the sun shone out again.
(A) Unless (B) With
(C) After (D) If

29. Make hay .... the sun shines.
(A) while (B) when
(C) whence (D) where

Direction (Q. No. 30 and 31): Fill in the blanks according to the subject-verb concord :

30. A pair of scissors .... necessary for craftwork.
(A) was (B) is
(C) are (D) were

31. There .... three girls in the car.
(A) was (B) is
(C) are (D) have

32. The heroic couplet generally is :
(A) Iambic dimeter (B) Iambic trimeter
(C) Iambic pentameter(D) Iambic tetrameter

33. State the emphatic of 'I am happy':
(A) I am really happy
(B) I am very happy
(C) I am so very happy
(D) I am so happy

34. Agitprop theatre, a well-known form in 20th century is :
(A) A form of folk theatre in rural England
(B) Brechtian drama
(C) Marxist and/or communist propaganda using the theatre form.
(D) A civil rights movement on the streets of Chicago, United States

35. What is the comparative form of 'beautiful' ?
(A) Beautifull
(B) More beautiful
(C) Beautifuller
(D) None of these

36. Who among the following was born first of all?
(A) William Shakespeare
(B) John Milton
(C) John Galsworthy
(D) William Wordsworth

37. Tick the correct one:
(A) Ram asked Shyam how are you.
(B) Ram asked Shyam how he was.
(C) Ram asked to Shyam how he was.
(D) Ram asked to Shyam how was he?

38. In his quest for true significance of life on its simpler levels, Wordsworth resembles :
(A) George Crabbe (B) William Cowper
(C) William Blake (D) Rober Burns

39. Granville Barker was responsible for the introduction to the English Stage of Galsworthy's following plays except one. Identify the odd one out:
(A) Justice (B) The Silver Box
(C) Strife (D) Loyalties

40. Which word cannot be formed from the letters of the words STRANGE ?
(A) Gangster (B) Angels
(C) Ranges (D) Grants

41. Which one word can be formed from the letters of the word REVERENCE ?
(A) Rare (B) Vear
(C) Never (D) Spear

42. Wordsworth learned that "verse may build a princely throne on humble truth" from:
(A) Robert Burton (B) Robert Burns
(C) Robert Bridges (D) Robert Blair

43. One of the following is not by Wordsworth :
(A) Michael
(B) Resolution and Independence
(C) It is a Beauteous Evening
(D) The May Queen

44. Wordsworth lived for 50 years among the :
(A) Cumberland dalesmen
(B) Alfoxden villagers
(C) Hawkshead countrymen
(D) French revolutionists

45. The true commencement of Wordsworth's poetic career was from:
(A) 1792-1793 (B) 1795-1796
(C) 1797-1798 (D) 1790-1791

Direction (Q. No. 46 to 50): Read the following passage and answer the questions based on it:

The chief condition of happiness, then barring certain physical prerequisites, is the life of reason the specific glory and power of man. Virtue, or rather excellence will depend on clear judgement, self-control, symmetry of desire, artistry of means; it is not the possession of the simple man, nor the gift of innocent intent, but the achievement of experience in the fully developed man. Yet there is a road to it, a guide to excellence, which may save many detours and delays: it is the middle way, the golden mean. The qualities of character can be arranged in triads in each of which can first and the last qualities will be extremes and vices, and the middle quality, a virtue or an excellence. So between cowardice and rashness is courage; between stinginess and extravagance is liberality; between sloth and greed is ambition; between humility and pride is modesty; between secrecy and loquacity is honesty; between quarrelsomeness and flattery is friendship; between Hamlet's indecisiveness and on Quixote's impulsiveness is self-control. The right in ethics or conduct is not different from right in mathematics or engineering; it means correct, fit, what works best to the best results.

46. Who, among the following is not the writer of either Hamlet or Don Quixote ?
(A) Ben Johnson (B) Shakespeare
(C) Cervantes (D) None of them

47. Which of the following is not the middle path of different qualities ?
(A) Liberality
(B) Ambition
(C) Friendship
(D) Secrecy

48. The author has not said :
(A) The middle path between humility and pride is modesty
(B) Middle path avoids delay in achieving excellence

(C) Right in ethics means that works to the best results

(D) Courage is the middle path of indecisiveness and impulsiveness

49. What is the implied meaning of the passage ?

(A) Happiness depends upon physical and mental qualities

(B) Self-control is necessary

(C) Excellence should be achieved

(D) Rational approach lies in following the middle path

50. What is the main idea of the passage?

(A) The qualities of character are three extremes and middle

(B) In some respects ethics and mathematics resemble

(C) Happiness can be achieved by following the middle path

(D) None of these

51. Heroic drama was a form mainly specific to :

(A) Anglo-Saxon Heroic Period

(B) Romantic Period

(C) Restoration Period

(D) Elizabethan Period

52. William Shakespeare was the third child of:

(A) Joseph Shakespeare and Mary John

(B) William Shakespeare and Mary Arden

(C) John Shakespeare and Mary Arden

(D) Jack Shakespeare and Mary William

53. Select the correct 'gerund form' from the following sentences :

(A) When painting stopped, the artist had looked up.

(B) Having painting stopped, the artist looking up.

(C) The paint stooped. The artist looked up.

(D) The painting had stopped, the artist looked up.

54. Julius Caesar falls in point of time between :

(A) the comedies and histories

(B) the comedies and tragedies

(C) the histories and tragedies

(D) the tragedies and romances

55. Which is the verb form in the underlined part of the sentence ?

She is going to <u>attend</u> a wedding :

(A) adverb (B) gerund

(C) infinitive (D) participle

56. John Milton's magnificent ode On the Morning of Christ's Nativity was written when the poet's age was :

(A) 24 years (B) 21 years

(C) 26 years (D) 35 years

57. Complete the sentence with the correct infinitive:

_____there is difficult.

(A) When reaching (B) Reaching to

(C) Reaching for (D) To reach

58. The Paradise Lost was completed by :

(A) 1666 (B) 1667

(C) 1665 (D) 1663

59. Identify the correct gerund form to rewrite the sentence –

"If a person cheats at business, he will never get anywhere, as business thrives only on honesty"

(A) cheated (B) by cheating

(C) cheating (D) as cheating

Direction (Q. No. 60 to 61): Insert the correct form of participle in the sentences below :

60. The ___ object turned out to be a spinning top.

(A) movementing (B) moved

(C) moving (D) movable

61. He is a______teacher.

(A) retiring (B) retired

(C) retire (D) retirant

Direction (Q. No. 62 to 66): Choose the correct preposition to fill the blanks in the following sentences :

62. Will you be here _______the weekend ?

(A) in (B) on

(C) about (D) at

63. Bob can run 100 metres ______20 minutes.

(A) at about (B) in about

(C) in around (D) at in

64. The Law is not concerned _____ political status of the accused.

(A) for (B) in
(C) about (D) of

65. A wise person always avail himself_____ opportunities provided.

(A) with (B) of
(C) about (D) in

66. We get out ____ life just what we put into it.

(A) from (B) to
(C) of (D) in

67. L'Allegro and Il Penseroso mean :

(A) 'the blind man' and 'the unhappy man'
(B) 'the desperate man' and 'the pensive man'
(C) 'the joyous man' and 'the meditative man'
(D) 'the philosopher' and 'the stalwart'

68. 'Pathetic Fallacy' is a phrase invented by :

(A) Shakespeare in 1591.
(B) John Ruskin in 1856
(C) Oliver Goldsmith in 1761
(D) Carlyle in 1823

Direction (Q. No. 69 to 70): Identify the type of underlined adverb in the following sentences:

69. I nearly had an accident.

(A) Adverb of Degree (B) Adverb of Manner
(C) Sentence Adverb (D) Adverb of Place

70. Rani rarely goes to the bazaar.

(A) Relative adverb
(B) Adverb of Time
(C) Adverb of Frequency
(D) Adverb of Manner

71. He was so tired that he just lay on the bed. Begin with: He was tired enough......

(A) He was tired enough he just lay on the bed.
(B) He was tired enough lying on the bed.
(C) He was tired enough just to lie on the bed.
(D) He was tired enough to lie on the bed.

72. To smoke cigarettes is injurious to health (Begin with: It is ....)

(A) It is injurious to health smoking cigarettes.
(B) It is injurious to health to smoke cigarettes.
(C) It is so injurious to smoke cigarettes.
(D) It is very injurious to health, to smoke cigarettes.

73. Samson Agonistes shows Milton's desire to bring over into English :

(A) the mythology of Samson for all to know
(B) the gravity and calm dignity of the Greek tragedies
(C) the story of Samson was akin to his own life
(D) the bitter irony with which he could write

74. The term for the novel in most European languages

(A) Epistolary (B) Roman
(C) Novelette (D) Picaresque

75. Milton was appointed to the position of Latin Secretary to Cromwell's Government chiefly due to his work:

(A) Paradise Lost
(B) Reason of Church Government
(C) On the Tenure of Kings and Magistrates
(D) Defensio Secunda

76. "He doesn't work. The underlined word in the sentence is used :

(A) to show emphasis in the positive degree
(B) to modify adverb.
(C) to modify verb in a negative sentence
(D) to show the comparative

77. Comus by John Milton is in the form of a :

(A) Masque (B) Hymn
(C) Epic (D) Lyric

Direction (Q. No. 78 to 80): Select the item nearest in meaning to the underlined word in the sentences below :

78. We are visiting a satellite town :

(A) a town near a satellite station
(B) a town economically or otherwise dependent on another town
(C) a town beside another town
(D) a town having scientists in the majority

79. The patient has been prescribed an emetic drug ;

(A) that induces sleep
(B) that induces allergy

(C) that induces vomiting
(D) that induces cramps

80. The residents are protesting against the move to set up an abattoir in their campus.
(A) a toilet complex
(B) a fish market
(C) a vegetable godown
(D) a slaughter-house

81. Shakespeare dedicated his youthful poems, Venus and Adonis, and Lucrece to :
(A) The Earl of Southey
(B) The Earl of Southampton
(C) The Earl of Surrey
(D) The Earl of Saxony

82. The Comedy of Errors is an adaptation of a Latin comedy which is :
(A) Novum organum
(B) Filostrato
(C) Cursor Mundi
(D) Menoechmi

83. Myth comes from Greek 'mythos' signifying :
(A) imagination
(B) children stories
(C) a story/plot, true or invented
(D) characters from the past

84. The ubi sunt motif means :
(A) the dawn song for the beloved
(B) a guiding motif
(C) the 'where-are' formula for lamenting the past
(D) the 'loathly lady' formula

85. William Wordsworth was in 1791 in France where he was witness to the middle stages :
(A) the French poetic practices
(B) the French drama
(C) the French culture of art
(D) the French Revolution

86. Persona, tone and voice reflect in recent criticism:
(A) the tendency to highlight characterisation
(B) the tendency to disregard plot in modern novels
(C) the tendency to infuse music as a major literary too
(D) the tendency to think of all narrative and lyric works of literature as discourse

Direction (Q. No. 87-93): Use the correct grammatic form in the following sentences :

87. The Chinese .... invented printing.
(A) have
(B) has
(C) hasn't
(D) none to be put in the blank

88. A bus crashed .... a car.
(A) to (B) with
(C) into (D) against

89. A bus collided .... a car.
(A) to (B) into
(C) against (D) with

90. Our house was .... a few days ago.
(A) broked into (B) broken into
(C) broke open (D) break into

91. I haven't been to the cinema for ages. We..............go a lot :
(A) were to (B) has to
(C) used to (D) are to

92. They are still working. They .... finished.
(A) haven't (B) hadn't
(C) hasn't (D) didn't

93. The baby has .... up.
(A) waken (B) awaken
(C) woken (D) awakened

94. The Prelude was written in :
(A) 1802 (B) 1805
(C) 1807 (D) 1806

95. The verse lines –
"She gave me eyes, she gave me ears; And humble cares, and delicate fears;....." were in reference to :
(A) River Wye
(B) Annette Vallon
(C) Dorothy Wordsworth
(D) Ancestral Scotland

96. 'De Doctrina Christiana' casts doubt on the orthodoxy of:
(A) Paradise Lost (B) History of Britain
(C) Paradise Regained (D) Pro Se Defensio

97. In metric movement, 'enjambement' means :
(A) jambing thoughts (B) a striding-over
(C) stopping short (D) a caesura

98. John Galsworthy's novels are chiefly occupied with the effect and conflict of:
(A) individual and the universe
(B) feudalism upon monarchy
(C) class traditions upon society
(D) class traditions upon religion.

99. Esha said, "Please lend me the book, Asha."
(A) Esha requested Asha to lend her the book.
(B) Esha said that the book be lent to her.
(C) Esha requested for the book.
(D) Esha demanded from Asha me book

100. Ram said, "Good morning Sir".
(A) Ram wished a good morning to Sir.
(B) Ram said Sir good morning.
(C) Ram declared it was a good morning.
(D) Ram wished his sir a good morning.

ANSWERS WITH EXPLANATION

1. (C)

2. (B) Pronouns of the direct speech are changed, where necessary, so that their relation with the reporter and his hearer, rather than the original speaker are indicated.

3. (C)

4. (D) A realisation dawned on her early that love and the assurance of being cared for were what people needed most.

5. (C) She disapproved of abortion because it signified double killing, of the fetus, and the conscience of the mother and for this belief of her she has been criticised severely.

6. (A) The saint of gutters that is Mother Teresa, was almost synonymous with slums and poverty of Calcutta. The slum dwellers and poor were her concern.

7. (A) Mother Teresa was target of criticism but was not defenceless. She defended herself but the intensity of criticism was more for her to defend yet it made no difference to her. Thus she was indifferent to it.

8. (D) Options 3 and 4 both are correct but the fourth one is more correct.

9. (D) Escape was published in 1926; The Pigeon in 1912; The Skin Game in 1920 and Loyalities of his later dramas.

10. (D) 'Escape' deals with faith and understanding; 'The Pigeon' with social deterioration. 'The skin Game' deals with the old established aristocracy and new rich manufacturing class whereas 'Loyalties' deals with racial pride and class convention.

11. (C) To put off means to evade or to satisfy and put off means postpone, so to turn down will be the answer.

12. (B) Distributive adjective is one which refers to each one of a number. Neither and each are distributive adjectives but neither is used in negative sense and in comparison between two.

13. (C)

14. (A) 'Turn on' means to switch on something; 'Turn off' means to switch off something. And turned in means to submit, to present to give.

15. (D) **16.** (D)

17. (B) 'The excursion' consist of nine books in blank verse. It is the middle portion of great philosophical poem. The recluse, but it clearly shows the decline of his genius.

18. (B) **19.** (A)

20. (B) Dash is used sometimes to elaborate the thing already said.

21. (C)

22. (A) 'Oh!, will be followed by a mark of exclamation and there will be no question mark.

23. (C) Shakespeare wrote 154 sonnets in all. Out of 154 first 126 were addressed to Earl of Southampton who was his friend and patron. His sonnets are the only direct expression of his own personal feelings.

24. (B) Not a single play by Shakespeare is completely in prose or completely in verse but is a mingling of both and major part of his plays are in blank verse.

25. (D) Total number of sonnets by Shakespeare is 154, published collectively in 1609.

26. (C) 'The Forsyte Saga' is a combination of six novels published in 1922, and are considered to be his masterpiece.

27. (A) 'The country House' analyses on a more detailed scale the little world which revolves round the traditional authority of the squire.

28. (C)

29. (A) It is an idiom hence there will be no change of words.

30. (B) A pair of shoes/scissors/gloves/trousers are singular. But when 'a pair of' is not used with them they are always treated as plural.

31. (C)

32. (C) Iambic pentameter is the most common English measure. It has five feet, each foot has two syllables of which the first is unaccented and the second is accented. The Heroic couplet consists of two Iambic pentameters lines rhyming together.

33. (D) **34.** (C)

35. (B) Adjectives of more than two syllables form the comparative and superlative by putting 'more' and 'most' before the positive.

36. (A) William Shakespeare – 1564
John Milton – 1608
John Galsworthy – 1867
William Wordsworth – 1770

37. (B)

38. (A) George Crabbe was a writer of common life. Robert Burns was lover of taverns. William Blake was mystic and William Cowper was a timid.

39. (B) **40.** (B)

41. (C)

42. (B) Robert Burton (1577–1640) is known for 'Anatomy of Melancholy' which is full of references and is difficult to understand for common readers. Robert Bridges (1844–1930) was born a few years before Wordsworth's death, hence no question of learning from him.

43. (D) 'The May Queen' is not written by Wordsworth whereas 'Michael' is a poem composed and published in 1800; 'Resolution and Independence' or 'The Leech Gatherer' is a poem composed in 1802 and published in 1807 and 'It is a Beauteous Evening' is a sonnet written in 1802 and published in 1807.

44. (A) Wordsworth stayed at Alfoxden with Coleridge and Dorothy, his sister, in between his return from France and publication of 'Lyrical Ballads'. He was sent to school at Hawkshead. He lived the last half century of his life in Cumberland at Rydal mount in Lake district.

45. (C) Wordsworth in 1798 published 'Lyrical, Ballads' with Coleridge which ultimately is the true commencement of his poetic career.

46. (A) 'Hamlet' is written by Shakespeare and 'Don Quixote' by Cervantes. Ben Johnson is the answer.

47. (D) 'Liberality' is middle path of stinginess and extravagance; 'Ambition' of sloth and greed; 'Friendship' of quarrelsomeness and flattery; whereas 'Secrecy' is one of the extremes.

48. (D) Courage is the middle path of cowardice and rashness and not of indecisiveness and impulsiveness.

49. (B) The main idea of the passage is how happiness can be achieved, i.e. by following the middle path. Middle path is all about self control that is avoiding extremes in every way.

50. (C)

51. (C) Another kind of tragedy, a tragedy which held the day in the later half of the 17th century, is the heroic tragedy. Later half of the 17th century that is from 1660 to 1700 is generally known as Restoration period.

52. (C) Shakespeare's father, John Shakespeare, was a farmer's son from the neighbouring village of Snitterfield. His mother, Mary Arden was the daughter of a prosperous farmer.

53. (A)

54. (C) Julius Caesar was a great Roman emperor. Shakespeare borrowed the plot of Julius Caesar, mainly from North's translation of plutarch's 'Lives of Caesar, Brutus and Antony'. Thus it has both elements of history and tragedy.

55. (c)

56. (B) He was at that time 21 years old. He composed this poem on the morning of 25th December, 1629.

57. (D)

58. (C) In 1658, Milton, in his darkness, (being blind), sat down to dictate the work which he had planned thirty years before. It was finished in 1665, after seven years of labour in darkness.

59. (B) **60.** (C)

61. (B) **62.** (B)

63. (B)

64. (A) Concerned is followed by 'for' regarding something.

65. (B) Verb avail is followed by preposition 'of'.

66. (C)

67. (C) L'Allegro and Il Penseroso are twin poems containing many lines and short descriptive passages which linger in the mind like strains of music, and which are known and loved wherever English is spoken. 'L' Allegro' which means the joyous or happy man is like an excursion into English fields. But in Il Penseroso, a quiet thoughtfulness takes the place of the pure joyous sensation of the morning.

68. (B)

69. (A) 'Adverb of Degree or Quantity' shows – how much or in what degree or to what extent.

70. (C) An Adverb is a word which modifies the meaning of a verb, an adjective or another adverb, adverb of Frequency shows how often. Here adverbs are normally put between the subject and the verb.

71. (C) **72.** (B)

73. (B) In Samson Agonistes, Milton turns to a more vital and personal theme and his genius transfigures the story of Samson, the mighty champion of Israel, now blind and scorned, working as a slave among the Philistines. The poet's aim was to present in English a pure tragedy, with all the passion, and restraint which marked the old Greek dramas.

74. (C) The term novel is now applied to a variety of writings that have in common only the attribute of being extended work of prose fiction. As an extended narrative, the novel is distinguished from the short story and from the work of middle length called the 'novelette'. The English name for the form is derived from the Italian 'novelle' meaning a little new world.

75. (C) Milton's "Tenure of kings and magistrates" was like the coming of a strong, not only to protect the child , but to justify his blow for liberty. Kings no less than people are subject to the eternal principle of law, Milton was called to secretary for foreign tongues in the new government.

76. (C)

77. (A) The 'Masque of comus' is in many respect is the most perfect of Milton's poems. It was written in 1634 to be performed at Ludlow castle before the earl of Bridge water and his friends.

78. (B) **79.** (C)

80. (D)

81. (B) Shakespeare dedicated his poems 'Venus and Adonis' and 'Lucrece' along with his first 126 sonnets to Carl of Southampton whose identity is a mystery till now.

82. (D) The Comedy of errors is a farce with a much evolved plot modelled on Plautus. He supplied less fastidious appetites with, a farce which was a free adaptation of the 'Menaechmi' by Plautus.

83. (C) A myth is a story in mythology – a system of hereditary stories which were once believed to be true by a particular cultural group.

84. (C)

85. (D) Wordsworth made his second trip to France in 1791 alongwith Young Oxford Republicans. He joined Girondists to participate in French Revolution.

86. (A)

87. (A) When article 'the' is used before the adjective form of a country name, then it is always plural so. The Chinese have invented printing.

88. (B) **89.** (C)

90. (B) Break into means to enter by force, e.g. His house was broken into last night.

91. (D) **92.** (A)

93. (B)

94. (B) The 'prelude' records the impressions made upon Wordsworth's mind from his earliest recollection until his full man-hood in 1805, when the poem was completed, though the poem was not published till after Wordsworth's death.

95. (C) **96.** (C)

97. (A)

98. (C) After tentative beginnings, the personality of Galsworthy shows itself in 'The Island Pharisee', in which the two main directions of his work appeared. The mental passivity, the lethargy of heart, and all the selfishness of a class, a nation, a tradition. This analysis of British society in the shortened perspective of a few figures and brief episodes, is of rare power.

99. (A) **100.** (D)

❑❑❑

PRACTICE SET–10

Direction For Questions 1-5: Choose the exact meaning of the idioms/phrases.

1. Flesh and blood
(A) Human nature
(B) Warning
(C) In life
(D) At the top speed

2. To cut a sorry figure
(A) A nominal head
(B) To fight to a finish
(C) To be ridiculed
(D) To struggle

3. Fair and square
(A) Successful (B) Honest means
(C) Honest (D) Worthy

4. To fly off the handle
(A) To break something
(B) To be indifferent
(C) To act foolishly
(D) To get into a rage and lose self-control

5. To bell the cat
(A) To take lead in danger
(B) To tie bell to cat's neck
(C) To be alert of the enemy
(D) To make noise

Direction For Questions 6-10: In these questions, arrange the given parts of the sentence in order so as to produce correct sentence.

6. (P) accidents are still bound to happen
(Q) Occasionally
(R) though
(S) despite everyone's best efforts
(A) SPRQ (B) RSPQ
(C) SRPQ (D) PQRS

7. (P) through the long, hot summer
(Q) If you plan to train hard
(R) cotinually
(S) you will need to acclimatise yourself
(A) QPRS (B) SRPQ
(C) QRSP (D) PQRS

8. (P) it becomes difficult
(Q) satisfying our desire
(R) but once we set about
(S) it is not impossible to restrain them
(A) RQPS (B) RQSP
(C) QRPS (D) PQRS

9. (P) four degree below normal
(Q) icy winds lashed Srinagar
(R) which minimum temperature registering
(S) which was already in grip of a grueline could wave conditions
(A) QSRP (B) SRPQ
(C) RPQS (D) PQSR

10. (P) when a chemical substance
(Q) the food poisoning occurred
(R) in the food preparations
(S) was mistaken for salt and used
(A) RQPS (B) Srqp
(C) QPSR (D) PSRQ

Direction For Questions 11-15: Out of the given alternatives, choose the one which can be substituted for the given sentence.

11. A place for keeping bees
(A) Aviary (B) Apiary
(C) Cage (D) Nest

12. One who lives among strangers
(A) Recluse (B) Alien
(C) Stoic (D) Rustic

13. A cure for all disease
(A) Panacea (B) Cure
(C) Antibiotic (D) Remedy

14. A speech made without preparation
(A) Prepared (B) Debate
(C) Extempore (D) Elocution

15. Too much official formality
(A) Delayed (B) Officiousness
(C) Formality (D) Red tapism

Direction For Questions 16-20: The following questions comprise two words which have a certain relationship between them, followed by four lettered pair of words. Select the lettered pair that has the same relationship as the original pair of words.

16. STARS : GALAXY
(A) Children : Paterfamilies
(B) Goose : Geese
(C) Ministers : Council
(D) Tree : Forest

17. HANDS : GLOVES
(A) Legs : Shoes (B) Fish : Water
(C) Socks: Feet (D) Bank : Fog

18. RUNG : LADDER
(A) Leaf : Leaflet
(B) Twig : Tree
(C) Land : Landlord
(D) Song : Singer

19. ANIMAL : ZOOLOGY
(A) Man : Philanthrophy
(B) Poems : Anthology
(C) Disease : Bacteriology
(D) Body : Physiology

20. BOOK : READER
(A) Cloth : Draper (B) School : Student
(C) Tea : Vendor (D) Play : Spectator

Direction For Questions 21-25: Read the following passage and answer these questions :

PASSAGE

For my own part, I have ever gained the most profit, and most pleasure also, from the books which have made me think the most and when the difficulties have once been overcome, these are the books which have struck deepest root, not only in my memory and understanding, but likewise in my affections. For this point too should be taken into account. We all want to win. When a maiden is too forward, her admirer deems it time, to draw back.

21. A maiden, like a good book, should
(A) Be easy to approach
(B) Respond to the admirers
(C) Not easily yield to the admirers
(D) Be forward before her admirers draw back

22. The point to be taken into account is that
(A) Anything for which we do not pay a price is taken lightly
(B) We would not make effort for what we get
(C) Slight effort makes us feel tired
(D) We think highly of what we win

23. Profit and pleasure come only after
(A) the books have struck deep roots
(B) the initial difficulty has been overcome
(C) the books have made me think
(D) the books that I have gotten for a small price

24. The author derives profit and pleasure from books that are
(A) difficult
(B) easy
(C) thought-provoking
(D) having deep roots

25. The author compares a book to
(A) a plant (B) a flower
(C) a maiden (D) an admirer

Direction For Questions 26 to 30: In these questions, choose the word, which is nearest in meaning to the given key words.

26. SMEAR
(A) Mark (B) Avoid
(C) Quarrel (D) economical

27. PRONE
(A) Thrown forward
(B) Disease

(C) Supine
(D) inactive

28. DEPLETE
(A) Take away (B) Fill
(C) Make greater (D) To exhaust

29. FIASCO
(A) Strength (B) Success
(C) Failure (D) Hope

30. WHIM
(A) Desire (B) Unnatural behaviour
(C) Clumsy (D) Fancy

Direction For Questions 31-35: In these questions, choose the word, opposite in meaning to the given key word.

31. NOMINAL
(A) Huge (B) Clear
(C) Real (D) Solid

32. MALIGN
(A) Disparage (B) Slander
(C) Praise (D) Purify

33. HYBRID
(A) Purebred (B) Composite
(C) Familiar (D) Ignorant

34. ECSTACY
(A) Raputure (B) Exaltation
(C) Oily (D) Misery

35. EXTRAVAGANT
(A) Developing (B) Wonderful
(C) Disappearing (D) Economical

36. Who among the following is an English Romantic poet?
(A) William Shakespeare
(B) John Milton
(C) William Wordsworth
(D) P. G. Wodehouse

37. Who among the following started his writing first ?
(A) William Shakespeare
(B) John Milton
(C) WilliamWordsworth
(D) P. G. Wodehouse

38. Who among the following was not a British citizen ?
(A) John Milton
(B) William Shakespeare
(C) William Wordsworth
(D) Katherine Frank

39. 'Paradise Regained' was the work of
(A) John Milton
(B) William Shakespeare
(C) William Wordsworth
(D) William Pitt

40. Who of the following became blind ?
(A) John Milton
(B) William Wordsworth
(C) P.G. Wodehouse
(D) A. Tennyson

41. Who among the following is the 'interpreter of nature in many moods' ?
(A) William Wordsworth
(B) William Shakespeare
(C) William Butler Yeats
(D) William Pitt

42. William Shakespeare has the sobriquet as
(A) Man of letters
(B) Bard of Avon
(C) Saint of the Gutters
(D) Father of Greek Tragedy

43. 'The Prelude' is the work of
(A) John Milton
(B) William Wordsworth
(C) William Shakespeare
(D) P. G. Wodehouse

44. 'The Comedy of Errors' is written by
(A) John Milton
(B) William Shakespeare
(C) William Wordsworth
(D) A. Tennyson

45. Which of the following is not authored by William Shakespeare ?
(A) Hamlet
(B) The Tempest

(C) Julies Caeser

(D) Docler Jekyll and Mr. Hyde

Direction For Questions: 46 to 50: Read the following passage and answer these questions.

PASSAGE

In the past man's worst enemy was nature. He lived under the continued threat of famine and pestilence, a wet summer could bring death to whole nations, and every winter was a menance. Mountains stood like a barrier between people and people, a sea was less a highway than an impassable division. Today nature, though still an enemy, is an enemy almost completely conquered. Modern agriculture assures us of an ample food supply. Modern transportation has made the resources of the entire planet accessible to all its inhabitants. Modern medicine and sanitation allow dense population to cover the ground without risk of pestilence. True, we are still at the mercy of the more violent natural convulsions. Against earthquake, flood and hurricane man has, as yet, devised no adequate protection. But these major cataclysms are rare. At most times, nature is no longer formidable, she has been subdued.

46. The modern transport system is a blessing as it

(A) has helped decrease the distances between towns and villages.

(B) has brought comfort to both towns and villages.

(C) has made all the commodities available to everyoné.

(D) has encouraged people to travel for pleasure.

47. In ancient times, man had an apprehension of

(A) Epidemics (B) Server droughts

(C) Floods (D) All of these

48. Which one of the following statements best reflects the underlying conviction of the passage ?

(A) Man can do wonders.

(B) Man's knowledge has no end.

(C) Man has been able to control nature to a great extent.

(D) Man has been able to control nature completely.

49. Man has not yet succeeded in controlling the furies of

(A) Earthquakes (B) Floods

(C) Hurricanes (D) All of these

50. Modern medicine has helped man

(A) To live longer every where in the world

(B) To live a healthy life in hygienic conditions

(C) To live in thickly populated areas without fear of epidemics

(D) Balance population with available resources

Direction For Questions 51-55: Read the following passage and answer these questions:

PASSAGE

A recent report in Newsweek says that in American colleges students of Asian origin out perform not only the minority group students but the majority whites as well. Many of these students must be of Indian origin and their achievement is something we can be proud of. It is unlikely that these, talented youngsters will come back to India and that is the familiar brain drain problem, However, recent statements by the. nation's policy makers indicate that the perception of this issue is changing. 'Brain bank' and not 'Brain drain' is the more appropriate idea, they suggest, since the expertise of Indians abroad is only deposited in other places and not lost.

This may be so, but this brain bank, like most of other banks, is one that primarily serves customers in its neighbourhood. The skills of the Asians now excelling in America's colleges will mainly help the USA. No matter how significant, what Non-Resident Indians do for India and what their counterparts do for other Asian lands is only a by-product. But it is also necessary to ask, or be reminded, why Indians study more fruitfully when abroad. The Asians whose accomplishments Newsweek records would have probably had a very different fate if they had studied in India. In America they found elbow room, books and facilities available and not likely to be available here. The need to prove themselves in their new country and the competition of an international standard they faced there must have cured mental and physical laziness, But other things helping them in America can be obtained here if we achieve a change in social attitudes, especially towards youth. We need to learn to value individuals and their unique qualities more than conformity and respectability. We need to learn the language of encouragement to add to out skill in flattery. We might also learn to be less liberal with blame, and less tight-fisted with appreciation, especially to those showing signs of independence.

51. The brain bank has limitations like all banks in the sense that
(A) a bank's services go mainly to those near it.
(B) small neighbourhood banks are not viable in this age of multinationals.
(C) only what is deposited can be with drawn and utilised.
(D) no one can be forced to put assets tn a bank.

52. There is a talk now of the 'brain bank'. This idea
(A) is a solution to the brain drain problem.
(B) is a new problem caused partly by the brain drain.
(C) is a new way of looking at the role of qualified Indians living abroad.
(D) is based on the plan to utilise foreign exchange remittances.

53. In general, the talented young Indians studying in America
(A) have a reputation for being hardworking.
(B) have the opportunity of contribute to India's development.
(C) will not return to pursue their careers India.
(D) can solve the brain drain problem because of recent changes in policy.

54. The students of Asian origin in America include
(A) a fair number from India
(B) a small group from India
(C) persons from India who are very proud
(D) Indians who are the most hardworking of all.

55. Among the many groups of students in American Colleges, Asian students
(A) are often written about in magazines like Newsweek.
(B) are the most successful academically.
(C) have proved that they are as good as the whites.
(D) have only a minority status like the blacks.

Direction for Questions 56-65: Fill in each of the numbered blanks in the following passage with the most suitable word from the choices provided under the passage :

PASSAGE

Kashmir is more than a territorial or political issue ...56... Indo-Pakistan relations and South Asian peace and stability. I have no intention of ...57... events and issues related to Kashmir in chronological..58.. nor do I intend to dilate on the political arguments put forward by India and Pakistan to ...59... their ...60... views on the present status or future of Kashmir.

The attempt is to analyse, to ..61.. impossible, the deeper historical memories, psychological, emotional...62...socio-economic...63...which contribute to the Kashmir policies of both the countries, policies which...64...the ...65... intractable.

56. (A) problem (B) problems
(C) attitude (D) attitudes

57. (A) become (B) becomes
(C) make (D) renders

58. (A) motivations (B) problems
(C) issues (D) issue

59. (A) but (B) yet
(C) and (D) as

60. (A) extent (B) extend
(C) level (D) levels

61. (A) Own (B) selfish
(C) personal (D) respective

62. (A) plan (B) enumerate
(C) narrate (D) substantiate

63. (A) pattern
(B) sequence
(C) manner
(D) background

64. (A) counting (B) calculating
(C) repeating (D) negotiating

65. (A) deteriorating (B) affecting
(C) effecting (D) spoiling

Direction For Questions 66-70: One of the words is misspelt. Find it out.

66. (A) Carer (B) Trumpery
(C) Scientific (D) Sonourous

67. (A) Twelth (B) Programme
(C) Cunning (D) Embarrassment

68. (A) Situation (B) Minicipal
(C) Samridhi (D) Pituitary

69. (A) Elaborate (B) Thoroughness
(C) Therapy (D) Instablily

70. (A) Supercilous (B) Parliament
(C) Benefactor (D) Testament

Direction For Questions 71-75: In these questions, the sentence is divided into three part (A), (B) and (C). Find out which parts of the sentence has an error. If there is no error, mark your answer as (D).

71. Can I lend/your pencil/for a minute please ?
(A) (B) (C)
No error
(D)

72. It is unfortunate that/many youngsters get/
(A) (B)
addicted to gamble./No error
(C) (D)

73. The conductor asked the passenger/why had
(A)
not he purchased a ticket/in advance to board
(B) (C)
the bus./No error
(D)

74. Neelima has scored a first class/in her final
(A) (B)
exams,/is not it ?/No error
(C) (D)

75. A lot of travel delay is caused/due to
(A)
inefficiency and lack of good management/
(B)
on behalf of the railway./No errors
(C) (D)

76. The sentence 'Why are you making a noise ?' is a
(A) Present perfect tense
(B) Present continous tense
(C) Simple present tense
(D) Simple past tense

77. The sentence 'In 2004, a disease destroyed the crops in one village', is a
(A) Present perfect tense
(B) Simple past tense
(C) Past perfect tense
(D) Future tense

78. The sentence 'I am going to be a teacher when grow up' is a
(A) Present tense
(B) Past tense
(C) Future tense
(D) Past perfect tense

79. The sentence 'However they had already been married outside the village' is a
(A) Present perfect tense
(B) Simple past tense
(C) Past perfect tense
(D) Future tense

80. The sentence 'Many Indians have settled abroad in recent years' is a
(A) Present perfect tense
(B) Simple past tense
(C) Past perfect tense
(D) Future tense

81. In the sentence 'I doubt whether she will meet him', 'whether' is:
(A) Pronoun
(B) Preposition
(C) Conjunction
(D) Adverb

82. In the sentence,'I want to hear the story in detail', 'story' is:

(A) Noun (B) Adjective
(C) Adverb (D) Verb

83. In the Sentence, "He demanded a thorough inquiry', 'thorough' is:

(A) Noun (B) Adjective
(C) Adverb (D) Verb

84. In the sentence, 'All the officers should respect one another', 'One another' is:

(A) Noun (B) Adjective
(C) Adverb (D) Pronoun

85. In the sentence, 'Athletics is his favourite sport', 'Athletics' is

(A) Noun (B) Adjective
(C) Adverb (D) Pronoun

Direction For Questions 86-90: In these questions, a sentence has been given where in a group of words have been underlined. Three alternatives (A), (B) and (C) are suggested to improve the sentence. Choose the alternative, which improves ths sentence. In case of no improvement, your answer is (D).

86. <u>In accordance to your instructions</u>, we have remitted the amount in the bank.

(A) for (B) by
(C) with (D) No improvement

87. Are you <u>more clever than us</u> ?

(A) more cleverer to us
(B) cleverer to us
(C) cleverer than us
(D) No improvement

88. Will you <u>lend me few rupees</u> in this hour or need ?

(A) lend me any rupees
(B) borrow me a few rupees
(C) lend me a few rupees
(D) No improvement

89. No sooner <u>he has returned home</u> then his mother felt happy.

(A) had he returned home when
(B) he had returned home then
(C) did he returned home than
(D) No improvement

90. <u>There is no more room</u> for you in this compartment.

(A) There is no more seat
(B) There is no more space
(C) There is no more accommodation
(D) No improvement

Direction For Questions 91-100: Choose the most appropriate word to fill the blank space in these sentences.

91. When an infant displayed signs of illness, the anxious parents called in a ....

(A) pediatrician (B) plagiarist
(C) pediatrist (D) practitioner

92. His book was marked by many .... which made us forget its main theme.

(A) idiotic (B) humorous
(C) slanted (D) digressive

93. He fielded the ball and threw it, but it missed the wicket ....

(A) by a long chalk
(B) by a distance
(C) to draw a blank
(D) by the way

94. The more Himanshu tried to find excuse for his coming late to his office regularly, the more he ....

(A) was confused
(B) tied the knot
(C) was in a flat spin
(D) cut above others

95. It was difficult to see through the .... of the headlights at the cars.

(A) brilliance (B) dazzle
(C) brightness (D) shine

96. Hem has no control .... his temper.

(A) in (B) over
(C) at (D) after

97. Keep clear .... wicked boys.

(A) of (B) from
(C) at (D) after

98. I am angry with him .... his carelessness.

(A) at (B) in
(C) for (D) of

99. Let this be an example .... the trublemakers.
(A) for
(B) about
(C) against
(D) to

100. A good judge never gropes .... the conclusions.
(A) to
(B) at
(C) on
(D) for

ANSWERS WITH EXPLANATION

1. (A) Flesh and blood means 'man' or 'human nature'.
2. (C) to cut a sorry figure means to put up a poor show or to be ridiculed.
3. (C) Fair and square means 'Just' Honest.
4. (D)
5. (A) To bell the cat means to do a risky job.
6. (A)
7. (A)
8. (D)
9. (A)
10. (D)
11. (B)
12. (B)
13. (A)
14. (C)
15. (D)
16. (D)
17. (C)
18. (B)
19. (D)
20. (B)
21. (C)
22. (D)
23. (B)
24. (C)
25. (C)
26. (A)
27. (A)
28. (D)
29. (C)
30. (D)
31. (A)
32. (C)
33. (A)
34. (D)
35. (D) Extravagant means wasteful.
36. (C) Wordsworth's 'Lyrical Ballads' with Coleridge in 1798 is said to be the beginning of Romantic period.
37. (A) As William Shakespeare is much older than other three, it is but natural that he started his writing first.
38. (D)
39. (A) 'Paradise Lost'and 'Paradise Regained' were written by John Milton
40. (A) Milton became blind and even wrote a poem titled – 'On His Blindness'.
41. (A) Wordsworth had a complete philosophy of nature. Under the influence of nature, he experienced a mystic mood.
42. (B) William Shakespeare was born in 1564 at Stratford on Avon and was so called – Bard of Avon.
43. (B) 'The prelude' is a epical, autobiographical poem by William Wordsworth, published after his death in 1850.
44. (B) The comedy of errors was written by the great English writer of drama in Elizabethan period.
45. (D)
46. (C)
47. (D)
48. (C)
49. (D)
50. (C)
51. (A)
52. (C)
53. (C)
54. (A)
55. (B)
56. (B)
57. (A)
58. (C)
59. (C)
60. (A)
61. (D)
62. (D)
63. (B)
64. (A)
65. (B) 'Affect' means 'to act on', whereas, 'effect' means 'result', outcome.
66. (D) Correctly spelt word will be 'sonorous' which means – giving out deep sounds.
67. (A) The correct spelling is 'Twelfth'.
68. (B) The correct spelling is 'municipal' which means – belonging to affairs of city or town.
69. (D) Correct spelling is instability' which means – fickleness or want of stability.
70. (A) The correet spelling is 'supercilious' which means – lofty with pride, disdainful.
71. (A)

72. (C) Addicted to gambling is the correct use.

73. (B) Why had he not purchased a ticket is the correct form.

74. (C)

75. (A) There should be 'a great deal of' in the place of 'a lots of'.

76. (B) When the action is going on at the time of speaking the tense is present continuous.

77. (B)

78. (C) We use the 'going to be' form when we have decided to do something before talking about it.

79. (C) The past perfect describe an action completed before a certain moment.

80. (A) The present perfect lense expresses on action begun in the past time and completed at present time.

81. (C) A conjunction is a word which is used to join words or sentences together.

82. (A)

83. (B) A word used with a noun to describe or point out the person, animal, place or thing which the noun names, or to tell the number or quantity is called an adjective.

84. (D) 'One another' is representing some persons so it is pronoun.

85. (A) Here Athletics is noun.

86. (C) Preposition 'with' is used with in accordance.

87. (C) More and clever both are comparative so there should be single comparative that is more clever or cleverer.

88. (C) 'A few' is the correct use, 'few' is almost nothing.

89. (C) It is a correlative conjunction. With 'No sooner' 'than' is used and not 'them' or but.

90. (D) There is no more room means there is no more seat.

91. (A) Pediatrics is the branch of medicine dealing with children and their diseases.

92. (D) Digressive means staying away from the main theme.

93. (C) **94.** (C)

95. (A) Dazzle means to be wilder with excess of light.

96. (B) **97.** (A)

98. (A) We are angry with a person, but at something he does or says.

99. (D) **100.** (D)

❑❑❑

PRACTICE SET–11

1. Punctuate the following lines:

   'as caesar loved me i weep for him as he was fortunate i rejoice at it as he was valiant i honour him but as he was ambitious i slew him

   Find out the correct one.

   (A) As Caesar loved me I weep for him. as he was fortunate I rejoice at it, as he was, valiant I honour him but as he was ambitious I slew him.

   (B) As Caesar loved me, I weep for him. As he was fortunate I rejoice at it. As he was valiant, I honour him but as he was ambitious, I slew him.

   (C) As Caesar Loved me, I weep for him : as he was fortunate. I rejoice at it ; as he was valiant. I honour him but as he was ambitious, I slew him.

   (D) As Caesar loved me I weep for him ; as he was fortunate I rejoice at it. as he was valiant I honour him but as he was ambitious I slew him.

2. The Restoration period was influenced by

   (A) French dramatists
   (B) The dramatists of England
   (C) Italian dramatists
   (D) Greek dramatists

3. 'Every great poet is a teacher' are the words of

   (A) Shelley (B) Keats
   (C) Byron (D) Wordsworth

4. Which of the following plays, is not written by Galsworthy ?

   (A) The Silver Box (B) Joy
   (C) Weavers (D) A Doll's House

5. Which of the following words means 'a place where the birds are kept'?

   (A) Aquarium (B) Zoo
   (C) Amensty (D) Aviary

6. Choose the correct spelling of the word.

   (A) restaurant (B) resturant
   (C) resteurant (D) restorant

7. Find out the mis-spelt word.

   (A) accompaniment
   (B) explaination
   (C) superstitious
   (D) miscellaneous

8. A figure of speech in which a qualifying adjective is sometimes transferred from a person to a thing or from one word to another, to which it does not strictly belong, is called

   (A) Metonymy (B) Transferred Epithet
   (C) Apostrophe (D) Personification

9. Choose the correct animal cry to complete the sentence :

   'Dogs bark, lions roar but frogs ....

   (A) coo (B) bleat
   (C) croak (D) cluck

10. Select from the following the correct meaning of the word 'Nostalgia' :

    (A) A fatal disease
    (B) Longing for things that were in past
    (C) An Allegorical story
    (D) A state of excessive fear and anxiety

11. What does the idiom, 'the pros and cons' mean?

    (A) Changes of life
    (B) The arguments urged for and against a thing

(C) Irregularly
(D) Repeatedly

12. Name the critic who remarks Justice (1910) is a commentary upon the prison administration of that period'
(A) Coasts (B) A.C. Ward
(C) A. Nicoll (D) Skemp

13. Who calls Milton 'God-gifted organ-voice of England' ?
(A) Arnold (B) Wordsworth
(C) Gray (D) Tennyson

14. Select the word with its correct spelling :
(A) Vaccum (B) Vaccume
(C) Vaccuum (D) Vacuum

15. Punctuate the following sentence :
'she called out angrily so you have been hitting makhan again phatik answered indignantly no I have not who told you that'
Find out the correct option -
(A) She called out angrily, so you have been hitting Makhan again,Phatik answered indignantly, 'No. I have not, who told you that'.
(B) She called out angrily, 'So you have been hitting Makhan again.' Phatik answered indignantly, 'No. haven't, who told you that'.
(C) She called out angrily, 'So you have been hitting Makhan again ?' Phatik answered indignantly, 'No I haven't; who told you that ?"
(D) She called out angrily, 'So you have been hitting Makhan ?' Again Phatik answered indignantly, 'No, I haven't. Who told you that ?"

16. The figure of speech in which the sound suggests the sense or meaning is known as
(A) Alliteration (B) Onomatopoeia
(C) Oxymoron (D) Transferred Epithet

17. Who wrote the following about Shakespeare? 'Others abide our question, thou art free'.
(A) T.S. Eliot (B) Arnold
(C) Blake (D) Wordsworth

18. The fall of ....in 1453 marks the beginning of Renaissance in Europe.
Choose the correct alternative to fill in the blank in the above sentence :
(A) Bastille
(B) The Roman Empire
(C) The Spanish Armada
(D) Constantinople

19. During his visit to France, Wordsworth fell in love with a girl named
(A) Catherine
(B) Mary Hutchinson
(C) Annette Vallon
(D) Simon Lee

20. Correct form of the sentence, 'I have often found him negligent................his work,' is
(A) I have often found him negligent in his work.
(B) I have often found him negligent of his work.
(C) I have often found him negligent to his work.
(D) I have often found him negligent with his work.

21. The following sentence has a blank space and four words given after the sentence. Select whichever word you consider most appropriate for the blank space.
'The doctor said that a small daily.........of the new drug would soon cure him.
(A) tablet (B) pill
(C) dose (D) quantity

22. Pick out the right option which expresses the meaning of word 'Invaluable'.
(A) Valueless
(B) priceless
(C) Useless
(D) Chear

23. 'A Bend in the Ganges' is a work of
(A) Anita Desai
(B) Amitav Ghosh
(C) Manohar Malgonkar
(D) M.R. Anand

24. 'For a handful of silver, he left us,' this line of Browning has a reference to
(A) Shakespeare (B) Wordsworth
(C) Tennyson (D) Dryden

25. 'Venus and Adonis' is a poetic composition of a poet who was a dramatist also
(A) Shakespeare (B) Milton
(C) Marlowe (D) Dryden

26. What figure of speech has been used in the following line ?
'Frailty, thy name is woman.!'
(A) Metaphor (B) Personification
(C) Apostrophe (D) Simile

27. What is the antonym of 'Manly' ?
(A) Feminine (B) Effeminate
(C) Masculine (D) Strong

28. Choose the correct word to complete the following:
'Barking dogs .... bite'.
(A) Sometimes (B) Seldom
(C) Always (D) Never

29. What figure of speech has been used in the following line ?
'Rascals and rogues ran a race round and round the rugged rock'.
(A) Hyperbole
(B) Alliteration
(C) Onomatopoeia
(D) Apostrophe

30. Which of the following is a work of Milton ?
(A) Novum Organum
(B) De Doctrina Christiana
(C) Endymion
(D) Prothalmion

31. 'On the Morning of Christ's Nativity' is a
(A) Sonnet (B) Ode
(C) Masque (D) Pastoral Elegy

32. Which play of Shakespeare portrays the character of Malvolio ?
(A) Love's Labour Lost
(B) Twelfth Night
(C) Hamlet
(D) As You Like It

33. 'When the assault was intended to the city' is a sonnet written by
(A) Milton (B) Wordsworth
(C) Shakespeare (D) Spenser

34. One of the following poets was nicknamed "the Lady of Christ's" by his fellow undergraduates. Spot the correct name of the poet.
(A) Milton (B) Spenser
(C) Shakespeare (D) Marlowe

35. Shakespeare is indebted to one of the following sources for the subject matter of his some plays. Choose the right one from the following :
(A) The Arabian Nights
(B) Holinshed's Chronicles
(C) Bewoulf
(D) The Arthuian Legends

Direction (Q. Nos. 36 to 40): Choose the correct alternatives to fill in the blanks in the following sentences :

36. Our college building has a good ....
(A) sight (B) site
(C) cite (D) side

37. It is not possible for everyone to .... an elephant.
(A) keep up (B) keep up with
(C) keep in (D) keep on

38. Laws grind the .... and rich man rule the law.
(A) criminals (B) poor
(C) innocents (D) destitutes

39. The road to Hell is .... with good intentions.
(A) decorated (B) engraved
(C) paved (D) crowded

40. A .... soldier fights for the sake of money.
(A) materialistic
(B) pioneer
(C) veteran
(D) mercenary

Direction (Q. No. 41 to 50): In questions 41 to 50 you have a brief passage with 10 questions. Read the passage carefully, and choose the best answer to each question out of the four alternatives.

You may think the sign of a good manager is to have a department where everybody is busy at work on their assigned tasks. But if your people are merely 'doing their jobs,' they're only working at about half their potential. A truly productive department is one in which every employee is actively thinking of better, more efficient methods of working ways in which to produce a higher quality product, in less time, at lower cost.

To get this kind of innovation from your people, you have to be receptive to new ideas: what's more, you have to encourage your people to produce new ideas. Incentives are one way to motivate employees to be more productive. You can offer a cash bonus, time off, or a gift, but a more powerful form of motivation is simply the employee's knowledge that management does listen to him or her, and does put employee suggestion and ideas to work.

When you listen to new ideas, be open minded. Don't shoot down a suggestion before you've heard it in full. Many of us are too quick, too eager, to show off our own experience and knowledge and say that something won't work because we've tried it before or 'we don't do it that way'. Well may be you did try it before but that doesn't mean it won't work now. And having done things a certain way in the past doesn't mean you've been doing them the best way. A good manager is open-minded and receptive to new ideas.

41. A good manager should
(A) be open-minded and receptive to new ideas.
(B) quickly shoot down innovative suggestions from an employee to asert supremacy of his experience and knowledge.
(C) discard innovative ideas dubbing them unworkable.
(D) be contented with the normal functioning of the department.

42. The innovative suggestions or new ideas from your employee can be obtained when
(A) you offer a cash bonus to him.
(B) you make him feel that management does listen to him or her and puts his ideas to work.
(C) you disturst his experience and knowledge.
(D) you pressurise him to tender new ideas or face the consequences.

43. A truly productive employee, according to their writer, is always
(A) busy at work on his assigned tasks.
(B) actively thinking of better and more efficient methods of working.
(C) has an eye on a cash bonus, time off, or a gift.
(D) suggesting but never busy at work.

44. The word 'incentives', in the context of the passage suggests
(A) to produce higher quality product in less time.
(B) to produce higher quality product at lower cost.
(C) an additional payment or additional facilities to employee to increase production.
(D) employee's faith that management does listen to his suggestions and ideas.

45. 'To be receptive to new ideas' in the passage suggests :
(A) readiness to receive new ideas
(B) to be cautious and careful about the new ideas
(C) to share, with your people the new ideas
(D) to think of better and more efficient methods of working.

46. The word 'motivation' in the passage means
(A) to impute a motive to an action
(B) the act of inspiring others
(C) to put a thing into action
(D) none of these

47. In a truly productive department
(A) people are busy at work on their assigned tasks

(B) people are busy at work to produce large quantity
(C) people always think of evolving better than more efficient methods of working
(D) people always make a show of their experience and knowledge.

48. People merely 'doing their jobs' in the passage means
(A) that people busy at work do not perform their assigned tasks
(B) that such people produce a higher quality product
(C) that such people are working at about half their potential
(D) that such people are innovative.

49. We understand from the passage that a good manager is one
(A) who has a department where everybody is busy at work
(B) who offers a cash bonus, time off or it gift to his workers
(C) who is open minded and receptive to new ideas
(D) who is too quick, too eager to show off his experience and knowledge.

50. The given passage speaks about
(A) the sign of a good manager
(B) the workers doing their job
(C) ways in which to produce a higher quality product
(D) the need to be open to new ideas.

51. A dramatic Monologue is
(A) a short play (B) a poem
(C) a novel (D) a prose story

52. Everyman is
(A) an interlude
(B) a comedy
(C) a tragi comedy
(D) a morality play

53. The statement, "Others abide our question, thou art free" refers to
(A) John Milton
(B) Edmund Spenser
(C) Christopher Marlowe
(D) Shakespeare

54. Who is the hero of Paradise Lost ?
(A) God (B) Satan
(C) Adam (D) None of them

55. Milton's Paradise Lost
(A) has no trace of personal element
(B) is notable for its autobiographical passages
(C) is quite objective
(D) has none of the above qualities

56. Shylock is a character in
(A) As You Like it
(B) The Merchant of Venice
(C) Twelfth Night
(D) Measure for Measure

57. In Twelfth Night, Olivia is over head and ears in love with
(A) Malvolio
(B) Duke Orshino
(C) The clown
(D) Viola disguised as Cesario

58. The dominating passion of Macbeth is
(A) jealousy (B) greed
(C) revenge (D) ambition

59. The name of Prospero's daughter in The Tempest is
(A) Desdemona (B) Cordelia
(C) Miranda (D) Olivia

60. Shakespeare's play 'Hamlet' is influenced by
(A) Marlowe (B) Kyd
(C) Peele (D) Nashe

61. Which of the following plays does not belong to the group of four great tragedies of Shakespeare ?
(A) King Lear (B) Hamlet
(C) Othello (D) Twelfth Night

62. The first play by John Galsworthy was
(A) Justice
(B) Loyalties
(C) The Skin Game
(D) The Silver Box

63. Shakespeare
(A) was a great scholar of Latin
(B) knew a lot in Greek
(C) had a great command over English
(D) knew little Latin and less Greek

64. One of the following works of Milton is a prose work Mention that.
(A) Lycidas
(B) Paradise Regained
(C) Paradise Lost
(D) Arepoagitica

65. From which book has it been taken ?
"To be weak is miserable
Doing or suffering ?"
(A) The Tempest (B) Paradise Regained
(C) The Prelude (D) Paradise Lost

66. Who has said it ?
"One impulse from a vernal wood
May teach us more of man,
Of moral evil and of good
Than all the sages can."
(A) Shakespeare (B) Milton
(C) Galsworthy (D) Wordsworth

67. Choose the correct name of the play (from those given) from which the following lines have been taken :
"We are such stuff As dreams are made on and our little life Is rounded with a sleep."
(A) The Tempest (B) Othello
(C) Macbeth (D) Cariolanus

68. In which play do the following lines occur ?
"Neither a borrower nor a lender be;
For loan oft loses both itself and friend, And borrowing dulls the edge of husbandry."
(A) Macbeth
(B) The Merchant of Venice
(C) Hamlet
(D) King Lear

69. The novel is
(A) one of the earliest forms of writing
(B) one of the latest forms of writing
(C) one of the discarded forms of writing
(D) none of these

70. Elegy began to be so called because
(A) it was written in the elegiac measure
(B) it was a poem of sorrow
(C) it was written by writers of elegies
(D) some expert critics named it so

71. Classical tragedy was a form of
(A) drama (B) novel
(C) prose (D) poetry

72. The sonnet is poem of
(A) ten lines (B) twelve lines
(C) fourteen lines (D) sixteen lines

73. Find out the correctly spelt word :
(A) aroplane (B) aroplain
(C) aeroplain (D) aeroplane

74. Find out the correctly spelt word :
(A) consumpshion (B) conjumption
(C) consumption (D) conjumpshan

75. Tick the correct sentence :
(A) Neither Ram of Shyam has done it.
(B) Either Ram nor Shyam has done it.
(C) Both Ram and Shyam has done it.
(D) Neither Ram nor Shyam had done it.

Direction (Q. No. 76 to 80): Choose the most appropriate preposition:

76. His story seems to be devoid............truth.
(A) from (B) of
(C) to (D) in

77. The Sarpanch turned..............the proposal without thinking properly.
(A) in (B) out
(C) up (D) down

78. Minority aspirations cannot forever be kept in check........... the gun.
(A) by (B) through
(C) with (D) from

79. Such remarks are certainly derogatory .... you.
(A) for (B) to
(C) with (D) on

80. A good judge never jumps..............the conclusion.

(A) at (B) for
(C) to (D) on

81. 'Inevitable' bears the opposite meaning of

(A) unavoidable (B) eatable
(C) uncertain (D) mutilated

82. 'Deviate' is the antonym of

(A) obliviate (B) break
(C) concentrate (D) follow

83. 'Alleviation' is the antonym of

(A) lessening (B) magnification
(C) aggravation (D) exaggeration

84. 'Enigmatic' is

(A) displeased (B) puzzling
(C) learned (D) short-sighted

85. 'Docile' means

(A) vague (B) gentle
(C) stupid (D) stubborn

Direction (Q. No. 86 to 95): Read each of the following sentences to trace the parts which are grammatically incorrect. The alphabet of the part is to be mentioned fix the answer :

86. Suresh asked Akbar/when could he/ reach Kanpur./No error.
(A) (B) (C) (D)

87. The Principal, along with teachers,/were invited/on the occasion./No error.
(A) (B) (C) (D)

88. No sooner the bell rang/than all students ran out/of their classes helter-skelter/No error.
(A) (B) (C) (D)

89. The price of this car/is higher than/your new car/No error.
(A) (B) (C) (D)

90. Nobody was prepared/to give up their seat/ to the old man bending on a stick./No error.
(A) (B) (C) (D)

91. You and your wife/appear to have seen/ much more happier days./No error.
(A) (B) (C) (D)

92. I am very thirsty/give me little water/to drink/ No error.
(A) (B) (C) (D)

93. What to talk of charity/you do not practise/ even ordinary humanity./No error.
(A) (B) (C) (D)

94. He could not give cattle/green fodder today because/he has broken his right hand a week ago./No error.
(A) (B) (C) (D)

95. The father as well as/the sons were/involved in in the murder/No error
(A) (B) (C) (D)

96. Select, from the following, the name of the author on whose grave, the words he choose himself, are carved :

'Here lies one whose name was writ in water'

(A) Keats (B) Byron
(C) Milton (D) Swinburne

97. Select the right meaning of the word 'Aristocracy' from the following :

(A) Government by the rich
(B) Government by the nobles
(C) Government by the officials
(D) Rule by mob

98. What is the antonym of 'consent' ?

(A) descent (B) dissent
(C) decent (D) assent

99. The first Indian author to win the prestigious Pulitzer Prize in the USA was

(A) Anita Desai
(B) Jhumpa Lahiri
(C) Vikram Seth
(D) Khushwant Singh

100. Find out the figure of speech in the following lines: 'Is this the face that launched a thousand ships, and burned the topless towers of Illium ?'

(A) Personification
(B) Hyperbole
(C) Metaphor
(D) Oxymoron

ANSWERS WITH EXPLANATION

1. (C) **2.** (B)

3. (D) Works of P.B. Shelley— To a Skylark, Ode to Westwind, Alastar etc.

4. (D) Work of Galsworthy are Silver Box, Strife, Weaver etc.

5. (D) **6.** (A)

7. (B)

8. (B) In 'Transferred Epithet' on epithet or qualifying an adjective is sometimes transferred from person to an object or from one word to another.

9. (C) Dogs bark, lions roar but frogs croak.

10. (B) **11.** (B)

12. (B)

13. (D) Works of John Milton are Paradise Lost, Paradise Regained, On his Blindness etc.

14. (D) **15.** (B)

16. (B) Onomatopoeia is a figure of speech in which the sound suggests the sense of meaning.

17. (B) Works of T.S. Eliot are Cocktail Party, Family Reunion, The Wasteland etc.

18. (D) The Renaissance is a French word which means rebirth, revival or re-awakening.

19. (C) William Wordsworth (1770-1856). His works—Tintern Abbey, The Prelude etc.

20. (A)

21. (C) 'Dose' means the amount of medicine to be taken by a patient at one time.

22. (B) **23.** (C)

24. (B) Works of William Wordsworth— The prelude, Tintern Abbey, To Skylark etc.

25. (A) Works of William Shakespear—Hamlet, King Lear, Twelfth Night, As You Like It etc.

26. (C) An apostrophe is a direct address to the dead, to the absent, or to the personified object or ideas.

27. (B)

28. (B) Barking dogs seldom bite.

29. (B) Alteration consist in the repetition of the letters of syllable or the same sound at the beginning of two or more words in a line.

30. (B) Francis Bacon, "the father of the English essay". His essays are of ambition, of suitors, of revenge, etc.

31. (B) Works of John Milton—Ode on the Nativity, Peneroso, Samson Agonistes etc.

32. (B) Works of William Shakespear—Love's Labour Lost, Twelfth Night, Hamlet, Julius Ceasar etc.

33. (A) Works of William Wordsworth—The Prelude, The Tintern Abbey, To a Skylark etc.

34. (A) Works of Milton—Paradise Lost, Comus, Paradise Regained.

35. (B) Hamlet, King Lear, Othello, Merchant of Venice etc.

36. (B) Cite—to quote, site—a place

37. (A) Keep up—carry on, maintain
Keep in—confine
Keep on—continue

38. (B) **39.** (C)

40. (D) 'Mercenary' means working merely for money.

41. (A) **42.** (B)

43. (B) **44.** (C)

45. (C) **46.** (B)

47. (C) **48.** (C)

49. (C) **50.** (A)

51. (B) Literary forms of Drama, Comedy, Tragedy, Problem Play, One Act play.

52. (D)

53. (D) John Milton was born on December 9, 1608 in London. At Christi's College, Cambridge, he was called the lady of the Christ's for his grace and beauty.

54. (B)

55. (B) Works of John Milton—Paradise Lost, Paradise Regained, On his Blindness etc.

56. (B) Works of William Shakespeare— As You Like It, The Merchant of Venice, Twelfth Night, Measure for Measure etc.

57. (D) Characters of Twelfth Night—Orisino, Sebastion, Valentine, Curio, Malvolio, Viola, Olivia etc.

58. (D)

59. (C) The characters in The Tempest-

Alonso	King of Naples
Prospero	The right duke of Milan
Ferdinand	Son to the king of Naples
Miranda	Daughter to Prospero

60. (B)

61. (D) King Lear, Hamlet and Othello are tragedies while Twelfth Night is a comedy.

62. (D) Works of John Galsworthy—Justice Loyalties, The Skin Game, The Silver Box, Strife etc.

63. (D)

64. (D) Works of John Milton—Lycidas, Paradise Lost, Paradise Regained etc.

65. (A)

66. (D) Works of Wordsworth—The Prelude, To a Skylark, Education of Nature, Tintern Abbey etc.

67. (A) Shakespeare (1564-1600) is known as the father of drama. His works—Merchant of Venice, Macbeth, Hamlet, King Lear etc.

68. (C) Macbeth, The Merchant of Venice, Hamlet, King Lear and Twelfth Night etc. by William Shakespeare.

69. (B)

70. (B) Milton's Lycidas, Gray's Elegy written in country churchyard, Shelley's Adonais etc.

71. (A) Forms of poetry—Lyric, ode, sonnet, elegy, ballad, epic.

72. (C) There are two important types of sonnet in English. The petrarchan sonnet, known after Petrarch. It is divided into two parts. The octave of eight lines and sestet of six lines. Another is English or the Shakespear sonnet.

73. (D)

74. (C) Consumption-consuming—purchase and use of goods etc.

75. (D) Neither Ram nor Shyam has done it.

76. (B)

77. (D)

Turn out	Get out
Turn down	Reject
Turn up	Appear/happen
Turn back	To drive back

78. (C) 'With' preposition is used for instrument.

79. (B) **80.** (A)

81. (C) **82.** (C)

83. (A) **84.** (B)

85. (B) **86.** (B)

87. (B)

88. (A) No sooner did the bell ring than all students ran out of their classes helter skelter.

89. (C) **90.** (B)

91. (C) Double comparative degree of adjective is considered wrong.

92. (B) Little means 'no.'

93. (D) **94.** (C)

95. (B) **96.** (A)

97. (B) **98.** (B)

99. (B)

100. (B) Hyperbole consists in representing things as much greater or smaller than they really are with an intention of producing a more striking effect than a plain statement can.

❑❑❑

PRACTICE SET–12

1. Next to, but not necessarily touching, means is :
   (A) Adjoin (B) Adjacent
   (C) Adhere (C) Adapt

Direction (Q. Nos. 2 to 6): The following sentences are given with blank spaces. Choose correct alternative to fill in the blank.

2. As sheep are to a flock, so are cattle to a ....
   (A) swarm (B) multitude
   (C) pack (D) herd
3. Our school library boasts of many .... editions of the .... classical writers.
   (A) old, ancient (B) ancient, ancient
   (C) ancient, new (D) old, old
4. He is repairing his car with a view .... it.
   (A) to sell (B) to selling
   (C) for selling (D) to have sold
5. He says he is not ....for the job of a doctor.
   (A) cup up (B) cut off
   (C) cut down (D) cut out
6. I am looking forward .... you.
   (A) to seeing (B) to see
   (C) to have seen (D) for seeing
7. Put in the correct prepositions :
   We heard .... it .... our meeting.
   (A) of, through (B) at, during
   (C) of, during (D) of, in
8. Which of the following is a masque written by Milton ?
   (A) Comus (B) Aereopagilica
   (C) Lycidas (D) None of the above
9. 'Novella' is a word from :
   (A) India (B) France
   (C) Italy (D) England
10. Galsworthy began his literary career as :
    (A) a journalist (B) a dramatist
    (C) a novelist (D) a poet
11. Tick the correct meaning of the idiom Rule:
    (A) gel (B) take place
    (C) happen (D) recover
12. Which is not Shakespeare's drama ?
    (A) Tilus Andronicus
    (B) Edward the Second
    (C) Hamlet
    (D) Richard III

Direction (Q. Nos. 13-14): Identify the type of adverb in the underlined word :

13. She <u>barely</u> left the room when the roof fell in.
    (A) Adverb of Time
    (B) Adverb of Degree
    (C) Adverb of Frequency
    (D) Adverb of Manner
14 She <u>often</u> goes to the cinema.
    (A) Adverb of Time
    (B) Adverb of Degree
    (C) Adverb of Frequency
    (D) Adverb of Manner
15. 'Dastard' means :
    (A) destitute (B) becoming
    (C) brave (D) coward
16. John Galsworthy was the son of a :
    (A) novelist
    (B) merchant
    (C) lawyer
    (D) doctor

17. The plural for 'handful' is :
(A) handfuls (B) handfulls
(C) handsful' (D) handsfulls

18. Fill the correct Infinitive :
.... is difficult for a sinner.
(A) Saying prayer (B) To pray
(C) Praying to (D) Being praying

19. Which is the correct meaning of the idiom backed up?
(A) sold (B) corroded
(C) supported (D) fabricated

20. 'The Dark Lady' appears in the sonnets of :
(A) Surrey (B) Wyatt
(C) Shakespeare (D) Spenser

21. Find the mis-spelt word:
(A) appropriate (B) title
(C) mission (D) passeg

22. 'Skilful' is :
(A) Advent (B) Adopt
(C) Adroit (D) Adverse

23. Gita .... hundred times everyday.
(A) skip (B) skips
(C) skipped (D) skipping

24. The regular ode is a close imitation of :
(A) Petrarch (B) Shelley
(C) Tata (D) Pindar

25. Wordsworth composed some of his finest poems during the years :
(A) 1798-99 (B) 1778-79
(C) 1788-89 (D) 1768-69

26. One who hates mankind is called :
(A) egoist (B) egotist
(C) introvert (D) misanthrope

27. Paradise Lost was written by Milton in the .... phase of his life.
(A) Middle (B) Last
(C) Student (D) First

28. We .... dinner at the Park Hotel yesterday.
(A) had eaten
(B) ate
(C) were eating
(D) got

29. Legitimate means :
(A) valid (B) correct
(C) rightful (D) possessive

30. Lyrical Ballad was written by Coleridge and
(A) Arnold (B) Keats
(C) Wordsworth (D) Blake

31. The age of Milton had three kinds of poets :
(A) Religious, Heroic, Puritan
(B) Metaphysical, Cavalier, Puritan
(C) Metaphysical, Romantic, Dramatic
(D) Cavalier, Religious, Classical

32. Which is the correct spelling ?
(A) rythym (B) ryhthm
(C) rhythm (D) rhithym

33. The originator and namer of 'deconstruction' is :
(A) Jacques Derrida
(B) Friedrich Nietzsche
(C) Martin Heidegger
(D) Sigmund Freud

Direction (Q.Nos. 34 and 35): Fill in the blanks with prepositions:

34. It is a translation .... Horace's Ars Poetica.
(A) to (B) in
(C) from (D) of

35. Ask .... me tomorrow and you shall find me a grave man.
(A) in (B) by
(C) for (D) from

36. The period known as the age of Milton is :
(A) 1621-1681 (B) 1620-1665
(C) 1625-1660 (D) 1628-1655

37. 'Incredible' means:
(A) surprising (B) interesting
(C) disgusting (D) unbelievable

38. The passive voice of "Jack was forcing through the crowd" is :
(A) Jack was being forced through the crowd
(B) The crowd was forcing through by Jack
(C) The crowd forced through Jack
(D) The crowd was being forced through by Jack

39. "Milton's poetry is a mirror in which the writer's character is very clearly reflected." Who made this statement ?
(A) Verity (B) Macmillan
(C) Pattison (D) Bush

Direction (Q. Nos. 40-41): Fill in the blanks with correct verb form :

40. We .... by a strange sound.
(A) were startled (B) was startled
(C) was startling (D) were startling

41. Yesterday at school, I .... the echo of a roar of laughter.
(A) were startled (B) was startled
(C) was startling (D) were startling

42. The Solitary Reaper is a :
(A) Ballad (B) Ode
(C) Lyric (D) Pastoral

43. Punctuate correctly :
At sunset the general taking decision marched forward.
(A) At sunset, the general, taking decision marched forward
(B) At sunset the general, taking decision, marched forward
(C) At sunset, the general, taking decision, marched forward
(D) At sunset, the general, taking decision, marched forward.

44. Which of the following is a pastoral poem by Milton ?
(A) Adonis (B) Thyrsis
(C) Lycidas (D) None of the above

45. Insert the correct verb form :
Barcelona.................the world to the Montjuic Stadium.
(A) brought (B) look
(C) welcomed (D) welcome

46. Choose the correct verb :
They .... to school by bus.
(A) going
(B) goes
(C) go
(D) None of these

47. Vers libre is :
(A) Colophon (B) Closed form
(C) Rhymed form (D) Open form

48. Pun is :
(A) Opposite word
(B) A play on words
(C) A funny word
(D) Identical words

49. Venus and Adonis is by :
(A) Shakespeare (B) Milton
(C) Galsworthy (D) Wordsworth

50. Which is the correct spelling ?
(A) Quintessence (B) Qintessence
(C) Quentesence (D) Quintesence

51. Give the meaning of the idiom:
The new play has fallen flat:
(A) The play is a success
(B) The play met with a cold reception
(C) The play received good review
(D) None of the above

52. He .... sitting beside a river.
(Fill in with the correct verb):
(A) shall find (B) is saw
(C) is finded (D) was found

53. Wordsworth, before his death, resided at:
(A) Rydal Mount (B) Gramere Parsonage
(C) Dove Cottage (D) Allan Bank

Direction (Q. Nos. 54 to 63): In Questions 54 to 63 you have a brief passage with 10 questions. Read the passage carefully and choose the best answer to each question out of the four alternatives.

We were in class when the headmaster came in, followed by a 'new fellow', not wearing the school uniform, and a school servant carrying a large desk. Those who had been asleep woke up, and everyone rose as if surprised at his work. The headmaster made a sign to us to sit down. Then turning to the class master, he said to him in a low voice : 'Mr. Roger, here is a pupil whom I recommend to your care. 'The new boy was wearing a tight green jacket, yellow trousers and a strange cap which soon attracted the attention of the whole class.

The new boy was still holding his strange cap on his knees even after the prayers were over.

'Rise', said the master. The boy stood up; his cap fell. The whole class began to laugh. He stood to pick it up, a neighbour knocked it down again with his elbow, he picked it up once more, 'Get rid of your helmet,' said the master, who was a bit of a joker. There was a burst of laughter from the boys, which so throughly shamed the boy that he didn't know whether to keep his cap in his hand, leave it on the ground, or put it on his head. He sat down again and placed it on his knee.

'Rise,' repeated the master, 'and tell me your name,' The new boy articulated in a stammering voice an unintelligible name, 'Again!' said the master, The same sputtering of syllables was heard, drowned by the tittering of the class. 'Louder!' cried the master; 'louder!' The new fellow opened a large mouth and shouted at the top of his voice as if calling someone the word 'Charbovari.'A hubbub broke out; they shouted, barked, stamped and repeated 'Charbovari! Charbovari!'

54. Which of the following would be the most suitable title for the passage?
(A) The mischievous master
(B) The mischievous class
(C) A funny boy in the class
(D) A new boy in the class

55. The word 'hubbub' in the last sentence of the passage means :
(A) complete silence
(B) noise and excitement
(C) dullness
(D) atmosphere

56. Which literary device has been used in the following sentence of last paragraph ?
'The same sputtering of syllables was heard, drowned by the tittering of the class.'
(A) Metaphor (B) Irony
(C) Apostrophe (D) Onomatopoeia

57. In the command of the master 'Get rid of your helmet' used in second paragraph :
(A) there is a cruel joke
(B) there is nothing cruel about it
(C) the master wants to help the boy
(D) the master wants to discipline the class

58. The boy was 'sputtering' syllables because he was :
(A) angry (B) sad
(C) shy (D) calm

59. The last part of the episode prove to be an anticlimax to :
(A) the class (B) the boy
(C) the teacher (D) all of them

60. Which of the following is true about the description of the new boy ?
(A) The boy has been sketched sympathetically.
(B) The boy has been caricatured.
(C) It is a serious description.
(D) The writer seems to hate the boy.

61. What contributed most to the misery of the new boy?
(A) the appearance of the boy
(B) his shyness
(C) the sadistic attitude of the master
(D) insenitive class-mates

62. What is the function of the clause 'a school servant carrying a large desk' in the opening sentence ?
(A) just to provide an extra information
(B) to describe the atmosphere
(C) to create seriousness
(D) to create humour

63. Who disturbed the peace of the class ?
(A) the new boy
(B) the mischievous boys of the class
(C) the master
(D) the headmaster

64. Wordsworth's poems, mostly, deal with :
(A) polities
(B) city life
(C) humble and rustic life
(D) revolution

65. Tick the correct auxiliary to indicate discontinued habit :
(A) There was a house there.
(B) There used-to be a house there.
(C) There is a house there.
(D) There was used to be a house there

66. Informal essay is also known as :
(A) Funny essay (B) Scholarly essay
(C) Familiar essay (D) Impersonal essay

67. Tick the correct one :
(A) Gita asked me where I lived.
(B) Gita asked to me where I lived.
(C) Gita asked me where did I live?
(D) Gita asked me where do you live ?

68. "A violet by a mossy stone/Half hidden from the eye!" is a quote from the :
(A) Ode to Duty
(B) Lucy Poems
(C) The Green Linnet
(D) The Solitary Reaper

Direction (Q. Nos. 69 to 73): Each of the following sentences is divided into four parts (A), (B), (C) and (D). Some of the sentences have errors is one part and some have none. Find out which part of the sentence has an error.

69. Few people know/that the climate of Shimla/
(A) (B)
is better than Srinagar./No error
(C) (D)

70. The examinations of the undergraduate
(A)
students/are likely to commence/
(B)
from Friday./No error
(C) (D)

71. The principal claimed that/there were less
(A)
than fifty students present in the building/
(B)
when it caught fire./No error
(C) (D)

72. We have lived/in this house ever since/
(A) (B)
my father has died./No error
(C) (D)

73. He explained to the government why/the
(A)
manufacturing of cars/have stopped in his
(B) (C)
new factory./No error
(D)

74. Find out the correct narration of the following direct speech :
"I know this area because I used to live here," he informed.
(A) He informed that he knew that area because he used to lived there
(B) He informed that The knew that area because he had lived there.
(C) He informed that he knew that area because he had been living there.
(D) He informed that he knew that area because he lived there.

75. Punctuate the following :
Dont worry father said he I'll soon leave the village and find a job in Delhi
(A) Dont worry father "said he" I'll soon leave the village and find a job in Delhi.
(B) Don't worry father, said he "I'll soon leave the village and find a job in Delhi"
(C) "Don't worry father," said he 'I'll soon leave the village and find a job in Delhi."
(D) "Don't worry father said he" I'II soon leave the village and find a job in Delhi.

76. The most common form of closing a letter to a close relative is :
(A) Yours sincerely
(B) Yours affectionately
(C) Yours faithfully
(D) Yours truly

77. Change the following simple sentence into a complex sentence :
His senior colleagues have been transferred lo Dehradun.
(A) His colleagues having a seniority over him have been transferred to Dehradun.
(B) His colleagues who are senior to him have been transferred to Dehradun.
(C) Some of his colleagues are senior to him therefore they have been transferred to Dehradun.
(D) Being senior some of his colleagues have been transferred to Dehradun.

78. Change the following into a complex sentence: He received the call of his friend and left for Delhi right away.
(A) Receiving the call of his friend, he left for Delhi right away.
(B) He received the call of his friend, therefore he left for Delhi right away.
(C) As soon as he received the call of his friend, he left for Delhi.
(D) He received the call of his friend and soon left for Delhi.

Direction (Q. Nos. 79-80) Choose the correct word for the blanks :

79. Songs .... sung in his memory.
(A) is (B) were
(C) had (D) been

80. .... the boy return to his village ?
(A) Shall (B) Will
(C) Was (D) Shan't

81. 'Compact' means :
(A) Face powder for women
(B) Computer software
(C) Put together in a small space
(D) None of the above

82. Select the correct spelling :
(A) Staff Quarters
(B) Stuff Quarters
(C) Staff Quaters
(D) None of the above

83. The meaning of 'solicited' is :
(A) advice requested
(B) to do a court case.
(C) to form a party
(D) none of the above

Direction (Q. Nos. 84-88): Read the following passage carefully and answer the questions that follow:

SANTINIKETAN, Aug. 17, 1998 : The rainy season has returned, and the man is back at his work. He is Pannalal Patel, the man who has completed 96 years, and is still going strong.

Pannalal was once a 'terrorist'. Then he turned into a Gandhian. At present his mission is "Meen Mangal" or "the well-being of fish", as he calls it.

Come the rains, and Pannalal would release millions of young salmons into rivers flowing through the neighbourhood. He says that water without fish is just as absurd as fish without water.

On Independence Day Eve he had an appointment with the Ajoy, the river he loves and adores choked up with silt and sand from bank to bank, the river remains almost dry throughout the year except in the rainy season. Once called 'the crazy river' for often changing its course; Ajoy is now better known for the great destruction it causes, at intervals of some years, by flooding the villages on its banks. It then washes away people and cattle and houses, and brings great misery.

The appointed day arrived. It was a cloudy afternoon at Palitpur, the venue of the programme where a new bridge has been built across the river.

Short speeches were made. Songs were sung. Mr. Patel took a handful of the young salmon and threw them into the water – once, twice, thrice. Others followed him. The hero of the day looked happy, and a smile lit up his wrinkled face.

But some fisherman in the crowd were rather sceptical about the usefulness of the programme. Will the fish, when grown up, return to the same waters and be caught in their nets. 'Perhaps not'. They talked among themselves,

Mr. Patel, however, does not bother himself about who catches how much fish in which waters. He himself is a complete vegetarian. His only concern is the well-being of fish.

84. The object of Pannalal's programme at Palitpur was the welfare of :
(A) the fishermen (B) the Ajoy
(C) society (D) fish

85. According to Pannalal, water without fish is :
(A) unthinkable
(B) tasteless
(C) impure
(D) unprofitable

86. The Ajoy floods its banks :
(A) every rainy season
(B) very rarely
(C) every few years
(D) quite often

87. Pannalal had an appointment with the river Ajoy :
(A) on 15th August
(B) on 14th August
(C) on 15th August morning
(D) on 14th August evening

88. Pannalal Patel, who is very old, is still :
(A) strong (B) fond of fishing
(C) very alert (D) can walk fast

89. Put in the correct verb form :
I know that you .... twenty on your last birthday.
(A) were (B) was
(C) are (D) is

90. Which is the correct spelling ?
(A) canceled (B) cancited
(C) cancelled (D) canscelled

91. Punctuate correctly :
Amrit sharma is a metro railway employee
(A) Amrit Sharma is a metro railway employee.
(B) Amrit Sharma is a Metro Railway employee.
(C) Amrit Sharma is a metro railway Employee.
(D) None of the above

92. To refurbish is :
(A) to repair (B) to survey
(C) to apply (D) to renovate

Direction (Q. Nos. 93-94) : Fill in the gaps with the correct prepositions

93. He vanished .... the darkness.
(A) to (B) in
(C) into (D) through

94. Chased by the dog, the thief ran .... the lawn.
(A) across (B) around
(C) over (D) through

95. She slept soundly Identify the nature of the underlined verb :
(A) Transitive verb
(B) Intransitive verb
(C) Regular verb
(D) Verb of complete predication

96. The plural for 'man-servant' is :
(A) man-workers (B) man-servants
(C) mans-servant (D) men-servant

97. In which poem does the following statement apear? "Solitude, sometimes is best society."
(A) Paradise Regained
(B) Lycidas
(C) Paradise Lost
(D) Comus

98. Shakespeare was born in :
(A) 1574 (B) 1563
(C) 1564 (D) 1589

99. Indicate the underlined word which is the correct Adverbial qualification:
(A) The flames spread everywhere
(B) The flames spread everywhere
(C) The flames spread everywhere
(D) The flames spread everywhere

100. 'Poetic Justice' was a term coined by :
(A) Samuel Johnson
(B) Geoffrey Leech
(C) John Dryden
(D) Thomas Rymer

ANSWERS WITH EXPLANATION

1. (B) 2. (D)
3. (A) 4. (A)
5. (D) 6. (B)
7. (C)

8. (A) The Masque of Comus' is in many respect the most perfect of Milton's Poems.
9. (C) The word novel is derived from the Italian 'novelle' which means, a Mule new thing, was a short table in prose.

10. (C) The, first published work of Galsworthy was a collection of stories in 1897. Then he wrote novels and success came to hin with his third novel.

11. (C)

12. (B) 'Edward The Second' is a drama by Christopher Marlowe.

13. (B) Adverbs of Degree or quantity answer the question 'how much' or 'in what degree' or 'to what' extent.

14. (C) **15.** (D)

16. (C) **17.** (A)

18. (B) When a verb merely make an action and is not limited by number and person to its subject it is called an infinitive. To + Verb is present infinitive.

19. (C) Back up means to support.

20. (C) Shakespeare's sounds are divided into two classes; one addressed to a man, his friend; and two to a woman who disdained his love and was called dark lady.

21. (D) The correct spelling of the word is 'Passage'.

22. (C)

23. (B) 's' and 'es' is used with the first form of the verb when the subject is in the third person singular.

24. (D) The 'Regular or Pindaric' ode in English is a learned imitation of Pindar's form, with all the 'Strophes' and 'antistrophes' written in one kind of stanza; and all the epodes in another.

25. (A) Wordsworth Published 'Lyrical Ballads', with Coleridge, in the year 1798. It contains some of his finest poems.

26. (D)

27. (B) Milton finished 'Paradise Lost' in 1665. His literary career is divided into three periods – (i) 1632 to 1637 (ii) 1640 to 1660 (iii) 1660 onwards.

28. (B) The sentence will be in past indefinite because there is only action thus it can't be in past perfect.

29. (A)

30. (C) 'Lyrical Ballads' was written by Coleridge and Wordsworth and Published in 1798.

31. (B) Miltonic Age covers the span of time between 1625 to 1660, which is dominated by metaphysical cavalier and poritan poets.

32. (C) **33.** (A)

34. (D) **35.** (C)

36. (C) The age of Milton that is 1625-1660 comprises the Caroline Age (1625-1649) and the Commonwealth (1649-1660).

37. (D)

38. (D) We change an active sentence into a passive by changing the object of the active in the subject of the passive, without changing the meaning.

39. (B) **40.** (A)

41. (B)

42. (C) Solitary Reaper is a lyric written in 1807. It was inspired, not by an actual sight, but by the description of a solitary Reaper given in Thomas Wilidngon's "Tour in Scotland".

43. (D)

44. (C). 'Lycidas' is a pastoral elegy written in 1637 in the memory of Milton's friend Edward King who drowned in the Irish sea.

45. (C) **46.** (C)

47. (D) Free verse or in French term 'verse libre' is a verse lacking regulare metre but depending for its effect upon nature speech rhythms.

48. (B) When we use the same word in two or more senses in order to make the people laugh, we employ the figure of speech called pun.

49. (A) Shakespeare's poems, rather than his dramatic work mark the beginning of his success. "Venus and Adonis" became immensely popular in London.

50. (A) **51.** (B)

52. (D)

53. (A) The last half century of Wordsworth's life, in which he retired to his beloved lake district and lived successively at grasmere and Rydal Mount.

54. (B)

55. (B)

56. (D) 'Sputtering' and 'Tittering one' are onomatopoeic.

57. (B) 58. (C)

59. (D) 60. (A)

61. (D) 62. (B)

63. (B) In fact the mischievous boys of the class were to blame for the disturbance of the class.

64. (C) Wordsworth always choose for his heroes & heroines, not famous men and women stupefied by victory, and intoxicated with story and power, but humble peasants, innocent farmers, artless shephard, lonely reapers.

65. (B) 66. (B)

67. (A)

68. (B) The title of the poem is – 'She Dwell Among the untroden Ways', and lines run as

A violet by a mossy stone
Half hidden from the eye!
Fair as a star, when only one
Is shining in the sky.

69. (C) It should be as 'is better than that of Srinagar'.

70. (C) It should be as 'On friday'.

71. (D)

72. (A) It should be as 'we have been living'.

73. (C) It should be 'have been stopped'.

74. (A) 75. (C)

76. (B) 77. (B)

78. (C) 79. (B)

80. (B) In Interrogative sentences "will" in the third person expresses simple future tense.

81. (*) Both option (A) and option (C) are correct.

82. (A) 83. (A)

84. (D) 85. (A)

86. (C)

87. (D) Meaning of the term, Independence Day Eve is the evening just before the Independence Day.

88. (A) 89. (A)

90. (C) 91. (B)

92. (D)

93. (C) 'In' is used when there is no action while 'into' is used to show action.

94. (A)

95. (B) The verb which does not require any object after it to complete the sense is called intransitive verb.

96. (D) Plural of a compound noun made of two nouns is made by changing the second noun into plural, but when the first noun of the compound noun is either man or woman then both the nouns are changed into plural to make the plural of compound noun.

97. (A)

98. (C) From the register of the Parish Church at Stratford on Avon. We learn that Shakespeare was baptised there on 26th April, 1564.

99. (A) An adverb is a word which modifies the meaning of a verb, an adjective or another adverb.

100. (A)

❑❑❑

PRACTICE SET–13

1. In which year was Justice published?
(A) 1905 (B) 1908
(C) 1912 (D) 1910

2. Pick out the correct antonym of the underlined word.
Extreme poverty had reduced them to a state of <u>apathy</u>.
(A) cooperation (B) friendship
(C) inspiration (D) enthusiasm

3. Find out the correct sentence:
(A) He was astonished at his success.
(B) He was astonished in his success.
(C) He was astonished on his success.
(D) He was astonished for his success.

4. Change the sentence into passive voice.
Do you not understand my meaning?
(A) I am not understood your meaning.
(B) I do not understanding meaning.
(C) Is your meaning understood?
(D) Is my meaning understood?

5. Find out the mistake in the sentence given below.
<u>The driver was</u> put/<u>in the prison</u>/<u>for exceeding</u>
(A) (B) (C)
<u>the speed limit</u>
(D)

6. Pick out the correct spelling of the word among the following words.
(A) platetude
(B) pllatitude
(C) pllattitude
(D) platitude

7. Choose the name of the Roman General who conquered England in 43 B.C.:
(A) Julius Caesar (B) Claudius
(C) Antony (D) None of these

8. Correct the following sentence.
It was bitter cold.
(A) It was cold bitterly.
(B) It was awful coldly.
(C) It was cold bitter.
(D) It was bitterly cold.

9. In which Shakespearean play does the following occur?
'The bright day is done
And we are for the dark'
(A) Antony and Clepatra
(B) Hamlet
(C) King Lear
(D) Measure for Measure

10. What does the idiom, 'smell a rat' means?
(A) to have reason to suspect
(B) to talk hoastfully
(C) to talk unfairly
(D) to discourage

11. Find out which part of the sentence has an error.
<u>If I am you</u>/<u>I would have seen to it</u>/
(A) (B)
<u>that I won the prize</u>/<u>No error</u>.
(C) (D)

12. Find out the correct proverb.
(A) diamond cuts iron
(B) diamond cuts gold
(C) diamond cuts silver
(D) diamond cuts diamond

13. In which country is the story of Othello set?
(A) Venice (B) Denmark
(C) England (D) Scotland

14. Who is the writer of '*History of Britain*'?
(A) William Shakespeare
(B) John Milton
(C) William Wordsworth
(D) John Galsworthy

15. Complete the sentence.
Ottava Rima is a ....stanza in Iambic Pentametres.
(A) four-lined (B) six-lined
(C) eight-lined (D) ten-lined

16. Put the following in indirect speech.
"How smart you are !" she said.
(A) She exclaimed that I am smart.
(B) She exclaimed that he was very smart.
(C) She exclaimed that she is smart.
(D) She exclaimed she was smart.

17. Select the correct option.
There was ....
(A) a fly in milk
(B) fly in the milk
(C) fly in milk
(D) a fly in the milk

18. Milton's Paradise Lost consists of ....books.
(A) twelve
(B) ten
(C) six
(D) eight

19. People have tried their best to *provoke* the flood victims.
Find out the correct antonym of the italicised word.
(A) gratify (B) convince
(C) pacify (D) attract

20. Choose the correct option.
'One impulse from a vernal wood'
The above line has been quoted from
(A) The Tables Turned
(B) Tintern Abbey
(C) The World is too Much With Us
(D) Ode to Duty

21. Complete the sentence.
Dirge means..............
(A) a song of wedding
(B) a song of pleasure
(C) a song of grief
(D) a song of unfulfilled desire

22. Find out which part of sentence has an error.
Even though the shirt is rather expensive/ (A)
but I wish to/ (B) purchase it with my own money/ (C)
No error (D)

23. Fill the gap with an appropriate preposition.
Volpone fell a victim ....his own greed.
(A) to (B) of
(C) about (D) for

24. Fill in the gap.
I will sit..............my desk to do my lesson.
(A) at (B) with
(C) for (D) in

25. Complete the sentence with correct option given below.
She gave him..............he wanted.
(A) what (B) that
(C) that which (D) that what

26. In which play of Shakespeare does Adam appear?
(A) Merry Wives of Windsor
(B) As You Like It
(C) Twelfth Night
(D) The Tempest

27. Find out which part of the sentence has an error.

Are you/lived alone/or married/No error
(A) (B) (C) (D)

28. Complete the sentence.

Milton became blind at the age of ....

(A) 46 (B) 47
(C) 44 (D) 48

29. Find in the gap with an appropriate word.

I am badly in need.............money.

(A) with (B) of
(C) for (D) on

30. Turn the following into indirect speech.

"Do you write a good hand?" he said.

(A) He asked whether I wrote a good hand.
(B) He asked whether they wrote a good hand.
(C) He asked whether I written a good hand.
(D) He asked whether I was written a good hand.

31. Complete the sentence.

Comus is ....

(A) a masque (B) a pastoral allegory
(C) poetic line (D) a farce

32. Name the 'figure of speech' in the following line. 'Boys will be boys.'

(A) epigram (B) personification
(C) litotes (D) metonymy

33. Who has written, *Jocelyn* among the following writers?

(A) Milton (B) Shakespeare
(C) Galsworthy (D) Wordsworth

34. Choose the correct meaning of the given word Craven.

(A) dishonest (B) cowardly
(C) dark (D) slavish

35. Complete the sentence

Galsworthy's play Strife deals with the subject of ....

(A) labour disputes
(B) Justice
(C) wars
(D) class distinction

36. How many parts are there in *The Prelude*?

(A) twelve (B) thirteen
(C) fourteen (D) eleven

37. Which of the following sentences is in passive voice?

(A) Always reach the school at time.
(B) Please bring me a glass of water.
(C) Let him read a book.
(D) Let the salary be given to these clerks.

38. Find out the correct option.

A sonnet consists of :

(A) 14 lines (B) 18 lines
(C) 20 lines (D) 12 lines

39. Elsinore in Denmark is the scene is a Shakespearean play—Which ?

(A) King Lear
(B) Coriolanus
(C) Hamlet
(D) Titus Andronicus

40. Change the sentence into passive voice.

I saw him opening the box.

(A) He was seen open the box.
(B) He was seen opening the box.
(C) He opened the box.
(D) He was seen opened the box.

41. What is 'Euphony'?

(A) Pleasant sound
(B) Serious sound
(C) Bitter sound
(D) Mixed sound

42. Who has written 'Cymbeline'?

(A) Milton (B) Wordsworth
(C) Shakespeare (D) Galsworthy

43. Find out the mis-spelt word.

(A) disparage (B) licentious
(C) Malleable (D) dillema

44. Change the following sentence into complex sentence.

He had to sign, or be executed.

(A) If he did not signed, he had not executed.
(B) If he had not signed, he would have been executed.

(C) If he had signed, he would not executed.
(D) If he was signed he did not executed.

45. Complete the sentence
Milton's Aeropagitica concerns with......
(A) liberty of human right
(B) liberty of press
(C) freedom of humanity
(D) freedom of politics

46. In the passage, the author is primarily concerned with
(A) moral conduct
(B) a humane approach to our problems
(C) the scientific point of view
(D) the acquisition of specialized knowledge

47. It is one's duty to resist
(A) all political propagandas
(B) religious practices
(C) unsatisfactory plans and programmes
(D) irrational ideas

48. When one does not think clearly and objectively
(A) one fails to achieve success
(B) one tends to believe in the wrong things
(C) one is considered a fool
(D) one tends to make mistakes in day-to-day life

49. If one does not observe restraint
(A) people around one will grow hostile
(B) one's friends will ignore one
(C) one's life will be miserable
(D) people will see it that one behaves responsibly

50. Choose the right option to complete the sentence.
Human obligations do not include
(A) behaving in a disciplined manner
(B) acquiring knowledge
(C) making others feel that you are always right
(D) thinking clearly

51. Fill in the gap :
King Lear had .... daughters.
(A) two (B) three
(C) four (D) five

52. Who is the writer of Descriptive Sketches?
(A) John Milton (B) Shakespeare
(C) Galsworthy (D) Wordsworth

53. Where was Wordsworth born?
(A) Cockerpate (B) Cockermouth
(C) Cocker Hill (D) Cockervalley

54. Complete the sentence.
'Aesthetic' means...........
(A) sorrow (B) despair
(C) beauty (D) pleasure

55. Who is the writer of 'Recluse'?
(A) Shakespeare (B) Milton
(C) Galsworthy (D) Wordsworth

56. Transform the following exclamatory sentence into assertion.
If only I had come one hour earlier !
(A) I wish I come one hour earlier.
(B) I wish I have come one hour earlier.
(C) I wish I had come one hour earlier.
(D) I wish I could come one hour earlier.

57. Choose the correct option.
'Little we see in Nature that is ours.'
The above line has been quoted from
(A) Tintern Abbey
(B) The World is too Much With Us
(C) Ode on Intimations of Immortality
(D) Lucy Grays.

58. 'Frailty, thy name is woman'; this remark is made by
(A) Macbeth
(B) King Lear
(C) Othello
(D) Hamlet

59. What is meaning of phrase, 'To count upon'?
(A) to be grateful
(B) to relax
(C) to clean a thing
(D) to depend upon

60. Fill in the gap with an appropriate conjunction.
.... you wish it, it shall be done.
(A) since
(B) having
(C) for
(D) with

61. Rearrange the sentence with correct order labeled as PQRS. Choose the proper sequence.
(P) only time will tell (Q) you credit the nation with (R) whether the great future (S) will turn out to be true
(A) QPRS (B) PRQS
(C) QRSP (D) RSQP

62. Change the direct sentence into indirect. Mohan said. "Alas ! I am undone."
(A) Mohan exclaimed sadly that he was undone.
(B) Mohan exclaimed that he was undone.
(C) Mohan exclaimed that he was not undone.
(D) Mohan exclimed that he is undone.

63. Who is known as the Fourth Witch in Shakespeare's women characters?
(A) Lady Macbeth (B) Gertude
(C) Cordelia (D) Desdemona

64. Fill in the gap with an appropriate preposition.
They were statesmen accustomed ....the management.........great affairs.
(A) of, to (B) in, to
(C) to, of (D) with, in

65. Complete the sentence.
Justice shows problems of
(A) British Society
(B) English legal system
(C) American legal system
(D) Scottish Society

66. Find out the correct spelling of the word.
(A) elixir (B) elesser
(C) eleseir (D) elixer

67. Complete the sentence.
The Island Pharisees has been written by ......
(A) Wordsworth (B) Galsworthy
(C) Milton (D) Shakespeare

68. A Lyric is ....
Find out the correct option.
(A) A long poem written in the form of an address.
(B) A poem written in praise of God.
(C) A short poem in which the poet express his/her intense personal feelings.
(D) A triumphal song

69. What is 'Baroque'?
(A) Jail
(B) style
(C) culture
(D) book

70. What is the synonym of 'wisdom'?
(A) swell (B) sagacity
(C) foolishness (D) surrender

71. Complete the sentence.
Shakespeare has written......historical plays.
(A) 4 (B) 6
(C) 7 (D) 10

72. Who invented and popularised the phrase, 'Poetic Justice'?
(A) Dryden (B) Johnson
(C) Rymer (D) Shakespeare

73. In which year, Milton's Lycidas was written?
(A) 1638 (B) 1632
(C) 1637 (D) 1636

74. Complete the sentence.
Milton's poetic style is generally regarded as.....
(A) plain (B) classical
(C) grand (D) ornamental

75. What is the meaning of 'Plagiarism'?
(A) poetic bankruptey
(B) literary theft
(C) writing crisis
(D) reading problem

76. How many sonnets are addressed to 'W.H.' by Shakespeare?
(A) 125 (B) 124
(C) 122 (D) 126

77. How many sonnets are addressed to 'Dark Lady' by Shakespeare?
(A) 27 (B) 28
(C) 29 (D) 26

78. Fill in the gap.
The title of the play, 'Justice' is.......
(A) satirical (B) vague
(C) inappropriate (D) problem

79. "Come, thou mortal wretch,
With thy sharp teeth this knot intrinsicate"
In which book do the above lines occur?
(A) Antony and Cleopatra
(B) Twelfth Night
(C) Hamlet
(D) Midsummer Night's Dream

80. Who wrote Metafiction?
(A) Roland Barthes
(B) Derrida
(C) Patricia Waugh
(D) Spivak

81. Choose the correct alternative.
You..........him since his childhood.
(A) have known
(B) know
(C) know
(D) am knowing

82. Which of the following flowers does the Mad Ophelia not give away?
(A) violets (B) Pansies
(C) reosemry (D) columbines

83. Find out which part of sentence has an error.
The two students walked/besides each other/in silence/No error
(A) (B) (C) (D)

84. What is the full name of Mr. W.H. in Shakespeare's Sonnets?
(A) William Herbert
(B) William Henry
(C) William Hartey
(D) William Harry

85. Complete the sentence.
The reversal of fortune of a tragic hero is called....
(A) catharsis (B) peripetia
(C) epistle (D) poesis

86. In which year, Milton's Paradise Lost was published?
(A) 1668 (B) 1670
(C) 1667 (D) 1665

87. Complete the sentence.
The error of Judgement in Tragedy is known as...
(A) hamartia (B) tragedy of blood
(C) catastrophe (D) catharsis

88. Complete the sentence.
The Globe Theatre was burned down in.........
(A) 1617 (B) 1619
(C) 1613 (D) 1609

89. Who has written 'Hamlet and His Problems'?
(A) Shelley (B) Eliot
(C) Shakespeare (D) Bacon

90. Complete the sentence.
Epiphany means..........
(A) manifestation of God's presence
(B) manifestation of Satan's presence
(C) fanciful world
(D) supernatural power

91. When was John Galsworthy awarded the Nobel Prize for literature?
(A) 1927 (B) 1929
(C) 1932 (D) 1935

92. Name the figure of speech in the following line. 'The more haste, the less speed'.
(A) Simile (B) Metaphor
(C) Irony (D) Epigram

93. In which play, Shakespeare has presented 'a royal criminal'?
(A) King Lear (B) Henry IV
(C) Richard III (D) Henry VIII

94. Change the voice
Why did he defraud you of your earnings?
(A) Why were you defrauded to your earnings by him.
(B) Why was he defrauded of his earnings.
(C) Why did he defraud you for his earnings.
(D) Why were you defrauded of your earnings by him.

95. Fill in the gap with an appropriate auxillary.
He was so tired that he ......scarcely stand.
(A) could (B) did
(C) should do (D) had

96. What is true of the form of Shakespeare's sonnet?
(A) it has an octave.
(B) it has in integrated from with no such divisions.
(C) it has three quatrains and couplet.
(D) it has the endings of alternate lines rhyming with each other.

97. 'Life of Milton' has been written by.......
Choose the right option from the given alternatives.
(A) Samuel Johnson
(B) Ben Jonson
(C) Charles Lamb (D) John Dryden

98. Who wrote, "Lilies that fester smell for worse than weeds'?
(A) Wordsworth
(B) Milton
(C) Galsworthy
(D) Shakespeare

99. In which year, Galsworthy refused the offer of a Knighthood?
(A) 1917
(B) 1918
(C) 1919
(D) 1920

100. Who is Harold Cleaver in Galsworthy's 'Justice'?
(A) Government Counsel
(B) Defence Counsel
(C) Judge
(D) Managing Clerk

ANSWERS WITH EXPLANATION

1. (D) 2. (D)
3. (A) He was astonished at his success. The word-astonished, surprised, alarmed, disappointed take 'at' in place of 'by'.
4. (D) Is my meaning understood?
5. (B) In the prison
There is no article before prison.
6. (D) 7. (D)
8. (D)
9. (A) Antony and Cleopatra

(1) Why then is none to you; for there is nothing either good or bad but thinking makes so.
To me it is a prison. **Hamlet**

(2) To be or not to be that is the question:
Whether' his nobler in the mind to suffer.
The slings and arrows of outrageous fortune. **Hamlet**

Good day, and happiness, dear Rosalind! Orland Farewell Monsieure Traveller look you lisp and wear strange suits, disable all the benefits of your own country.

10. (A) 'Smell a rat' means to suspect that something is wrong about a situation.

11. (A) If I am you

It is a part of imagination, I takes 'were' in place of 'am'.

12. (D)

13. (A) Venice

Following his experimental work there came a succession of wonderful plays: Merchant of Venice, As you like It, Twelfth Night, Julius Caesar, Hamlet, Macbeth, Othello, King Lear, Antony and Cleopatra. The great tragedies of this period are associated with a period of gloom as sorrow in the poet's life; but of its cause we have no knowledge. It may have been this unknown sorrow which turned his thoughts back to Stratford and caused apparently, a disatisfaction with his work and profession, but the letter is generally attributed to other causes.

14. (C) John Milton

Milton's famous works:

Paradise Lost (1667)

Paradise Regained (1671)

Samson Agonistes (1671)

Ode On the Morning of Christ's Nativity (1929)

On Shakespeare (1630)

On Arriving to the Age of twenty-three (1631)

History of Britain (Incompleted)

15. (C) Eight lined

It is a stanza of eight lines in Jamkic pentametres with a rhyme scheme a b ab ab cc. Like the Terza Rima it is of Italian origin. It was introduced into England by Sir Thomos Wyatt in the 16th century. Byron made an effective use of Ottava Rima in Don Juan, but he introduced into it a slight variation of his own instead of using eleven syllables in the original Italian form he used a ten syllabled line. The following is an example from Byron's Don Juan.

16. (B) She exclaimed that he was very smart.

17. (D)

18. (C) Twelve

The theme of Fall and Expulsion from Eden had been in Milton's mind from the 1640s. His ambition was to compose an epic poem to rival the ancient poets such as Homer and Virgil, whose grand vision in Aeneid left traces in his work. Originally, it was issued in 10 books in 1667, and in 12 books in the second edition of 1674. Milton, who wanted to be a great poet had also to cope with the towering figure of Shakespeare, who had died in 1616. Milton was seven at that time. In his own hierarchy, Milton placed highest in the scale. The epic, below it was the drama.

19. (C) **20.** (A)

21. (C) A song of grief

22. (B) **23.** (A)

24. (A) **25.** (A)

26. (B) As You Like It

Famous Characters

Antonio	Gratiano
Portia	Jessica
Shylock	Nerissa
Bassanio	Leorenzo

Play- The Merchant of Venice

Famous Characters

Hamlet	Ophelia
Polonious	Gertude
Horatio	Claudius
Laertes	

Play-Hamlet

Famous Characters

Orlando	Adam
Oliver	Jaques Junior
Rosalind	Sir Oliver Martext

Celia	Corin
Frederick	William
Touchstone	Audrey
Jaques	

27. (B)

28. (C) 44

In 1651 Milton became blind at the age of 44 but like Jorge Luis Borges Centuries later, blindness helped him to stimulate his verbal richness. He sacrificed his sight and then he remembered his first desire, that of being a poet. Borges wrote one of his lectures. One of his assistants was the poet and satirist Andew Marvell, who spoke for him in parliament, when his political opinions stirred much controversy. After the Restoration of Charles II in 1660 Milton was arrested as a noted defender of the commonwealth, but was soon released. However for his opposition, Milton was forced to play a massive fine. Besides public burning of Eikonklastes and the first Defensio in Paris and Toulouse Milton escaped from more punishment, but be became a relatively poor man.

29. (B)

30. (A) He asked whether I wrote a good hand.

31. (A) A masque

The "Masque of Comus" is in many respects the most perfect of Milton's poem. It was written in 1634 to be performed at Ludlow Castle before the earl of Bridge water and his friends while there are undoubted traces of Jonson and John Fletcher in Milton's "Comus". The poem for surpasses its predecessors in the airy beauty and melody of its verses.

32. (A) Epigram

An Epigram is a brief pointed saying frequently introducing antithetical ideas which excite, surprise and arrest attention.

Examples :

1. The child is father of the man
2. He makes no fried. Who never made a foe.
3. Know then thyself presume not God to scan. The proper study of mankind is man.
4. A man can't be too careful in the choice of his enemies.

33. (C) Galsworthy

Galsworthy's famous plays are Island Pharisees (1904), The Pigen (1922), Escape (1926), Justice (1910), The Silver Box (1909), Loyalties (1922).

34. (B)

35. (A) 'Strife' was the third of Galsworthy's plays. It was written in 1907. It was first performed in 1909. Galsworthy's first play 'The Silver Box' which was called a 'play of ideas'. Galsworthy wrote his plays to create such an illusion of actual life passing on the stage as to compell the spectator to pass through an experience of his own to think and talk and move with the people he sees thinking and talking and moving infront of him.

36. (C) Fourteen

Wordsworth's autobiographical poem, The Prelude was begun in 1799 and was completed in 1805. However it was published only after his death in 1850. The first version containing two books was published in 1799. The second version which was published in 1805 and the final revised version came out in 1850 with 14 books.

37. (D)

38. (A) 14 lines

The Sonnet is a poem of fourteen lambric Pentameter (five foot line) build usually of the two traditional patterns the Petrarchan form and the Shakespearen form. The petrachan Sonnet invented in

Italy and introduced into England by Sir Thomas Wyatt in the sixteenth century is built in two parts. The first part is known as octave consists of eight lines and the last six lines are known as sestet. There is a break in thought after the eight line. The octave always rhymes a b ba abba, while liberties have been allowed in the sestet, It may rhyme cd cd ee or cdd eee.

39. (C) Hamlet

It is evident that in writing Hamlet, Shakespeare to some extent adopted the dramatic tradition of the Revenge Tragedy. Revenge implies the individual taking the law into his own hands in order to satisfy an inner urge, although in civilized society the function of rights and wrongs done to individuals belong to the state or the government. This matter of vengeance for wrongs done played a significant role in the history of drama in Europe.

40. (B)

41. (A)

42. (C) Shakespeare

Fourth Period Late experiment

Coriolanus, Pericles, (1608;)

Cymbeline (1609), Winter's tale (1610-1611).

The Tempest (1611). Henry VIII unfinished.

43. (D) **44.** (B)

45. (B) Liberty of Press

Johns Milton [1608-74]

L' Allegro (1632). II Penseroso (1632). Comus (1634), Lycidas (1637).

Paradise Lost (1667), Paradise Regained (1671)

Samson Agonistes (1671)

'Ode on the Morning of Christ's Nativity (1629)

'On Shakespeare' (1630)

'On Arriving at the Age of twenty-three (1631)

'Of Education' (1644), Areopgitica (1644) History of Britain (Incomplete)

46. (C) **47.** (D)

48. (B) **49.** (D)

50. (B)

51. (A) 1623

The first printed collection of his plays, now called the First Folio (1623), was made by two actors, Heming and Condell, who asserted that they had access to the papers of the poet and had made a perfect edition, in order to keep the memory of so worthy friend and follow alive. This contains thirty-six of the thirty-seven plays generally attributed to Shakespeare Pericles being omitted. This celebrated First Folio was printed from play house manuscripts and from printed quartos containing many notes and changes by individual actors and stage manager.

52. (D) Wordsworth

Descriptive Sketches was written in France Commemorating walking tour in the Alps in the summer of 1790. Though the two poems are imitative and immature, but it is said that even if Wordsworth had not written anything more he would still have a place as poet of some note. They are the most minute and copious inventories of the aspects he saw of the noises he heard in his native lakes An Evening walk or in his sanderings through Switzerland Descriptive sketches.

53. (B) Cockermouth

William Wordsworth was born on the 7th of April, 1770 at Cockermouth on the Derwent in Cumberland. His father John Wordsworth was an attorney at Cockermouth and agent to Sir James Lowther towards the first earl of Lonsdale. His mother Anne Cookson was the only daughter of William Cookson a well to do mercer at Penrith and of Dorothy Crackanthorpe, whose ancestors had been lords of the manner of new biggin near Penrith. So Wordsworth came of gentle kin. He was the second of five children of his parents, the others being Richard, Dorothy, John and Christopher.

54. (C) Beauty

Asthetic—The Science of study of the beautiful things in nature or art.

55. (D) William Wordsworth

[1770-1850]

Famous works : The Prelude (1805)

The Excursion, we are seven Lucy Gray, Simon Lee, The Leech Gatherer, Michael, The Rainbow, Lines Written in March, The Daffodials, lines written in Early spring To the Cockoo, The Solitary Reper, Laodamia, Dion, ode to Duty, Ode one Intimations of Immortality, The World is too much with us, Milton upon westminister Bridge, Tintem Abbey, The Old Cumberland Beggar, An Evening Walk (1793), Descriptive Sketches (1793), She dwelt among the untrodden ways, strange Fits of Ression have I known.

56. (C)

57. (B) The world is too much with us Bliss was it in that dawn to be alive, But to be young was very heaven; 10 times.

No Nightingale did ever chaunt more welcome notes to weary bands of travellers in some shady haunt, Among Arabian sands :

A voice so thrilling ne'er was heard in spring time from the Cuckoo-bird, breaking the silence of the seas among the farthest Hebrides.

58. (D) **59.** (D)

60. (A)

61. (B) **62.** (A)

63. (A) **64.** (C)

65. (B) **66.** (A)

67. (B)

68. (C) A short poem in which the poet expresses his/her intense personal feelings. In the beginning the word 'Lyre' was used for any song meant to be sung with the 'Lyre' a stringed musical instrument known to the Greeks. In course of time this musical accompaniment of the lyric was dropped and the word came to signify and short poem or song expressing the personal emotions and experience of the poet.

69. (B) Style

Baroqe- A style in architecutre and its chief characteristic is over-elaboration which almost obscures the underlying order or pattern. The term is extended to apply to and extravagant and luxirious literary style.

70. (B) **71.** (D)

72. (C)

73. (C) 1637

In the next poem, "Lycidas" a pastoral elegy written in 1637, and the lost of his Horton poems, Milton is no longer the inheritor of the old age, but the prophet of a new. A college friend, Edward King has been drowned in the Irish sea and Milton follows the poetic custom of his age by representating both his friends and himself in the lives of shepherds leading the pastoral life.

74. (C) Grand

Milton is the most sublime of the English poets and the acknowledged master of grand style. In everything he wrote a proud and commanding genius mainfests itself and he is one of those masters who inspire reverence rather than affection. His hand and temper were firm enough to weave together into one system the wearing tendencies of poetry and to give theme sureness accuracy and variety. The next generation, lacking the inspiration of the Elizabethan found in him the necessary stimulus to order and accuracy; and from him, to a great extent; sprang the new classicism' that what to be the rule for more than a century.

75. (B)

76. (D) **77.** (B)

78. (D) 'Justice' is called a problem play. Other famous plays of Galsworthy are : Loyalties and 'Escape'.

79. (A)

80. (C)

81. (A) **82.** (A)

83. (B)

84. (A) William Herbert

Shakespeare's sonnets one hundred and fifty four in number are the only direct expression of the poet's own feelings that we possess : for his plays are the most impersonal in all literature. He dedicated his sonnet to W.H. (William Herbert) and Dark lady. It is generally asserted that; If Shakespeare had written no plays his poems alone would have given him commanding place in the Elizabethan Age.

85. (B) **Peripetia**–Sudden change of fortune in a play or story e.g. the downfall of shylock in The Merchant of Venice.

86. (C) 1667

Milton is the poet of steadfast will and purpose, who moves like a God amid the fears and hopes and changing impulses of the world. Regarding them as trivial and momentary things that can never serve a great soul from its coarse Paradise Lost was published in 1667. It was a great epic in the field of English Literature.

87. (A) Hamartia

The defect in a tragic hero/heroine which leads to his/her downfall as; Hamlet's indecision. Othello's over-credulousness.

88. (C)

89. (B) T.S. Eliot

T.S. Eliot's remarks are momentous to reflect the obscurity of modern poetry. He has stated "We can only say that it appears likely that poets in our Civilization as it exists at present, must be difficult. Our civilization comprehends great variety and complexity and this variety and complexity playing upon a refined sensibility, must produce various and complex results. The post must become more and more comprehensive more allusive more indirect in order to force to dislocate if necessary language into his meaning."

90. (A)

91. (C) 1932

John Galsworthy was born at Kingston, near London, on August 14th, 1867 as the son of a wealthy London Solicitor and property owner. He was educated at Harrow, and at New College, Oxford, he studied law. He went on to Kincoin's Inn. In 1890 he was called to the Bar. Galsworthy got Nobel Prize for Literature in 1932.

92. (D)

93. (C) Richard III

It is pleasing to the fancy to imagine that Shakespeare had his full quota of a school boy's experience and pranks. He must have gone bird's nesting and joined in Mayday, christmas and new year's game; helped made hay, gone to harvest homes and sheep-Shearings (The winter Tale. (IV, II), fished. Much Ado, ran out with barriers and loved a God and horse; A Midsummer Night's Dream; Richard III.

94. (D)

95. (A) Could

Principal clause was given in past so subordinate clause should be in past also.

96. (C)

97. (A) Samuel Johnson (1709-84)

Famous works—London (1738), The Vanity of Human Wishes (1749), The Life of Sagave (1744), The Lives of the Poets (1781); Dictionary of the English Language (1755), Shakespeare (1765), A Journey to the Western Islands of Scotland (1775), The Rambeer, Russelas,

Prince of Abyssinia (1759) and Life of Milton.

98. (D) Shakespeare soon broke away from his apprentice work and then appeared in guide succession. Love's Labour's Lost, Comedy of Errots, Two Gentlemen of Verona. The English chronic plays (Henry & Richard III, Richard II, King John), A Midsummer Night's Dream, and Romeo and Juliet. The wide variety of these plays as well as their frequent crudities marks the first or experimental stage of Shakespeare's works. It is as if the author were trying the temper of his audience for, to please his audience was the ruling motive of Shakespeare.

99. (A) 1917

Galsworthy refused knighthood in 1917.

100. (A) Government Counsel

Galsworthy's thirty plays are nearly all of the problem type. His favorite method is to stage two contrasting individuals as in Justice or two constrasting groups as in Loyalties and let the audience weight their conflicting claims as in the balance. In explanation he wrote : "Every grouping of life has its inherent moral and the business of the dramatist is to bring that moral poignantly to the light of day." Plot or story element was to him of no consequence.

❑❑❑

PRACTICE SET–14

Direction (Q. Nos. 1 to 5: In questions 1 to 5 you have a passage. Read the passage carefully and choose the best answer to each question out of the four alternatives.

Though fond of many acquaintances. I desire an intimacy only with a few. The Man in Black, whom I have often mentioned, is one whose friendship I could wish to acquire, because he possesses my esteem. His manners, it is true, are tinctured with some strange inconsistencies: and he may be justly termed a humorist in a nation of humorists. Though he is generous even to profusion, lie effects to he thought a prodigy of parsimony and prudence: though his conversation be replete with the most sordid and selfish maxims, his heart is dilated with the most unbounded love. I have known him profess himself a man-hater, while his cheek was glowing with compassion : and while his looks were softened into pity, I have heard him use the language of the most ill-bounded ill nature. Some affect humanity and tenderness, others boast of having such disposition from nature; but he is the only man I ever knew who seemed ashamed of his natural benevolence. He lakes as much pains to hide his feelings, as any hypocrite would to conceal his indifference but on every unguarded moment the mask drops off, and reveals him to the most superficial observer.

1. 'Reveals him' means

(A) exposes his shameful conduct

(B) evidences his irritability

(C) makes his latent goodness evident

(D) manifests his attempt to hide his shameful conduct.

2. 'Glowing with compassion' implies

(A) full of pity

(B) red with anger

(C) blushing

(D) shamefacedly

3. 'Parsimony' refers to

(A) the money that parses use for donation

(B) avoidance of excess

(C) the quality of being a spendthrift

(D) the money that does not belong to the user

4. 'Humorist' has been used for

(A) one who loves creating humour

(B) one who writes comedies of humours

(C) one who is capricious

(D) one who loves humorous people

5. 'Because he possesses my esteem' means

(A) I hate him

(B) I have great regard for him

(C) He occupies my room unlawfully

(D) He does not like me

Direction (Q. Nos. 6 – 15): In questions 6 to 15 you have a passage. Read the passage carefully and choose the best answer to each question out of the four alternatives.

He is a very skilled man. Sometimes he sends his drill more than a mile into the earth. There is a lot of luck in drilling for oil. The drill may just miss the oil although it is near; on the other hand, it may strike oil at a fairly high level. When the drill goes down, it brings up soil. The samples of solid from various depths are examined for traces of oil. When we buy a few gallons of petrol for our cars, we pay not only the cost of the petrol but also part of the cost of the petrol cost of the search that is always going on.

6. The cost of unsuccessful drilling
   (A) is borne by the driller
   (B) is borne by the refineries
   (C) is borne by the government
   (D) is borne by the consumer of petrol or other petroleum products
7. The oil drill
   (A) should invariably go at least a mile into the earth
   (B) cannot go more than a mile into the earth
   (C) often goes about a mile into the earth
   (D) occasionally goes more than a mile into the earth
8. The author opines that where there is shale, there is likely to be oil because
   (A) oil was first formed under the sea
   (B) shale is a sedimentary rock
   (C) oil was made from shale
   (D) shale is a sort of oil
9. Scientists are of the opinion
   (A) coal was formed from shale lying under the surface of the earth
   (B) large deposits of mud on the sea between to form oil
   (C) the sea creatures caught between layers of rock went to form oil
   (D) oil was formed from sea water when it was added by the process of chemistry, pressure and temperature.
10. Mineral oil became very important only when
   (A) engineers invented the internal combustion engine
   (B) scientists in Pennsylvania developed oil wells
   (C) lubricating oils were made from it.
   (D) American Indians promoted its use
11. The purpose of lubrication is
   (A) production of heat
   (B) reduction of heat and friction
   (C) to reach all part of a machine
   (D) production of the oil having the right thickness
12. Oil-burning lamps
   (A) are in use in more and more homes these days
   (B) are not very much is use now
   (C) burn more brightly than any other type of lamps
   (D) are used by a large number of people- although not so many as previously
13. The term 'mineral oil' refers here to
   (A) the oil from which petrol is made
   (B) petrol only
   (C) diesel only
   (D) any oil that burns brightly
14. Vegetable oil
   (A) was not known to people in ancient times
   (B) was well known to people long ago
   (C) was known only in ancient times
   (D) is known only to old people
15. Whales are
   (A) the largest animals ever existing in the world
   (B) the largest animals living on land at present
   (C) the largest animals now living in the world
   (D) the largest animals living in the Caspian Sea
16. 'Let us go then, you and I, When the evening is spread out against the sky Like a patient etherised upon a table.
   The above lines have been written in
   (A) Unrhymed Verse
   (B) Blank Verse
   (C) Free Verse
   (D) lambic Meter
17. Robert Southey was succeeded by ....as the poet Laureate of England.
   (A) Tennyson
   (B) Arnold
   (C) Wordsworth
   (D) Shelley

18. 'Our bodies are our gardens, to which our wills are gardeners.'
The above words form the speech of
(A) Hamlet
(B) lago
(C) Viola
(D) Brutus

19. Complete the following sentence by selecting the correct option :
Shakespeare was born at ....
(A) Stratford-at-Avon
(B) Stratford-upon-Avon
(C) Stratford-in-Avon
(D) Stratford-on-Avon

20. 'The wisest, the brightest and the meanest' is said of :
(A) Defoe
(B) Bacon
(C) Milton
(D) Dryden

21. Shakespeare wrote
(A) romantic comedies
(B) comedies of humours
(C) comedies of manners
(D) sentimental comedies

22. Othello killed Desdemona out of
(A) anger (B) hatred
(C) love (D) ignorance

23. Tick the correctly punctuated sentence:
(A) The ganga rises form the Himalayas
(B) The Ganga rises from the Himalayas.
(C) The ganga rises from the Himalayas
(D) The Ganga rises from the Himalayas

24. Tick the correctly punctuated sentence :
(A) They involved Gods who blessed them
(B) They invoked Gods who blessed them
(C) They invoked Gods who blessed them.
(D) They invoked Gods who blessed them.

25. Rewrite the following sentence using 'too' :
He was so excited that he could not think.
(A) He was too excited and so he could not think
(B) He was very too excited to think
(C) He was too excited to think
(D) He was much too excited to think

26. Find out the figure of speech in the following line:
'The waves thundered on the shore.'
(A) Personification
(B) Onomatopoeia
(C) Hyperbole
(D) Metaphor

27. The sounding cataract
Haunted me like passion,'
These lines occur in the poem
(A) Resolution and independence
(B) The Tables Turned
(C) The River Dudden
(D) Tintern Abbey

28. Who made the following remark about Milton? "Milton was of the Devil's party without knowing it."
(A) Tilliard (B) Coleridge
(C) Blake (D) Christopher Hill

29. 'Death of a Salesman' is written by
(A) Faulkner (B) Arthur Miller
(C) O' Neill (D) Hemingway

30. 'Will no one tell me what she sings, Perhaps the plaintive numbers flow, For old unhappy far off things, And battles long ago.'
The above lines occurs in
(A) The Solitary Reper
(B) Three Years She Grew
(C) Michael
(D) An Evening Walk

31. Galsworthy was awarded the Nobel Prize for Literature in
(A) 1931 (B) 1929
(C) 1930 (D) 1932

32. The woman character Delilah appears in
(A) Dr. Faustus (B) Samson Agonistes
(C) Twelfth Night (D) Macbeth

33. 'As files to wanton boys are we to the gods, They kill us for sport'.

The above lines by Shakespeare occur in the play

(A) Julius Caesar (B) Macbeth

(C) Hamlet (D) King Lear

34. In the year 1637 Milton confided to his friend that he had fixed his mind upon writing some monumental poetical work.

Select among the following, the name of his friend to whom this information was given :

(A) Richard Powell

(B) Edward King

(C) Henry Lawes

(D) Diodati

35. 'Sartor Resartus' is a thought provoking work of

(A) Carlyle (B) William Morris

(C) Ruskin (D) Ibsen

36. The phrase 'objective co-relative' has been coined by :

(A) Ezra Pound

(B) Walt Whitman

(C) T.S. Eliot

(D) I.A. Richards

37. Who, among the following, was the first poet laureate officially appointed by the British sovereign?

(A) Ben Jonson

(B) Robert Southey

(C) Dryden

(D) Wordsworth

38. 'A sudden and ridiculous descent from the exalted to the common-place and ordinary, especially when a write, striving for the noble or pathetic, achieves the ludicrous' is best expressed by the term.

(A) The comic relief

(B) Bathos

(C) Melodrama

(D) Paradox

39. The Little Man ' written by Galsworthy is a/an

(A) Poem (B) Novel

(C) Play (D) One Act play

40. The Chaucerian Stanza or Rhyme Royal Comprises

(A) 7 lines

(B) 8 lines

(C) 9 lines

(D) 4 lines

41. 'Willing suspension of disbelief' is a phrase coined by :

(A) Dryden (B) Coleridge

(C) T.S. Eliot (D) Arnold

42. To use another person's thought, writings as one's own is called

(A) Plagiarism (B) Pantheism

(C) Syllogism (D) Parody

43. In which Charles Dickens' novel we come across a character called Mr. Micawber ?

(A) A Tale of Two Cities

(B) David Copperfield

(C) Great Expectations

(D) Oliver Twist

44. The beginning of the modern realistic drama in England took place with the writing of Caste, a play written by

(A) Pinero

(B) Arthur Jones

(C) Robertson

(D) Ibsen

Direction (Q. No. 45 to 46): Tick the correct expression :

45. (A) Look before you do

(B) Look before you work

(C) Look before you leap

(D) Look first and then leap

46. (A) I am fed with you

(B) I am fed up with you

(C) I am fed of you

(D) I am fed of with you

Direction (Q. No. 47 to 50): Each of the following sentences is divided into three parts (A), (B) & (C). Some of the sentences have errors in one part and some have none. Find out which part of the sentence has on error. If there is no error mark (D).

47. He told me/that he is not/interested in games
(A) (B)
and sports/No error
(C) (D)

48. Many things/have happened since/
(A) (B)
I have left the school./No error
(C) (D)

49. It is really strange/that he has not/
(A) (B)
replied my letter./No error.
(C) (D)

50. Both Ram and Shyam/were not present/
(A) (B)
in the classroom./No error
(C) (D)

51. 'Hypothetical' means
(A) practical (B) philosophical
(C) sensitive (D) supposed

52. 'Nauseous' means
(A) gaseous (B) venomous
(C) sickening (D) generous

53. 'Reticent' means
(A) outspoken (B) reserved
(C) quarrelsome (D) benevolent

54. 'Tumultuous' means
(A) causing disturbance
(B) causing fear
(C) causing illness
(D) causing grief

55. 'Vindictive' means
(A) windy (B) stormy
(C) revengeful (D) peace loving

56. 'Bucolic' refers to
(A) the poets who wrote in praise of wine
(B) the poets who wrote pastoral poetry
(C) the poets who imitated pope
(D) the poets who imitated Wordsworth

57. Beat writers
(A) wrote in the 1950s
(B) wrote in the 1940s.
(C) wrote in the 1960s.
(D) wrote in the 1980s.

58. E.M. Forster belonged to
(A) The Fleshly School of Poetry
(B) The Georgains
(C) The Bloomsbury Group
(D) The Age of Interrogation

59. Who of the following poets belongs to the Fleshly School of Poetry?
(A) Edmund Spenser(B) John Keats
(C) J.S. Eliot (D) D.G. Rossetti

60. The author of "Samson Agonistes" was
(A) John Fletcher (B) John Webster
(C) John Milton (D) Ben Jonson

61. "Loyalties-criss-cross each other" is a dialogue in a play by
(A) Shakespeare
(B) Galsworthy
(C) Milton
(D) Shaw

62. The lines "Bliss was it in that dawn to be alive, But to be young was very heaven" occur in the poem of
(A) William Wordsworth
(B) William Shakespeare
(C) John Milton
(D) Christopher Marlowe

63. The line "The mind is its own place, and in itself can make a heav'n of bell, a hell of heaven" occur in
(A) Lycidas
(B) Paradise Regained
(C) Comus
(D) Paradise Lost

64. The lines, "Age cannot wither her, nor Custom stale Her infinite variety" occur in
(A) All for Love
(B) Hamlet
(C) Antony and Cleopatra
(D) As You like it

65. Portia is the heroine of the play

(A) Hamlet

(B) The Merry Wives of Windsor

(C) The Tempest

(D) The Merchant of Venice

66. 'Parable' is

(A) a poem in paragraphs

(B) a book in an epic

(C) a brief tale illustrating some moral

(D) a cure of paralysis

67. Name the figure of speach in the following line : Why then, O brawling love, O loving hate.

(A) Metaphor

(B) Simile

(C) Apostrophe

(D) Oxymoron

68. Morality plays were

(A) produced in the 15th the 16th centuries

(B) produced in the 17th century

(C) produced in the 18th century

(D) produced in the 19th century

69. 'Comic Relief' implies

(A) the interval in the play or film

(B) a hilarious comedy

(C) a short humorous episode interrupting a tragedy

(D) the effect of Catharsis.

70. 'Chorus'

(A) is a brand of writing inks

(B) is a group of singers in drama

(C) is a group of beautiful actresses

(D) is a group D.J. dancers.

71. 'Catharsis'

(A) is related to tragedy

(B) is related to comedy

(C) is related to sonneteering

(D) is related to farce

72. "Cambridge School" refers to

(A) a group of early twentieth century poets

(B) a group of early twentieth century novelists

(C) a group of early twentieth century dramatists

(D) a group of early twentieth century critics

Direction (Q. No. 73 to 77): Change the narration.

73. I invited Rama to come for a drive the following day

(A) I said to Rama. "Will you come for a drive the following day?"

(B) I said to Rama. "Will you come for a drive the next day?

(C) I put a question to Rama. "Will you come for a drive the day following"

(D) I said, "Rama would you like to come for a drive tomorrow?"

74. "You used to be good at Grammar," said I, "Why have you neglected it ?

(A) I said that be used to be good at Grammar and said why he had neglected it.

(B) I said to him that he had been good at grammar and wanted to know why he had neglected it.

(C) I reminded him that he used to be good at grammar and asked why he has neglected it.

(D) I asked him that why had he neglected grammar when he used to be good at it.

75. "I hope you" II have a good journey." I said, I also said, "Good bye".

(A) I bade him good bye and hoped that he would have a good journey.

(B) I said that I hoped with good bye that he will have a good journey.

(C) I was hopeful that he will have a good journey and bade him good bye.

(D) I said him good bye and wished him a good journey.

76. "Ugh! There's a slug in my lettuce. Waiter!" he cried.

(A) He said ugh that there was a slug in his lettuce and asked the waiter to come.

(B) He exclaimed with disgust that there was a slug in his lettuce and called the waiter.

(C) He said to the waiter that ugh there was a slug in his lettuce.

(D) He asked the waiter that there was a slug in his lettuce.

77. The kidnappers said, "If you do not pay the ransom, we'll kill the boy."

(A) The kidnappers threatened to kill the boy if they did not pay the ransom.

(B) The kidnappers said that if they paid not the ransom, they will kill the boy.

(C) The kidnappers said to them that if you do not pay the ransom, we shall kill the boy.

(D) The kidnappers threatened that if the parents of the boy did not pay the ransom, the boy will be killed.

78. He was made to surrender his passport.

(A) I made him to surrender his passport.

(B) The authorities made him to surrender his passport.

(C) They made him surrender his passport.

(D) We made him to surrender his passport.

79. An uneasy silence succeeded the shot.

(A) The shot was successful after an uneasy silence.

(B) The shot was succeeded by an uneasy silence.

(C) The shot was succeeded by an uneasy silence among them.

(D) There was an uneasy silence after the shot had been fired.

80. The P.M. was to have opened the dry dock.

(A) The dry dock was to have been opened by the P.M.

(B) It was expected that the P.M. would open the dry dock.

(C) The opening of the dry dock was to be done by the P.M.

(D) The P.M. was scheduled to open the dry dock.

81. He expected us to offer him the job.

(A) A job was expected by us to be offered him.

(B) He expected to be offered a job.

(C) An offer of a job by us was expected by him.

(D) An offer of a job was being expected by him.

82. The organizers will exhibit the painting till the end of the month.

(A) The painting will be exhibiting by the organizers till the end of the month.

(B) The paintings will be presented in an exhibition till the end of the month.

(C) An exhibition of the paintings will be held till the end of the month.

(D) The painting will be exhibited by the organizers till the end of the month.

83. They are pulling down the old theatre.

(A) The old theatre is being pulled down.

(B) The old theatre is being pulled down by them.

(C) The old theatre is pulling down.

(D) The old theatre has been pulling down.

Question Nos. 84 to 87: Select the correctly punctuated sentences.

84. There is a slavery that no legislation can abolish the slavery of caste.

(A) there is a slavery that no legislation can abolish: The slavery of caste.

(B) There is a slavery that no legislation can abolish: the slavery of caste.

(C) There is a slavery, that no legislation can abolish, the slavery of caste.

(D) There is a slavery, that no legislation can abolish, The Slavery of Caste.

85. Perhaps cried he there may be such monsters that you describe

(A) "Perhaps" cried he, "there may be such monsters as you describe."

(B) "Perhaps," cried he. "There may be such monsters as you describe."

(C) "Perhaps." cried he. " There may be such monsters as you describe.

(D) "Perhaps," cried he. "there may be such monsters as you describe.

86. Wealth may seek us but wisdom must be sought.
(A) Wealth may seek us, but wisdom must be sought.
(B) Wealth may seek us, but wisdom must be sought
(C) Wealth may seek us. But wisdom must be sought
(D) Wealth may seek us, but wisdom must be sought

87. Speak clearly if you would be understood
(A) Speak clearly if you would be understood
(B) Speak clearly, if you would be understood.
(C) Speak clearly If you would be understood
(D) Speak clearly If you would be understood.

Questions Nos. 88 to 93: Fill in the blanks with correct prepositions from those given after every sentence :

88. The police accused the young man .... murder.
(A) of
(B) about
(C) for
(D) amid

89. You must account to the manager..........the money you used.
(A) of
(B) with
(C) about
(D) for

90. We set.............as soon as the old man pointed out the way to us.
(A) of (B) off
(C) towards (D) for

91. She is going to have another blouse made to go with her costume, as her old one is quite worn....
(A) to (B) of
(C) out (D) within

92. He shook me...........the hand and helped me off with my coat.
(A) on (B) by
(C) with (D) off

93. I don't understand; what you are getting...........
(A) on (B) in
(C) at (D) with

94. Who is known as "the poet's poet"?
(A) John Milton
(B) John Dryden
(C) Edmund Spenser
(D) T.S. Eliot

Question Nos. (95 to 100): In questions 95 to 100 you have a passage. Read the passage carefully, and choose the best answer to each question out of the four alternatives.

Truth and non-violence are our goals. Non-violence is the supreme dharma, there is no discovery of greater import than this. So long as we engage in mundane actions, so long as soul and body are together, some violence will continue to occur through our agency. But we must renounce at least the violence that it is possible for us to renounce. We should understand that the less violence a religion permits, the more is the truth contained in it. If we can ensure the deliverance of India, it is only through truth and non-violence. Many people have the habit of hiding their own sentiments when in the presence of an important person and suiting their talk to his pleasure. They do not realise how cruelly they deceive themselves and harm the truth. One must say what one feels, It is impertinence to go against the reason. One must not hesitate: the least to tell what one feels to anyone, be he a Minister of the Government or even a more exalted person. Deal with all with truth and non-violence.

95. "Allusion"
(A) is another spelling of illusion
(B) is a grammatical device
(C) is an indirect or passing reference to an event, person, place or artistic work
(D) is a dramatic device

96. Which is the most truthful dharma?
(A) That which encourages violence
(B) That which discourages violence

(C) That which has nothing to do with non-violence

(D) That which is amoral

97. People hide their own sentiments before an important person

(A) because they are afraid of him

(B) because they do not want to let him know the real position

(C) because they are secretive by nature

(D) because they want to flatter and please him

98. Deliverance implies

(A) the release of the soul from the body

(B) freedom from the British domination

(C) the author's release from the jail

(D) authoritative opinion

99. 'So long as soul and body are together' means.

(A) so long as we are alive

(B) so long as we are able to meet our expenses

(C) so long as we keep ourselves away from religious disputes

(D) so long as we do not support the fight for freedom

100. 'Import' here means

(A) to bring from abroad

(B) that which is brought from abroad

(C) importance

(D) to be of consequence to

ANSWERS WITH EXPLANATION

1. (C) **2.** (A)
3. (C) **4.** (A)
5. (B) **6.** (D)
7. (D) **8.** (B)
9. (C) **10.** (A)
11. (B) **12.** (D)
13. (D) **14.** (B)
15. (B) **16.** (C)
17. (C) **18.** (B)

19. (D) Stratford-on-Avon.

20. (B) Bacon, Alexander Pope said this statement of Bacon.

21. (A) The Romantic comedy written by Shakespeare. The comedy humours written by Ben Jonson. The comedy of manners written by Congreve. The sentimental comedy written by Oliver Goldmith and Richard Sheridan.

22. (D) 'Othello' is one of the four great tragedies of Shakespeare.

23. (B) **24.** (B)
25. (C) **26.** (B)

27. (D) Tintern Abbey by Wordsworth.

28. (C) Blake, his famous poems are 'Songs of Innocence' (1789), 'Songs of Experience' (1794). Marriage of Heaven and Hell' (1790) is his famous prose work.

29. (B) Arthur Miller, famous for his play : All my Sons (1947).

30. (A) The Solitary Reaper, one of the most famous lyrics of Wordsworth, the other important lines: Some natural sorrow loss, of pain that has been and may be again.

31. (D)

32. (B) Samson Agonistes, a tragedy by Milton, Published in 1971 in the same volume as 'Paradise Regained.'

33. (D) "As flies to wanton by are we to the gods; they kill us for their sport." This lines has been taken from "King Lear" written by Shakespeare.

34. (B)

35. (A) Carlyle, his full name is Thomas Carlyle. His other notable works are- French Revolution (1937), Post and Present (1843), History of Fredrick the Coreat.

36. (C) T.S. Elliot. He was awarded Nobel Prize for Literature in 1948. His famous works are-The Waste Land (1922), Burnt Norton (1936), Murder in the Cathedral (1935) etc.

37. (C) Dryden. He was awarded poet Laureate in 1668.

38. (B)

39. (C) His other famous plays are Strife (1909), "The Skin Game' (1920). 'Justice' (1910), The Silver Box' (1906),' Loyalties (1922).

40. (A)

Ryme royal	– seven (7) lines
Ottava rima	– eight (8) lines
Spenseria stanza	– nine (9) lines
The guatrain stanza	– four (4) lines

41. (B) Coleridge, one of the famous Romantic Poets.

42. (A)

43. (B) The other notable characters of the same novel are : David Copper Field, Mr. Murdstone, Betsey Trotwood, Mr. Dick etc.

44. (C) The beginning of the modern realistic drama England place with the writing of caste, a play written by Robertson.

45. (C) **46.** (B)

47. (B) There must be 'was' in place of 'is' according to the rules of narration.

48. (C) **49.** (B)

50. (D) **51.** (D)

52. (C) **53.** (B)

54. (A) **55.** (C)

56. (B) **57.** (A)

58. (C) **59.** (D)

60. (C)

61. (B) The dialogue is from Galsworthy's play, Loyalties (1922).

62. (A) These lines are from Wordsworth's poem: 'French Revolution.'

63. (D) 'Paradise Lost' is an epic by Milton. It was began in 1958, completed in 1663 and published in 1667.

64. (C) 'Antony and Cleoptra' an historical tragedy by Shakespear, probably written in about (1606-7).

65. (D) The 'Merchant of Venice' is a famous tragicomedy written by Shakespeare.

66. (C)

67. (D) 'Why then O brawling love O loving hate, in this lines figure of speech Oxymoron, Oxymoron in oxymoron two opposite words or ideas are put together.

68. (A) Morality plays are dramatized 'allegories' of the life of man, his temptation and sinning his guest for salvation and his confrontation by death. The best known morality play in the fifteenth century Everyman.

69. (C) 'Comic Relief' is the use of humorous characters, speeches, or scenes in a serious or tragic work, especially a dramatic work.

70. (D) Among the ancient Greeks the chorus was a group, wearing masks, who sang or chauted verse while performing dance like maneuvers at religious festivals.

71. (D) 'Catharsis' is related to tragedy. Catharsis refers to the effect of tragedy in the human heart.

72. (D) **73.** (B)

74. (C) **75.** (A)

76. (B) **77.** (A)

78. (B) **79.** (B)

80. (A) **81.** (B)

82. (D) **83.** (A)

84. (B) **85.** (C)

86. (A) **87.** (B)

88. (A) **89.** (D)

90. (B) **91.** (C)

92. (C) **93.** (A)

94. (C)

95. (C) Allusion - A reference to a familiar thing or person or event often mythical resulting in provision of further meaning in compressed form.

96. (B) **97.** (D)

98. (B) **99.** (C)

100. (C)

❑❑❑

PRACTICE SET–15

Direction (Q. Nos. 1-9): Read the given passage and answer the questions that follow by selecting the most appropriate option.

Raja Ravi Verma was the Indian King and painter whose paintings brought a momentous turn in Indian art. His works on great Indian epics Ramayana and Mahabharata brought the omnipresent deities to the surroundings of earthy world. This showed excellent fusion of Indian traditional art with European realism. These paintings influenced future generation artists and also influenced the literature and films. His representation of mythological characters has become a part of the Indian imagination of the classics. His style is criticized for being too gaudy and sentimental.

Ravi Verma was born on April 29th, 1848 in Killimanoor Palace in Kerala. Ravi Verma was brought up in an environment of art and culture. At the age of seven he started painting the figures of animals, acts and scenes from daily life on the wall with charcoal. As he grew up, he was exposed to the famous paintings of Italian painters. Here, he was using indigenous paints made from leaves, flowers. He enhanced his creativity by listening to the music of veterans, watching Kathakali, a folk dance form, going through the manuscripts preserved in ancient families and listening to the artistic interpretation of the epics.

Raja Ravi Verma is most remembered for his paintings of beautifully sari-clad women, who were depicted as graceful and shapely.

1. In the extract, 'artistic interpretation of the epics' means he was interested in :
   (A) popular writing of his time
   (B) unique rendering of old mythologies
   (C) standard interpretation of the Indian epics
   (D) unusual and rare myths found in legends

2. He was especially able to access historical documents in the possession of :
   (A) national museums that curate them
   (B) certain individuals
   (C) families who inherited them
   (D) his family members in Kilimanoor

3. Find a word in the passage which is opposite of 'minimized' :
   (A) influenced (B) criticized
   (C) exposed (D) enhanced

4. A synonym for 'Omnipresent' is :
   (A) Conspicuous
   (B) Universal
   (C) Partly invisible
   (D) Magnificent

5. 'His style is criticized for being too gaudy and sentimental' means that his work was characterized by :
   (A) pale colours and sad atmosphere
   (B) unrealistic images
   (C) lacking intellectual and emotional depth
   (D) strong colours and emotionally appealing

6. The article is a/an :
   (A) fiction (B) essay
   (C) biography (D) autobiography

7. As he matured in his craft, Ravi Verma's skills were influenced by :
   (A) Italian artists
   (B) Indian cinema
   (C) ancient manuscripts
   (D) None of these

8. The focus is on the subject's association with :
(A) sculpture (B) painting
(C) music (D) dance (Kathakali)

9. The themes of Ravi Verma's famous paintings were :
(A) deities
(B) animals and habitats
(C) natural scenery
(D) female figures

10. Examples of irregular verbs are :
(A) break-broke (B) train-trainer
(C) walk-walked (D) happy-happier

11. The gathering skill while reading is :
(A) note-taking (B) note-making
(C) puzzling out (D) analysis

12. A self-contained unit of a discourse in writing dealing with a particular point or idea is :
(A) an essay (B) a poem
(C) a paragraph (D) a statement

13. Encouraging the students to love the world and to imagine a peaceful future and caring for the student and encouraging the student to care for other is .... education.
(A) distance (B) academic
(C) values (D) vocational

14. In the word 'flower', the phonetic transcription is:
(A) /fleur/ (B) /flaevr/
(C) /flauer/ (D) /flovr/

15. Communication technology that enable sharing of educational resources within an institution :
(A) internet (B) intranet
(C) telephone (D) audio-video cassette

16. Standardized assessment means .... assessment.
(A) formative (B) summative
(C) frequent (D) alternative

17. The following is a conditional sentence :
(A) I have to go to work
(B) If the sea is stormy, the waves are high
(C) Shut the door
(D) It's a sunny day, isn't it ?

Direction (Q. Nos. 18-20): in the following questions, choose the word opposite in meaning to the given word.

18. Indict
(A) Accuse (B) Exonerate
(C) Incriminate (D) Impeach

19. Suppress
(A) Reveal (B) Increase
(C) Open (D) Explain

20. Vocal
(A) Voluble (B) Calm
(C) Quite (D) Silent

Direction (Q. No. 21-24): Some parts of the sentences have errors and some are correct. Find out which part of a sentence has an error and blacken the oval (•) corresponding to the appropriate letter (A, B, C). If a sentence is free from error, blacken the oval corresponding to (D) in the Answer Sheet.

21. Subha/is living/in Chennai since 1987/No error
(A) (B) (C) (D)

22. He studied/so hardly/he was sure of passing/No error
(A) (B) (C) (D)

23. Every child in the class/are wearing/sandals today/No error
(A) (B) (C) (D)

24. This errors/are made/by foreigners/No error
(A) (B) (C) (D)

Direction (Q. No. 25-28): Sentences are given with blanks to be filled in with an appropriate word(s). Four alternatives are suggested for each question. Choose the correct alternative out of the four and indicate it by blackening the appropriate oval (•) in the Answer Sheet.

25. Will all of you .... up for prayer ?
(A) race (B) raise
(C) rise (D) raze

26. A technology - starved customer would only be .... to be presented with a new product.
(A) thrilled (B) thriving
(C) declarative (D) irritable

27. A number of refugees .... been turned back at the border.
(A) have (B) are
(C) has (D) is

28. Neither Shyam .... Rohit came to the school today.
(A) and (B) but
(C) or (D) nor

Direction (Q. No. 29-31): Out of the four alternatives, choose the one which best expresses the meaning of the given word and mark it in the Answer Sheet.

29. CLANDESTINE
(A) Secret (B) Family
(C) Useful (D) Dangerous

30. ECSTASY
(A) Extremism (B) Economy
(C) Eclipse (D) joy

31. FETCH
(A) Take
(B) Order
(C) Bring
(D) Scoop

Directions (Q. No. 32-34): Choose the word opposite in meaning to the given word and mark it in the Answer Sheet.

32. Aggressive
(A) Inactive
(B) Dull
(C) Peaceful
(D) Doleful

33. Stationary
(A) Writing
(B) Slowing
(C) Standing
(D) Moving

34. Doleful
(A) Beautiful
(B) Mournful
(C) Cheerful
(D) Deceitful

Direction (Q. No. 35): Four alternatives are given for the Idiom/Phrase bold in the sentence. Choose the alternative which best expresses the meaning of the Idiom/Phrase and mark it in the Answer Sheet.

35. The music group **broke up** unceremoniously.
(A) Disbanded itself
(B) Went bankrupt
(C) Broke each other's instruments
(D) Disturbed the neighbourhood

Direction (Q. Nos. 36-37): In these questions, out of the four alterntives choose the one, which can be substituted for the given words/sentence.

36. To free anything from germs.
(A) Cauterise
(B) Sterilise
(C) Antiseptic
(D) Antivirus

37. One who leaves one's country in order to settle permanently in another.
(A) Emigrant
(B) Omnipresent
(C) Celibate
(D) Bigot

Direction (Q. Nos. 38-40): In these questions, a sentence/part of the sentence is underlined. Below are given alternatives to the underlined part as (A), (B) and (C), which may improve the sentece. Choose the correct alternative. In case no improvement is needed, your answer is (d).

38. <u>To contact the police he tried hard</u>.
(A) He tried to contact the police hard.
(B) He tried hard to contact the police.
(C) He tried the police to contact hard.
(D) No improvement

39. He is reputed to be a <u>closed fisted</u> man.
(A) claw fisted
(B) clasped fisted
(C) close fisted
(D) No improvement

40. Dust is a problem particular to India.

(A) Pathetic
(B) Pollution
(C) Peculiar
(D) No improvement

Directions (41–45): In the following questions some of the sentences have errors and some have none. Find out which part of the sentence has an error. The number of that part is your answer. If there is no error, the answer is (D).

41. I don't (A)/ want to (B)/ loose it. (C)/ No error. (D)

42. Do not (A)/ get panicked (B)/ in emergencies. (C)/ No error. (D)

43. Sometimes (A)/ I get angry (B)/ on her. (C)/ No error. (D)

44. I use (A)/ to go out (B)/ to work earlier. (C)/ No error. (D)

45. The teacher (A)/ has took (B)/ the responsibility. (C)/ No error. (D)

Directions (46–50): In the following questions sentences are given with blanks to be filled in with an appropriate word(s). Four alternatives are suggested for each question. Choose the correct alternative out of the four.

46. I have ...... Lakshmi for the past twelve years.

(A) Know (B) Knew
(C) Known (D) Knows

47. He did not qualify ...... the job.

(A) For (B) To
(C) Against (D) With

48. ...... the last ten years we have been victims of abuse.

(A) From (B) For
(C) Before (D) Since

49. The strike has been called ....

(A) of (B) at
(C) off (D) up

50. He is always angry ...... his children

(A) with (B) on
(C) over (D) at

Directions (51–60): In the following questions four alternatives are given for the idiom/ phrase printed in bold the sentence. Choose the alternative which best expresses the meaning of the idiom/phrase.

51. The angry hockey players **gave vent to their feelings.**

(A) to express (B) to emphasise
(C) to suppress (D) to dismiss

52. I trust you will **bear with** me a few minutes more.

(A) have patience with
(B) support
(C) carry the burden for
(D) be in control for

53. As usual he is **blowing his own trumpet.**

(A) Refusing to use anybody else's trumpet
(B) Playing a tune on the trumpet
(C) Praising himself
(D) Praising himself and others

54. When trade was brisk, he worked hard and made his fortune; he believes in **making hay while the sun shines.**

(A) Taking advantage of a favourable opportunity
(B) Earning money through dishonest means
(C) Earning money at the cost of others
(D) Taking advantage of the inflationary trends

55. When they were surrounded from all sides, the dacoits **laid down their arms.**

(A) Put their arms on the ground
(B) Fought bravely
(C) Surrendered
(D) Became nervous

Directions (56–60): In the following questions a part of the sentence is printed in bold. Below are given alternatives to the bold part at (A), (B) and (C) which may improve the sentence. Choose the correct alternative. In case no improvement is needed your answer is (D).

56. He behaves **like coward.**
(A) Cowardly
(B) In a cowardly manner
(C) As if he was a coward
(D) No improvement

57. **Neither of them went** to the cinema.
(A) Both of them did not go
(B) Both did not go
(C) Neither went
(D) No improvement

58. **I used to have** very thick hair.
(A) Use to have
(B) Used to having
(C) Used to had
(D) No improvement

59. They **reached at Kolkata** on Monday last.
(A) reached to Kolkata
(B) reached on Kolkata
(C) reached Kolkata
(D) No improvement

60. I **did not saw** my cousin in Chennai.
(A) not seen
(B) did not see
(C) did not seen
(D) No improvement

61. In the following question, out of the four alternatives, choose the word which best expresses the meaning of the given word.
Panacea
(A) Praise (B) Cure-all
(C) Poison (D) Ambrosia

62. In the following question, out of the four alternatives, choose the word which is opposite in meaning to the given word.
Detest
(A) Denounce (B) Ignore
(C) Adore (D) Castigate

63. Four words are given, out of which only one word is spelt correctly. Choose the correctly spelt word.
(A) Debilitate (B) Impecable
(C) Inkulcate (D) Harrass

Directions (64–66): The sentences given with blanks are to be filled with an appropriate word(s). Four alternatives are suggested for each question. For each question, choose the correct alternative.

64. What a .... holiday!
(A) Momentous (B) Memorable
(C) Momentary (D) Immortal

65. Many important projects have reached the final stage of ....
(A) Accomplishment
(B) Initiation
(C) Resolution
(D) Implementation

66. .... you live long!
(A) Might (B) May
(C) Shall (D) Should

Directions (67–69): In the following questions, some parts of the sentences have errors and some are correct. Find out which part of a sentence has an error. The number of that part is your answer. If a sentence is free from errors, your answer is No error.

67. Each of the girls (A)/ have come (B)/ with her books. (C)/ No Error (D)

68. Me and my wife (A)/ were at home (B)/ last night. (C)/ No Error (D)

69. Essay writing is an art (A)/ that requires many planning (B)/ on the part of the writer. (C)/ No Error (D)

Directions (70–72): In these questions, four alternatives are given for the idiom/ phrase printed in bold. Choose the alternative which best expresses the meaning of the idiom/phrase given in bold.

70. **Caught red-handed**
(A) Caught by mistake
(B) Caught with a red-handkerchief
(C) Found wounded
(D) Discovered in the act of doing

71. Gate crasher

(A) Invader
(B) Thief
(C) Uninvited guest
(D) Children

72. To angle

(A) To measure the river breadth
(B) To fish with a net
(C) To fish
(D) To sit and watch the river

Directions (73–75): In each of the following questions, out of the four alternatives, choose the one which can be substituted for the given words/ sentence.

73. Favouritism shown by a person in power to his relatives.

(A) Formalism (B) Red-tapism
(C) Nepotism (D) Bureaucracy

74. A round-about way of expression

(A) Verbosity
(B) Talkativeness
(C) Circumlocution
(D) Locquacious

75. Suitable or intended for only young persons

(A) Youthful (B) Puerile
(C) Adolescent (D) Juvenile

Directions (76–80): In each of the following questions, a sentence/part of the sentence is printed in bold. Four alternatives are given to the bold part which will improve the sentence. Choose the correct alternative. In case no improvement is needed, select option corresponding to "No improvement".

76. Each self is unique, and therefore **cannot be compared.**

(A) Incomparable
(B) Non comparable
(C) Incomparably
(D) No Improvement

77. Shall I sit **between** you at the concert?

(A) Beside
(B) Besides
(C) Next
(D) No Improvement

78. No one other reason than poverty is hampering India's progress.

(A) No other
(B) None other
(C) No another
(D) No Improvement

79. The custom has **took root** in the society.

(A) Taken root
(B) Take root
(C) Takes root
(D) No Improvement

80. We will **take care of** your children when you are away at Mumbai.

(A) Be looking for
(B) Look after
(C) Take care after
(D) No Improvement

Directions (81–82): Choose the word, which is most similar in meaning to the given words.

81. Dishevelled

(A) Tidy (B) Clean
(C) Neat (D) Untidy

82. Venerate

(A) Despise (B) Disobey
(C) Disregard (D) Revere

Directions (83–84): Choose the word, which is most opposite in meaning to the given words.

83. Congenial

(A) Accord (B) Snug
(C) Engaging (D) Unpleasant

84. Abjure

(A) Renounce (B) Relinquish
(C) Abnegate (D) Acquire

Directions (85–87): In the following questions, out of the four alternatives, choose the one which can be substituted for the given words/sentence.

85. Highly skilled
(A) Consummate (B) Inveterate
(C) Notorious (D) Maladroit

86. Identification with the feelings of another
(A) Sympathy (B) Empathy
(C) Apathy (D) Compassion

87. Insatiable desire for wealth
(A) Selfish (B) Avarice
(C) Egoist (D) Generosity

Directions (88–90): In these questions, four alternatives are given for the idiom/phrase given in bold. Choose the alternative which best expresses the meaning of the idiom/phrase.

88. **Cut the mustard**
(A) To get under expectations
(B) To score average
(C) To perform well
(D) To underperform

89. **A chip off the old block**
(A) Reminds them of one's father
(B) To remind one's sin
(C) Reminds them of one's son
(D) Reminds of previous memories

90. **To fish in troubled waters**
(A) To indulge in evil conspiracies
(B) To make a profit out of disturbance
(C) To aggravate the situation
(D) To make the most of bad bargain

Directions (91–92): In these questions, a part of sentence is underlined. Below are given alternatives to the underlined part, which may improve the sentence. Choose the correct alternative. In case to improvement is needed, mark 'No improvement' as your answer.

91. What <u>you have been doing</u> since the workshop last month?
(A) have you done
(B) you have done
(C) have you been doing
(D) No improvement

92. Corruption is <u>the most serious</u> problem in India.
(A) the more serious
(B) very serious
(C) serious
(D) No improvement

Directions (93–97): Each of the following sentences has a blank space and four words given after the sentence. Select whichever word you consider most appropriate for the blank space.

93. Sid and Harsh are ...... unable to complete the task.
(A) neither (B) either
(C) each (D) both

94. The examinee could guess ...... the answer correctly.
(A) at (B) about
(C) through (D) to

95. Be ...... and always look to the comfort of others.
(A) considerate (B) cautious
(C) considerable (D) consider

96. As usual, a lot of people were ...... in the king's darbar.
(A) their (B) possess
(C) past (D) present

97. In this question, four words are given out of which one is incorrectly spelt. Find the incorrectly spelt word.
(A) Ommineous (B) Omineous
(C) Ominous (D) Omenous

Directions (98–100): In the following questions, a sentence has been given in parts, out of which a part contains an error. The part with the error is your answer. In case there is no error, then your answer is 'No error'.

98. He ought not/have done such/a filthy thing.
(A) He ought not
(B) have done such
(C) filthy thing
(D) No error

99. The reason for/his failure is because/he did not work hard.
(A) The reason for
(B) His failure is because
(C) He did not work hard
(D) No error

100. I have reached/the office before/the rain started.
(A) I have reached
(B) The office before
(C) The rain started
(D) No error

ANSWERS WITH EXPLANATION

1. (B)
2. (C) He was able to access historical documents in the possession of families who inherited them.
3. (D)
4. (B)
5. (D)
6. (C)
7. (A) Ravi Verma's skills were highly influenced by Italian artists.
8. (B)
9. (D)
10. (A) Here, irregular verbs are break-broke.
11. (B)
12. (C)
13. (C)
14. (D)
15. (B)
16. (B)
17. (B)
18. (B)
19. (A)
20. (D)
21. (B)
22. (B)
23. (B)
24. (A)
25. (C)
26. (A)
27. (C)
28. (D)
29. (A)
30. (D)
31. (C)
32. (C)
33. (D)
34. (C)
35. (A)
36. (B)
37. (A)
38. (B)
39. (C)
40. (C)
41. (C) Replace **loose** it by **lose** it, the word **Loose (Verb)** means: loosen; to release something.
The word **lose (Verb)** means: to be unable to find something/somebody; mislay.
42. (B) Here, get panicky (Adjective) should be used.
43. (C) Here, angry will be followed by 'with'. Hence, **with her** should be used.
44. (A) Here, **I used to** should be used.
Sentence → **I used to** go there every Sunday.
45. (B) Here, has taken (V_3) should be used.
Structure of a sentence in Present Perfect is:
Subject + have/has + V_3 (Past Participle)
46. (C) I have **known** Lakshmi for the past twelve years.
47. (A) He did not qualify **for** the job.
48. (B) **For** the last ten years we have been victims of abuse.
49. (C) Phrase **call off** means: to cancel something.
50. (A) He is always angry **with** his children.
51. (A) Idiom **give (full) vent to** something means: to express a feeling especially anger, strongly.
52. (A) Phrase **bear with** means: to be patient with somebody/something.
53. (C) Idiom **blow your own trumpet** means: boast; to praise your own abilities and achievements.
54. (A) Idiom **make hay while the sun shines** means: to make good use of opportunities, good conditions.
55. (C) Idiom **lay down your arms** means: to stop fighting; surrender.
56. (C) 'As if he was a coward' in place of 'like coward'.
57. (D) No improvement required.
58. (B) 'Having' in place of 'have'.

59. (C) Delete 'at' before Kolkata.

60. (B) 'See' in place of 'saw'.

61. (B) **Panacea** (Noun): Something that will solve all the problems of a particular situation.

62. (C) **Detest** (Verb): To hate somebody/ something very much; loathe.

Adore (Verb): To love somebody very much.

63. (A) Correctly Spelt Word: Debilitate

64. (B) **Memorable (Adjective):** Unforgettable, special, good or unusual.

65. (D) **Implementation (Noun):** Carrying out; enactment; execution; application.

66. (B) **May** is used to express a wish.

67. (B) Error in part (B), 'has come' in place of 'have come' should be used here.

68. (A) Error in part (A), 'I and my wife' in place of 'Me and my wife' should be used here.

69. (B) Error in part (B), 'that requires much planning' in place of 'that requires many planning' should be used here.

70. (D) **Catch somebody redhanded:** To catch somebody in the act of doing something wrong or committing a crime.

71. (C) **Gate crasher:** One who goes to a party or social event without being invited.

72. (C) **To angle (go angling):** To catch fish with a line and a hook.

73. (C) **Nepotism:** Unfair advantages for members of your own family.

Sentence → He was guilty of nepotism and corruption.

74. (C) **Circumlocution:** Using more words than are necessary; instead of speaking or writing in a clear, direct way.

75. (D) **Juvenile:** is a young person who is not yet old enough to be regarded as a adult.

Sentence → Juvenile crime is increasing at a terrifying rate.

76. (A) **Incomparable (Adjective):** So good or impressive that nothing can be compared to it; matchless.

77. (A) **Beside:** Next to or at the side of somebody.

Sentence → He sat beside her all night.

78. (A) **No other reason** is a correct usage.

79. (A) Took root = taken root

80. (B) **Take care of:** look after.

81. (D) 'Dishevelled' means untidy.

82. (D) 'Venerate' means to show a lot of respect. All other options means to dislike or have no respect.

83. (D) 'Congenial' means pleasant or welcoming.

84. (D) 'Abjure' means to promise to reject a belief or a way of behaving. All other options mean to reject, deny or give up.

85. (A) 'Consummate' means complete and its synonym is highly skilled.

86. (B) 'Empathy' means the ability to understand and share the feelings of another.

87. (B) 'Avarice' means extreme or insatiable desire for wealth.

88. (C) The idiom 'cut the mustard' means to perform well and succeed.

89. (A) The idiom 'a chip off the old block' means someone who closely resembles their parent in character or appearance.

90. (B) The idiom 'to fish in troubled waters' means to take advantage or to make a profit out of disturbance.

91. (C) The helping verb (have) will come before the subject (you) in case of an interrogative sentence.

92. (D) No improvement required for this sentence.

93. (D) Sid and Harsh are **both** unable to complete the task.

94. (A) The examinee could guess **at** the answer correctly.

95. (A) Be **considerate** and always look to the comfort of others.

96. (D) As usual, a lot of people were present in the king's darbar.

97. (C) Correct spelling → Ominous

98. (A) Part (A) has error. The correct expression should be 'He ought not to'.

99. (B) Part (B) has error. Using the word 'because' with the word 'reason' is not required. It should be 'The reason for his failure is that he did not work hard'.

100. (A) Part (A) has error. The sentence is in Past Perfect Tense. It should be 'I had reached the office before the rain started.'

❑❑❑